CU00923382

THE BIOPOLITICS OF INTELLECTUAL PROPERTY

As a central part of the regulation of contemporary economies, intellectual property is central to all aspects of our lives. It matters for the works we create, the brands we prefer and the medicines we consume. But if IP is power, what kind of power is it, and what does it do? Building on the work of Michel Foucault, Gordon Hull examines different ways of understanding power in copyright, trademark, and patent policy: as law, as promotion of public welfare, and as promotion of neoliberal privatization. He argues that intellectual property policy is moving toward neoliberalism, even as that move is broadly contested in everything from resistance movements to Supreme Court decisions. This work should be read by anyone interested in understanding why the struggle to conceptualize IP matters.

GORDON HULL is Associate Professor of Philosophy and Public Policy at the University of North Carolina at Charlotte. He has published numerous articles on contemporary philosophical and political theory, intellectual property, privacy, and the history of philosophy. He is also the author of *Hobbes and the Making of Modern Political Thought* (2009).

The Biopolitics of Intellectual Property

REGULATING INNOVATION AND PERSONHOOD IN THE INFORMATION AGE

GORDON HULL

University of North Carolina, Charlotte

CAMBRIDGE
UNIVERSITY PRESS

University Printing House, Cambridge CB2 8BS, United Kingdom

One Liberty Plaza, 20th Floor, New York, NY 10006, USA

477 Williamstown Road, Port Melbourne, VIC 3207, Australia

314–321, 3rd Floor, Plot 3, Splendor Forum, Jasola District Centre, New Delhi – 110025, India

79 Anson Road, #06–04/06, Singapore 079906

Cambridge University Press is part of the University of Cambridge.

It furthers the University's mission by disseminating knowledge in the pursuit of
education, learning, and research at the highest international levels of excellence.

www.cambridge.org
Information on this title: www.cambridge.org/9781108482356
DOI: 10.1017/9781108687232

© Gordon Hull 2019

First published 2019

Printed and bound in Great Britain by Clays Ltd, Elcograf S.p.A.

A catalogue record for this publication is available from the British Library.

Library of Congress Cataloging-in-Publication Data
NAMES: Hull, Gordon, 1972– author.
TITLE: The biopolitics of intellectual property : regulating innovation and personhood in the
information age / Gordon Hull, University of North Carolina, Charlotte.
DESCRIPTION: Cambridge, United Kingdom ; New York, NY, USA : Cambridge University Press, 2019. |
Includes index.
IDENTIFIERS: LCCN 2019021286 | ISBN 9781108482356 (hardback) | ISBN 9781108712057 (pbk.)
SUBJECTS: LCSH: Intellectual property–Philosophy. | Biopolitics–Philosophy.
CLASSIFICATION: LCC K1401 .H85 2019 | DDC 346.04/8–dc23
LC record available at https://lccn.loc.gov/2019021286

ISBN 978-1-108-48235-6 Hardback
ISBN 978-1-108-71205-7 Paperback

Contents

Preface

As one might expect of a genealogy, the origins of this book are diffuse. My disciplinary training and academic home are in philosophy, and I began with a combination of history and a heavy dose of contemporary French and German theory. I began learning about intellectual property (IP) as part of teaching, and soon found myself regularly reading from law reviews. This somewhat eclectic nexus of history, law, and contemporary philosophy is both where I remain and where this book is located. In it, I want to show that how one understands power has a lot to do with how one understands intellectual property. Not only that, the socially dominant model of power is changing, and with it the structure of intellectual property policy. I draw the "power" part from the work of Michel Foucault, whose research into the contingent historical bases of some of our most deeply held concepts turns philosophy away from itself and towards the world of politics. It is perhaps not surprising that in intellectual property I have been particularly drawn to the theorists – people like Lawrence Lessig, Yochai Benkler, Julie Cohen, James Boyle, Sonia Katyal, and Madhavi Sunder – who emphasize some of the same entanglements between theory and law.

I view my own contribution as genealogical in the sense that I take a step back and frame what is at stake in a number of contemporary IP debates, show that deeply held convictions about what IP does both shape and animate some very specific policies and institutional decisions, and that all of that is fundamentally important for understanding who we are. I will argue that there are three basic ways of understanding power involved. One is typical of the social contract theorists, and speaks in the language of rights and state powers. Another is typical of modern liberalism, and tries to situate an account of markets into a larger narrative about civil society or the public. The third inverts the second, situating civil society into a narrative governed by the logic of markets. In areas as diverse as fashion advertising and genomics, a regulatory model structured by this third version is ascendant across a number of registers. That said, if the third version is ascendant, it is not despotic, and I also study how institutional actors like the Supreme Court invoke other understandings of power in an effort to push back.

How these struggles turn out matters enormously. Modern economies are heavily driven by immaterial goods, and contemporary economic theory heavily emphasizes innovation. At a more individual level, the natural human impulse to creative and imaginative play intersects continuously with intellectual property, whether in the form of copyright that structures how we create and access cultural goods like books and videos, of trademark that structures how we interact with brands and corporate logos, or of patents that structure such basic amenities as how we access medical care. This interaction is an important part of what determines who we are as people, and so it is not a stretch to say that IP is in the business of making people.

The theorists who say creativity is a social process are right, and no academic work exists without the benefit of countless interactions, large and small, both in writing and in person. This is doubly true of interdisciplinary work, which simply cannot happen in a vacuum. I have been fortunate to work in a department that encourages interdisciplinarity, and to intersect with academic communities that are willing to engage it. I have had many conversations over the years developing the ideas in this book, and am grateful for all of them. Various parts of the argument have benefitted from presentation at UNC Charlotte, the Society for the Philosophy of Technology (SPT) and the Society for Phenomenology and Existential Philosophy (SPEP). I would like especially to thank Julie Cohen, Brett Frischmann, Ben Hippen, Robin James, Sonia Katyal, Lisa Rasmussen, Madhavi Sunder, and two anonymous readers at Cambridge University Press for reading portions of the manuscript and offering much appreciated feedback. The initial stages of the work were supported by a research leave at UNC Charlotte, and I am grateful for the time that afforded. My greatest debt, as always, is to my family: my partner, Maya Socolovsky, who both pushed me to complete the project and supported it in countless ways, and my children – Ilan, Amia, and Gali – who live the joy of creativity and imagination every day.

An earlier version of the incentives discussion in Chapter 3 appeared as "Copyright between Economic and Cultural Models of Creativity," in *Spaces for the Future: A Companion to Philosophy of Technology*, eds. Joseph C. Pitt and Ashley Shew (New York: Routledge, 2018), 130–140. An earlier version of the discussion of DRM in Chapter 3 appeared as "Coding the Dictatorship of 'the They:' A Phenomenological Critique of Digital Rights Management," in *Ethics and Phenomenology*, eds. Mark Sanders and Jeremy Wisnewski (Lanham, MD: Lexington Books, 2012), 197–219. An earlier version of parts of Chapter 4 appeared as "Cultural Branding, Geographic Source Indicators and Commodification," *Theory, Culture & Society* 33:2 (2016), 125–145. In all three cases, the present argument is thoroughly revised. I am grateful for the publishers' permission to rework that material here.

1

Introduction

1.1 GOD AND COPYRIGHT

In 1984, at the age of 92, Herbert W. Armstrong, founder and leader of the Worldwide Church of God (WCG), penned his last work, *Mystery of the Ages*. *Mystery* begins by proposing that we live in "a world ridden with escalating crime and violence, immorality, injustice (even in its courts of law), dishonesty, corruption in government and business, and continual wars, pointing now to the final nuclear World War III" (Armstrong, 1985).[1] The world would be better, and saved from this "paradox of progress and degeneration," he proposes, by a proper, literal reading of the Bible. Armstrong perceived two primary obstacles to acceptance of such a reading: the general acceptance of evolutionary theory and an incorrect interpretation of Scripture by established Christianity.

In the remainder of the introduction, Armstrong recounts his own 1926 conversion from the world of business – advertising specifically – to religion, a conversion that culminated in the founding of WCG in 1968. Originally challenged by his wife's decision to celebrate the Sabbath on Saturday, he read both evolutionary theory and the Bible, deciding along the way that the Biblical text seemed to promise "death" and not damnation for those who were not saved. In this and other ways, he came to believe that established Christianity departed substantially from the Bible. Armstrong also wrote with millenarian urgency: As he argues in the last chapter, the Kingdom of God was to be a literal kingdom on earth, since "man has proven his utter incapability of ruling himself." The arrival of this kingdom was near, as "the last, final, brief resurrection of the Roman Empire by ten European groups or nations" had already begun. This final reincarnation of what he later calls the

---

[1] I refer to the online versions of these works, as they are readily available. All Armstrong references are from this edition of *Mystery*.

"United States of Europe," he says, "is to endure but a very short time. It is to fight against Christ at his Second Coming! That will be its end."

Armstrong had a very idiosyncratic vision of messianic time. For example, over-population would be solved by God's increase of the amount of arable land. In addition, "once the returning Christ conquers this earth, he will usher in an era of total literacy, total education – and give the world one, new, pure language." So too, the world's economy will be done with capitalism and wage labor (although Armstrong does not use those words): "never again will any person become rich from investing in the labors and creative ability of another person. No more stock markets, world banks, financing centers, insurance companies, mortgage com-panies, loan agencies, or time payments." Armstrong's description of the world to come is at times remarkably granular; in one passage, for example, he proposes that "Job will be director of worldwide urban renewal." He concludes by arguing that, after a thousand years of the Kingdom of God on earth and a final judgment in which those who are not saved die a final death, God will open the entire universe to humanity, and "we shall impart life to billions and billions of dead planets, as life has been imparted to this earth. We shall create, as God directs and instructs. We shall rule through all eternity!"

In the ensuing few years, WCG put over nine million copies of *Mystery* into circulation at no charge (WCG, p. 1113). Two years after Armstrong's death, how-ever, WCG undertook substantial doctrinal revision. Many points of the theology of *Mystery* were abandoned, and seeking to "prevent a transgression of conscience by proclaiming what the Church considered to be ecclesiastical error," and in defer-ence to "cultural standards of social sensitivity," the Church under the leadership of Joseph Tkach, Sr. both ceased publication of *Mystery* and destroyed excess inventory copies (Tkach, 1997b). The doctrinal revisions indeed affected core beliefs of WCG. For example, in Tkach's son's version of events, a central problem related precisely to Armstrong's embrace of the Sabbath on Saturday, which was connected in his mind to "Anglo-Israelism," the view that parts of Europe and the United States represented the lost Israeli tribes, and that they were accordingly going to receive preferential treatment when Christ returned.[2]

Tkach's son called Anglo-Israelism a "central plank" of WCG doctrine. He also thought that it "silently worked to foster racial prejudice" (Tkach, 1997a). Anglo-Israelite doctrine appears in the fifth chapter of *Mystery*; in it, Armstrong proposes that "the probability is that these [ancient Hebrew, chosen] people were all – or nearly all – of the white racial strain, unchanged since creation." (They were not, he argues repeatedly, all Jewish.) He then suggests that when God came to govern the Israelites by way of Moses, "one reason was to preserve the original physical racial

[2] "The peoples of the United States, the British Commonwealth nations, and the nations of Northwestern Europe are, in fact, the peoples of the Ten Tribes of the House of Israel. The Jewish people are the House of Judah" (qt. in Tkach, 1997a).

strain." The Biblical lost tribes reemerged in the years 1800–1804, "when national supremacy and economic dominance was to become theirs" as promised to Abraham (Armstrong, 1985). WCG officially abandoned Anglo-Israelism in 1995.

Not everyone thought Anglo-Israelism was problematic. In 1989, two former WCG ministers, Gerald Flurry and John Amos, formed their own Church, the Philadelphia Church of God (PCG), committed to the literal teachings of Armstrong. Flurry began work on a manuscript and started meeting with other disaffected church members, including Amos. Many of their concerns had to do with finances and other institutional arrangements, but Flurry was apparently particularly bothered by the withdrawal of *Mystery*. After an apparently contentious meeting on December 7, 1989, Tkach, Jr., fired Flurry and Amos. Flurry's son later referred to WCG doctrinal revisions as the "WORST SPIRITUAL SHIPWRECK SINCE THE FIRST-CENTURY CHURCH SPLINTERED ON THE ROCKS OF APOSTACY" (Flurry, 2006).

At this point, what otherwise might seem to be a story about internecine politics in fringe religious movements took an unusual turn. PCG faced a problem: access to *Mystery*, which not only was WCG no longer publishing, but for which it also owned the rights. By 1997, PCG had run out of available copies, and so it began making its own copies of *Mystery*, distributing them to its members free of charge. When PCG ignored a cease and desist demand from WCG, WCG sued for copyright infringement. PCG claimed the right to distribute the work under the First Amendment's Free Exercise clause, the Religious Freedom Restoration Act, and as Fair Use under the Copyright Act. In 2000, the Ninth Circuit issued a split ruling in favor of WCG, denying PCG's request for an injunction.

Several years later, after a protracted negotiating process, WCG sold the rights to *Mystery* and a number of Armstrong's other texts to PCG for $3 million (Flurry, 2006). In his own recounting of the litigation, Flurry's son could hardly contain himself:

> What did happen is this: They [WCG] sold us a storehouse of literature for an amount of money that, by our estimate, barely covered their legal costs, if even that. They retrieved no "profits" or "damages" from us. All their "overwhelming" victories in court were conditioned on them making Mr. Armstrong's works available. And in the end, they were exactly where they started before the case, money-wise, but having forfeited ownership of all 19 copyrights.
>
> (Flurry, 2006)

In recounting WCG's efforts to prevent his attendance at some of the proceedings, Flurry's son framed the issue as one of ethics:

> [WCG] wanted to strip away all the *historical* intrigue – the PASSIONATE spiritual and emotional involvement we had invested in this case, in this *way of life* under Mr. Armstrong. They knew we were righteously indignant – even angry – about

what Tkachism had done. They knew we would intensely fight for our spiritual livelihood – so they didn't want us around. They wanted this battle to be fought between lawyers only – and over what they considered to be purely a legal matter involving the Copyright Act and "stolen" property.

(Flurry, 2006)

In Flurry's view, the question was one of a way of life. The opposing view, he suggests, was merely a matter of "law."

In arguing that PCG was trying to preserve a way of life, Flurry calls attention to two things. The first is of course the way that PCG members used Armstrong's writings as part of what French philosopher Michel Foucault would call a "technology of the self" or an "ethos" – in this case, a coordinated set of doctrinal beliefs and material practices that constituted those who followed them as members of PCG. The second is the role of law – in this case Copyright – in fostering or inhibiting that form of life. As Flurry suggests, a decision in PCG's favor would foster PCG by enabling the easy dissemination of a text central to its members' beliefs. *Mystery* and the associated Armstrong writings that PCG obtained with it are not only central to PCG doctrine; as Flurry repeatedly emphasizes in his memoir, in PCG's view, they define its specificity, especially in relation to WCG and mainline evangelical Protestantism. On the other hand, what Flurry calls the "purely legal" construal of the dispute as being about the theft of property also had implications for PCG's way of life. A decision that PCG's use of *Mystery* was not a fair use would mean that PCG's ability to access that text would depend on both WCG's willingness to license or sell the rights to it and the successful negotiation of a price or fee. As Flurry's narrative makes apparent, neither of those conditions was guaranteed.

A copyright decision, in either direction, would thus necessarily be involved in the most intimate details of how members of PCG – and possibly WCG – understood themselves as people. In that way, the litigation illustrates the way that intellectual property (IP) law is deeply imbricated in shaping ways of life. In short, IP law is part of making people.[3] In a variety of ways, and in a broad set of social contexts, IP is intimately tied to how all of us understand ourselves as people, as well as the sorts of people we become. Religious practice and belief (or their absence) are central to most people's understanding of what it means to be human. Particularly with contemporary religious practices, there exists the real possibility that the foundational works would be under copyright, as original authorship would be both attributable and recent. The WCG case is not isolated; Scientology's use of copyright is most well-known in this regard. The Church claims that copyright can be used to preserve its doctrine and its use; critics see a bad faith effort to stifle dissent.[4]

[3] I draw the term from Hacking (1986); Hacking is working in a broadly Foucauldian spirit.
[4] For the Church, see its own statement on IP: "Scientology and Dianetics are technologies that work if applied exactly. If they are altered, the results will not be uniform. To safeguard the scripture and ensure it could never be altered or misused, Mr. Hubbard copyrighted all the

However, in any case where texts are involved, there are potential questions of copyright and originality, even in cases, such as the Dead Sea Scrolls, where the ancient text in question was reconstructed from fragments (for a summary and critical discussion, see Nimmer, 2001).

IP is also, on this account, a kind of power. At one level, it interacts with First Amendment discourse about the limits of state power to regulate expression or to regulate access to property. It is this sense of power that Flurry dismisses as mere lawyering. As Flurry recognizes, however, its ability to modulate ways of life is also an exercise of power. Of course, this view requires that we see power as more than the capacity of the state to repress. Instead, as I will develop over the course of the book, we need to see power in broader, social terms, where the repressive state apparatus is only one version. As Foucault puts it in a famous passage, "power produces: it produces reality; it produces domains of objects and rituals of truth. The individual and the knowledge that may be gained of him belong to this production" (1977, p. 194). In this regard, copyright can be seen as operating in at least two ways: as a regulation by law of traditional, judicial things like rights, and as an intervention into ways of life.

Interestingly, the Ninth Circuit's opinion in the WCG litigation evidenced both ways that copyright functioned. The majority proceeded in relatively formal legal analysis of the doctrinal requirements for fair use, finding that all four factors tended to push toward a ruling against fair use.[5] In particular, the Court noted that the first factor – the nature of use – which is generally the most important one in fair use litigation, worked against PCG. After all, there was nothing even remotely transformative about PCG's use of *Mystery*, since it was for religious instruction. The Court also found that the use, though perhaps instructive for individuals, nonetheless profited PCG by "providing it at no cost with the core text essential to its members' religious observance, by attracting through distribution of MOA

---

materials of the religion. While to guarantee that Dianetics and Scientology could not be misrepresented, he further trademarked many of the religion's identifying words and symbols. These copyrights and trademarks provide a legal mechanism by which to ensure Scientology's religious technologies are standardly ministered in exact accordance with scriptures and not altered by misappropriation or improper use. Over the years, unscrupulous persons have attempted, through dishonest conduct, to profit from the technologies of Dianetics and Scientology. The subjects were developed for spiritual salvation, not for anyone's personal enrichment. By owning the trademarks and copyrights of the religion and enforcing their proper use, the Church can ensure such ill-intentioned actions will never occur" (www.scientology.org/faq/scientology-in-society/why-is-everything-copyrighted-and-trademarked-in-scientology.html, accessed June 2018).

5   In determining if a use is fair, and thus not infringement, Courts are to consider four statutory factors on a case-by-case basis: "(1) the purpose and character of the use, including whether such use is of a commercial nature or is for nonprofit educational purposes; (2) the nature of the copyrighted work; (3) the amount and substantiality of the portion used in relation to the copyrighted work as a whole; and (4) the effect of the use upon the potential market for or value of the copyrighted work." 17 U.S.C. §107.

[*Mystery*] new members who tithe ten percent of their income to PCG, and by enabling the ministry's growth" (WCG, p. 1118).

The Court then makes fairly short work of the second and third factors, finding that *Mystery* is a creative (not factual) work, that PCG copies the entirety of it, and that such copying is not like the home recording of a TV program to watch it later. Instead, "PCG uses the MOA as a central element of its members' religious observance; a reasonable person would expect PCG to pay WCG for the right to copy and distribute MOA created by WCG with its resources" (WCG, pp. 1118–1119).

Finally, the Court finds that PCG appropriation of the text damages WCG's market for those who might be interested in the Church because of *Mystery*, arguing that "PCG's distribution of its unauthorized version of MOA thus harms WCG's goodwill by diverting potential members and contributions from WCG" (WCG, p. 1119). That WCG did not plan to publish the book did not mean it no longer retained rights over the material, which it now found heretical.[6] WCG argued that it planned to produce an annotated version of the work (presumably with errors noted and explained); when PCG replied that the annotated text would not be the same and could not serve the same purpose as the original, the Court reiterated its original point: "the argument . . . misses the point. The fact remains that PCG has unfairly appropriated MOA in its entirety for the very purposes for which WCG created MOA" (WCG, p. 1120).

The fair use analysis, whatever one thinks of the outcome, is notable for its application of the four statutory standards and the effort to interpret the litigation in the terms suggested by traditional copyright analysis in terms of markets and market harm. Judge Melvin Brunetti's dissent, on the other hand, proposes that fair use be understood as an "equitable rule of reason." For the first factor, Brunetti argues that "the noncommercial and religious elements of PCG's use overwhelm any commercial aspects" and push toward a finding of fair use. After suggesting that the second and third are irrelevant in this case, he turns to the fourth. Here, he finds WCG's objections to continuing to distribute *Mystery* as dispositive in ruling that PCG is not depriving WCG of present or future market value, since "WCG's decision to cease publication of MOA, destroy inventory copies, and disavow MOA's religious message in the context of its doctrinal shift as a church demonstrates that MOA is no longer of value to WCG for" attracting tithing members (WCG, p. 1124). He then dissects the claim about a future annotated version:

> In contrast to PCG's evangelical use, the central purpose behind WCG's proposed annotated version of MOA is to identify Armstrong's historical, doctrinal, and social errors. The target markets for the two versions of MOA are different because it simply does not make sense for WCG to widely distribute an annotated MOA

[6] John Tehranian (2012) suggests that texts which occupy a "sacralized" social status (his example is J. D. Salinger's *Catcher in the Rye*) are more likely to succeed in warding off fair use claims. Here that is literally true.

highlighting the errors of the original MOA to the general public in order to recruit new members.

(WCG, p. 1124)

In short, as he concludes, "WCG appears less interested in protecting its rights to exploit MOA than in suppressing Armstrong's ideas which now run counter to church doctrine" (WCG, p. 1125). Unlike the analysis in the majority opinion, the dissent foregrounds precisely the questions of religion as a way of life, and the role that access to *Mystery* plays in it.

I do not wish to assess the validity of either argument. What I do want to emphasize is that their logics are subtly different. In ways that I will make explicit, the majority's focus on economic power and markets evidences one background set of assumptions about the social role of IP, and the dissent's emphasis on communal religious practices evidences another.

1.2 THEORIZING THE EXPANSION OF IP

In a general sense, IP – principally copyright, patent and trademark – seems to have insinuated itself into all aspects of life. It is in the mundane – the proliferation of brand logos on everything, or the sudden disappearance of videos from YouTube – and it is in the vital, as in the price of prescription drugs. This observation is reflected in academic work, where it has been commonplace over the last twenty years or so to claim that IP is rapidly growing in legal and social importance. For example, after citing debates around the patentability of the human genome, James Boyle puts matters this way:

> The genome is not the only area to be partially "enclosed" during this second enclosure movement. The expansion of intellectual property rights has been remarkable – from business method patents, to the Digital Millennium Copyright Act, to trademark "anti-dilution" rulings, to the European Database Protection Directive. The old limits to intellectual property rights – the anti-erosion walls around the public domain – are also under attack. The annual process of updating my syllabus for a basic intellectual property course provides a nice snapshot of what is going on. I can wax nostalgic looking back to a five-year-old text, with its confident list of subject matter that intellectual property rights could not cover, the privileges that circumscribed the rights that did exist, and the length of time before a work falls into the public domain. In each case, the limits have been eaten away.

(2008, p. 46)

Boyle is one of the most prominent critics of the expansion of IP, and three of the expansions Boyle cites – patents on genetic code, the anti-circumvention provisions of the Copyright Act, and the expansion of trademark into anti-dilution – will be among the principal case studies of this book.

Legal developments do not occur in a vacuum, and there are technological, political, and larger economic forces at play. One of the most significant technological factors is digitization, as the move to digital technologies means that more aspects of daily life are covered by IP. For example, to read something on a computer requires making a copy of it in the computer's memory, so virtually anything done online involves copyright. More consequentially, perhaps, the Digital Millennium Copyright Act of 1998 made it illegal to tamper with copyright protection schemes built into things like DVD players, making it illegal to evade regional coding, copyright notices, and (frequently) advertising. Both the easy copying that the DMCA provision was designed to thwart and the way it tries to do so are affordances of digital technologies. On the political side, pressure by content owners is a significant factor in driving a steady upward ratcheting of IP law itself, which now lasts longer, covers more areas, and is treated as more important than ever before. For example, the Copyright Term Extension Act of 1998 retroactively extended copyright protections for twenty years, keeping Mickey Mouse out of the public domain for that period. In a more general sense, Susan Sell (2003) argued that the current expansion in IP was at the initiative of twelve pharma executives who engaged in a sustained campaign to make IP important to Congress, first as an international trade and competitiveness issue. Finally, the development of neoliberalism in the larger economy is, as I will demonstrate in detail, a significant factor both in driving changes in IP and in what those changes are. Neoliberalism has accompanied a relative decline in the importance of traditional, Fordist manufacturing to the economy, and the rising importance of immaterial goods and services.[7]

The expansion of IP is important to track and understand. But, as the story of Armstrong and *Mystery* indicates, behind it there is another question: what, exactly, does IP law *do*? More precisely, as an exercise in law, it is also an exercise in sociopolitical power.[8] Power comes in a variety of forms, of course, from social norms against smoking to spending by corporations to influence legislation. Law is thus only one institutional structure through which power operates, but it is nonetheless an important one, especially where, as here, IP is so central to culture. A moment's reflection will validate the further intuition that even legal power operates in different ways. A law requiring the installation of speed bumps, for example, operates on different premises from a law appropriating funds to hire more police officers,

---

[7] For neoliberalism, see the discussion in Chapter 2. For a succinct history, see Harvey (2005).

[8] The analysis here thus has much in common with critical legal studies and other critical or "postmodern" accounts of law. There is a rich literature, much of it important to what follows, on the nexus of IP and critical legal theories. For a survey, see, e.g., Craig (2019) (including a substantial literature review); Goodrich, Katyal, and Tushnet (2013) (giving their own theoretical backgrounds); and Tehranian (2012) (arguing that IP is central in preserving hegemonic social structures and norms). My emphasis on Foucault's later work, in particular on the different kinds of forms of power expressed by law, and on the ways that power exists as a process of subjectification, has received less emphasis (but not none, of course: see the discussion of Coombe, later).

even if the goal in both cases is to reduce speeding. An eighteenth-century public torture and execution is clearly premised on a different understanding of legal punishment than current debates about minimizing the pain experienced during an execution. It is that kind of question, about the nature of power expressed in IP, that this book addresses.

The core of my argument is that the kind of power expressed in IP is subtly changing. Initial evidence for this claim is that new doctrinal developments have been difficult to incorporate into traditional models of IP. For example, retroactive copyright extension is hard to square with a theory that says copyright is about incentives to create new works. Presumably, Walt Disney will be unmotivated by any changes in IP today. Trademark dilution, which allows action against expression that damages a brand's image in consumers' minds, is difficult to square with the standard theory that says that trademark is about avoiding consumer confusion. And the patentability of living organisms and (until recently) isolated genetic fragments is difficult to reconcile with the traditional view that products of nature should not receive patent protections. In cases such as these, I will argue, it is necessary to recognize that IP is performing a different and new social function, one that requires a rethinking of the kind of power expressed by IP laws and regulations.

I take my theoretical starting point from the work of Michel Foucault, for whom modern power has operated in two basic forms.[9] The first, associated with the social contract tradition, conceptualizes a rights-bearing, juridical subject, for whom law operates as a system of constraint and coercion. That which law does not prohibit is allowed, and the most important questions revolve around the limits to law's ability to prohibit. The second, associated with the modern, administrative state, Foucault calls "biopower" or "biopolitics," and it is concerned with productively managing and even optimizing populations through such measures as public health and education programs. Biopower is thus fundamentally generative. Closely aligned with the rise of capitalism, biopower has emerged as central to the operation of the modern state, which tends to emphasize regulatory agencies and administrative law, even if it also retains a framework of judicial rights.

In the years since Foucault's death in 1984, it has become clear that biopower has at least two forms. One is concerned with the productivity of populations in a general sense, and can be seen in large-scale, publicly funded infrastructure programs. The second, a neoliberal variant, attempts to achieve many of the same results by directly incentivizing individual behaviors. The strategies and techniques of neoliberal biopolitics derive from an extension of economic reasoning to all factors of life. If classical liberalism attempted to allow markets to function,

---

[9] I offer a detailed analysis in the following chapter; the primary Foucault texts on this topic are all initially from the mid-late 1970s: *Discipline and Punish* [1975], *History of Sexuality, Vol. I* [1976], *Society Must Be Defended* [lectures from 1975–1976] and *Security, Territory, Population* [lectures from 1977–1978]. Foucault offers an initial reading of neoliberal theory, especially Gary Becker, in *Birth of Biopolitics* [lectures from 1978–1979].

neoliberalism not only tries to create markets where previously there had been none, it also understands problems and regulations only insofar as they are presented in market-oriented terms. Individuals are no longer rights-bearing subjects or equivalent members of a population; instead, they are understood to be economically rational agents, seeking to maximize their own outcomes. Good policies are those which are efficient in facilitating this process. For example, if developing human capital is a goal of government, then citizens need to understand themselves as involved in developing their human capital; a decision to pursue education or good health practices should be something that people make on the basis of expected returns on that investment. Similarly, people should avoid behaviors that are likely to damage their future earning capacity. This process of subject formation, accomplished through a complex web of nudges, pushes, legal strictures, environmental and architectural restraints, works to create the sorts of individuals who most easily work toward neoliberal biopolitical aims.

A quick look at the US Constitutional text suggests that IP exists at the nexus of juridical and public biopower.[10] The goal – progress in the arts and sciences – is clearly biopolitical, but the mechanism – property rights – is juridical. It is my central contention that IP has shifted markedly (if unevenly) in the last twenty years or so in the direction of neoliberal biopolitics. Even when they were economically justified, earlier iterations of IP functioned much more along the public biopower model, attempting to improve the welfare of the public as a whole, with provisions such as limits on term length designed to ensure that the public benefited as much and as quickly as possible. Neoliberal IP maintains the idea of welfare enhancement, but it grants many more rights to producers, and instead of benefiting the public at large, it increasingly targets individuals in the public directly, reconceptualizing them as consumers and their welfare in strictly economic terms.

At the same time, the expression of power in IP is deeply contested within the very institutions through which it operates. For example, the Supreme Court's patent jurisprudence has repeatedly insisted that IP is to be treated juridically, through standard judicial norms and vocabularies. Similarly, §1201 of the Copyright Act, which prohibits the circumvention of copyright protection technologies, has operated in practice to allow copyright owners to regulate how copyrighted material is consumed, strongly nudging individuals to approach this material only as paying customers, not as members of a more amorphous public. At the same time, the Copyright Office carves out periodic exemptions to the law for such public functions as education.

I thus trace, primarily through a series of studies of IP litigation, the contours of both the shift in statutory IP toward a neoliberal biopolitics and the various forms of

---

[10] Among the enumerated Congressional powers is: "To promote the progress of science and useful arts, by securing for limited times to authors and inventors the exclusive right to their respective writings and discoveries" (U.S. Constitution, Art. 1, §8, clause 8).

resistance and contestation that it has produced. The book's case studies cross a range of interdisciplinary sites, from the permissibility of music sampling, to whether association with sex damages the brand of Victoria's Secret lingerie, to the metaphysical status of isolated gene fragments. Drawing on the resources of law, philosophy, and critical social theory, I develop the vocabulary and theory for a more nuanced understanding of both IP law's development and what it actually does. As it moves unevenly toward expressing neoliberal biopower, IP becomes more immediately involved in producing and directing the lives of individuals. Specifically, it moves toward fostering forms of subjectivity that take market-relations as normal, that approach issues of culture and life as appropriately mediated by markets, and that treat the appropriate relation to cultural goods as that of consumer. This is in sharp contrast to earlier understandings of IP, which spoke in terms of the rights of creators, or of the need to remove obstacles to markets, or which worried about the deleterious effects of artificial monopolies. IP, then, makes people. Its current, neoliberal version increasingly tries to make people conform to the image of idealized economic agent, always and already participating in a society which is intelligible only in market terms.

I make no attempt to write a comprehensive history of IP or any of its component parts. Others have done that far better than I could. Rather, the focus is on detailed analysis of specific cases that I take to be illustrative of the emergence of neoliberal biopower and the way it functions as a form of subjectification. Some aspects of IP, which have been central to recent discussions, receive relatively little treatment here. So too, I will put considerable emphasis on Court decisions when discussing concrete legal developments. This is in part for the sake of convenience, insofar as these decisions present well-publicized treatments of often difficult or controversial issues. It is also because judicial opinions both track and contribute to social and institutional understandings of what law is. This is not just in the basic sense of the Court's role in articulating what statutory requirements are, or whether they conflict with constitutional strictures. Court decisions also offer a window into the kind of thinking that animates concrete decisions about how IP functions as a form of law. In other words, because of their role in framing what IP law does, court opinions offer a readily legible index to how IP functions socially, and how institutional structures debate and articulate differing models of power.

The book is also limited in that it does not attempt to treat innovation policy as a whole. This is partly for reasons of scope, but there are also two substantive reasons why I limit my attention to IP theory, copyright, trademark, and patents. First, treating innovation policy more generally risks putting the cart before the horse: the centrality of "innovation" to economic policy and its subsequent centrality to neoliberal IP policy is a historically specific phenomenon, dating roughly to Schumpeter. The centrality of innovation has been instrumental to the rise of neoliberalism. To start with innovation is to risk assuming the neoliberal frame the contingency of which I aim to demonstrate. That said, I do more in Chapter 2 to

situate innovation in the context of neoliberalism, and return briefly in the conclusion to questions of innovation policy and the role of IP within it.

Second, the treatment here is specific to property theory and developments in the
understanding of property. Copyright, trademark, and patents can all readily be
treated this way. First Amendment theory, although clearly important insofar as it
interacts with IP, is not generally treated as a question of property. As a result,
I approach First Amendment issues only when directly relevant to the topic at hand.
More significantly, framing the discussion as a question of property necessarily
leaves trade secrets largely to the side. Content owners often pursue a mix of IP
and trade secret claims to protect their interests, as Orly Lobel's (2018) discussion of
litigation surrounding Barbie vividly illustrates. That said, trade secrets have historically been a poor fit with IP. Most fundamentally, trade secrets protect information
only insofar as they are both generally not known and their owner make reasonable
efforts to keep them secret. IP regimes, on the other hand, generally require
disclosure of the protected content. In addition, because the cause for action
involves the illegitimate acquisition of information, and because that most often
happens when employees leave a job or someone violates a contract, trade secret law
tends to rely for enforcement on torts about confidentiality and on contract law. It
seems to me that the social meaning of contracts has changed substantially since the
emergence of social contract theory and texts like the US Constitution, but to
properly trace that genealogy (with attention to such topics as mandatory arbitration,
the *Lochner* era, adhesion contracts, and so forth) and its implications for our
current understanding of IP is well beyond the scope of what can be attempted
here.[11] Thus, trade secrets do make the occasional appearance here, but a more
thorough treatment remains for another time.

1.3 THE CORE THEORY

Although I will articulate a much more precise version of the argument in Chapter 2,
it will perhaps be useful here to put my primary theoretical apparatus on the table.
It has two components. One is a thesis about power and the other is a thesis about
people.

The thesis about power is that it is possible to see, in a variety of institutional and
social practices, the functioning of an implicit understanding of what power is and

---

[11] It would also attend to critical work on contracts that emerges in the wake of Carole Pateman's
Sexual Contract. Social contract theory has been enormously important in the history of
political philosophy; one task of a genealogy of contract would be to trace the interaction
between the emergence of social contract theory and developments in court systems, especially
in England. For evidence that there is a story to tell here, see Kary (1999/2000). I have also
argued that the earliest modern social contract theory is biopolitical in underappreciated ways;
see Hull (2009b). For the history of trade secret doctrine, see, e.g., Bone (1998). In the
conclusion, I return to the status of trade secrets in the context of public biopolitics.

does. It's a thesis that is best introduced by its most famous example, presented in Michel Foucault's *Discipline and Punish*. Foucault opens the book with graphic newspaper accounts of an eighteenth-century execution. The unfortunate inmate is carted to a public scaffold (erected specially for the occasion) and systematically dismembered with red-hot pincers (again, specially made). Still alive, he was to be drawn and quartered; when that proved impossible, the executioner manually cut his body into pieces. His body was then burned and the ashes scattered. Foucault then cites, by way of contrast, a rules manual for a prison in Paris some seventy years later. There, the entire focus was on micromanaging the prisoners' every move with a goal toward their rehabilitation. Whatever else one thinks of the differences between the scenarios, it seems clear that they can be distinguished by the thought that they operationalize very different views of what "punishment" is and what it is supposed to achieve.

Moving outside Foucault's discussion makes the point even clearer. In a late dialogue on law by Thomas Hobbes, a lawyer (who is an Edward Coke stand-in) proposes that the punishment for high treason is:

> To be drawn upon a Hurdle from the Prison to the Gallows, and there to be hanged by the Neck, and laid upon the ground alive, and have his bowels taken out, and burnt, whilst he is yet living; to have his Head cut off, his Body to be divided into four parts, and his Head, and Quarters to be placed as the King shall assign.

(1971, p. 163)

In the ensuing discussion, the lawyer defends both a variety of forms of execution for different offenses and different forms of execution for different instances of the same offense. The contrast is stark between the seventeenth-century lawyer's catalog of punishments and a context in which the Supreme Court can rule on whether a sedative designed to minimize pain during a lethal injection is sufficiently reliable, and debate whether execution is itself excessively cruel.[12]

The second point is that current models of IP are about making people. Here I want to assemble enough examples to make the claim seem coherent as a topic; later chapters will develop both the examples and the argument in more detail. One way to put the point is to contrast two kinds of questions. One, frequently invoked in debates around the price of patented medicines, concerns access: how do we understand questions about who has access to IP? This question is vitally important, and undergirds a growing body of literature that approaches IP from a point of social justice.

The second approaches similar material, but somewhat orthogonally, and asks: how does IP shape who we are as people? The litigation surrounding WCG offers one example. In becoming a primary mechanism through which access to a religious text could be mediated, copyright became an important aspect of how

---

[12] *Glossip v. Gross*, 135 S.Ct. 2726 (2015).

the affected people would be able to understand their own religious identity, and thus one of the most intimate aspects of themselves. Copyright became a very real part of who they were. As discussed earlier, the WCG example is not isolated, even in terms of access to religious texts; both Scientology texts and the Dead Sea Scrolls have been the subjects of copyright litigation. Copyright also influences our racial self-understandings. The family of Martin Luther King, Jr., has used copyright to control dissemination of his texts and images, and the discovery of a trove of Malcolm X's papers in 2002 led to further litigation about who could curate them. Rosa Parks sued the band Outkast in an unsuccessful effort to remove a reference to her from one of their songs (Schur, 2011, pp. 19–23). Insofar as King, Malcoim, and Parks are partly constitutive of how Americans understand race, that understanding is at least partly mediated through IP. As I will argue in Chapter 3 on copyright, hip hop in particular has an uneasy relation with copyright, and litigation against music sampling has had substantial impacts on the aesthetic of the medium.

IP's framing of our culture and thus our identities is not limited to copyright. If the question of access to medicine in patents is sufficiently obvious as a matter of life and death, consider the view of medical personhood implicit in genetic medicine. I will develop the point in much greater detail in Chapter 5 on patents, but dealing with cancer is no longer just a matter of finding and treating physiological evidence of a problem in the form of a tumor (as under older models); it is also about understanding one's genetic risk, the odds that one might be a future patient, and what one ought to do now (including such fundamental choices as whether to have children). Consider also trademark. Decisions about what to eat are fundamental to who we are. Under developing geographic-indicator rules, it will be impossible to purchase "parmesan" cheese from any place except that region. Toys also matter. Barbie is widely seen, for better or worse, as a fundamental image of womanhood that girls have to navigate as they mature. Mattel Corp. has spent tremendous resources over the years, using IP and other laws, to prevent the emergence of competing dolls in the toy market, culminating in a (failed) several hundred million dollar expenditure to stop the emergence of Bratz dolls (Lobel, 2018).

In all of these ways, the claim is that who we are is substantially a function of our environment, that IP is a fundamental feature of that environment, and so IP is a fundamental feature of who we are. The argument of this book is that it is increasingly, if unevenly, deliberately so, and that it is deliberately so in a direction designed to make us good subjects of contemporary neoliberal capitalism. This view of personhood as a function of one's environment may seem strange, especially to those of us who grew up in a theoretical tradition of social contract or classical liberalism: Is not a person a rational agent who can make free choices? I am drawing my critique of that position from French theory, but you do not need to go there to find support for it. Even a quick survey of marketing literature or behavioral economics will suffice to suggest that the view of the person as a rational, freely choosing individual who is exogenous to his or her social and cultural milieu is at best a theoretical abstraction, and one with a very tenuous relation to reality.

I am of course not the first person to bring subjectification and law together, even if one narrows the scope to IP. As Rosemary Coombe – situating her work in a rich body of literature at the intersection of "law" and "culture" – argued some twenty years ago:

> Law is an authoritative medium of a cultural politics in which the social is itself articulated. By recognizing that the social world must be represented, performatively expressed, and institutionally inscribed, we can avoid a metaphysics of political presence that presupposes a realm of self-evidently "political" practices ... Law is not simply an institutional forum or legitimating discourse to which social groups turn to have preexisting differences recognized, but, more crucially, it is a central locus for the control and dissemination of those signifying forms with which identities and differences are made and remade.
>
> (1998, pp. 28–29)

The present study exists in the space opened by work such as Coombe's, as well as more recent work such as that of Julie Cohen (see especially 2012). The framing here allows emphasis on two additional contributions that I hope to make. First, in situating the discussion at the level of cultural models of power, I draw attention to a neglected aspect of subjectification. It is not just that power is an important part of cultural processes; it is that different understandings of power work in very different ways to create very different kinds of subjects. This point is important because it enables one to see the ways that IP tracks broader cultural and economic movements toward neoliberalism. Many of the most contentious or apparently aberrant developments in IP become legible as aspects of this movement.

Second, the scholarship around Foucault, perhaps inspired by his rejection of excessive theoretical focus on the state and his remarks about the relative decline of juridical power, tends to ignore law and legal institutions as sites of power and contestation.[13] As I will emphasize, and as IP illustrates very clearly, the decline of juridical power does not mean that the state ceases to be a site of power, and the important caution against statism does not mean that the state is not important in understanding power, especially in contexts where state regulation intervenes directly into culturally important areas. At a very minimum, the neoliberal state is understood by its most coherent advocates to enable the function of markets. This is also the standard view of IP: It is a branch of law that spurs innovation by enabling

---

[13] For my argument, see Chapter 2. Much of the relevant earlier scholarship is contained in Golder and Fitzpatrick (2010). See also Golder and Fitzpatrick (2009). For the earlier view that Foucault argues that law and juridical power disappear with biopower, see Hunt (1992) and for a critique, see Tadros (1998). On law as a viable strategy for resistance even under biopower, see Bloom (2012), and for some theoretical commonalities between legal realism and Foucault, see Kennedy (1993). My own initial contribution to the Foucault/Law literature as it pertains to courts and biopower is Hull (2017).

markets in intangible goods to function. The scholarship that reads Foucault and moves too quickly away from law risks throwing out the baby with the bath water. The present text is intended as a corrective.

1.4 OUTLINE OF THE BOOK

In what follows, I briefly outline the structure of the book and its argument. In Chapter 2, I set out in detail the theoretical framework for the rest of the book, and show how that framework can illuminate previously under-theorized aspects of IP. I introduce the framing of IP in terms of Foucault's models of power, and the application of that frame to contemporary IP theory. Accordingly, the first section introduces the models of power I use in the book: juridical power (sovereignty and rights-based), public biopower (promoting the productivity and health of the population in a general way), and neoliberal biopower (same objective as biopower, but working on individuals and treating everything as part of the economy). I particularly emphasize the way that neoliberal biopower works to make a certain kind of subject, a *homo economicus* who behaves according to the dictates of economic rationality in all aspects of life. This concern with subject-formation – making people – emerges primarily in Foucault's late writings, but it is, I argue, central to understanding the models of power drawn from his work more broadly. To put the point bluntly, one of the most important ways that power functions is through techniques of subjectification.

I then trace IP from its emergence at the intersection of classical liberalism and juridical power, to the current neoliberal form. My focus is on the contrast between the early, public biopower version of IP and the current, neoliberal one. The earlier version relies on the notion of benefits to an amorphous public and worries about the effects of monopolies; the newer drops the aversion to monopoly and attempts to use property rights to capture and internalize public benefits, while putting pressure on individuals in the public to view their interaction with culture economically. I then analyze the current dominant theorization of IP in Demsetzian property theory, showing how it advances core claims of neoliberalism.

The book then turns to analyses of developments in specific areas of IP law. I begin with copyright because it is the area of IP law that is most neoliberal, by which I mean it is the branch of IP where there has been the least resistance to the law treating the interaction with culture as an economic exchange, and less a matter of either public benefit or individual rights. The chapter offers an account of why this is, as well as the limitations of the economic account in explaining it. The opening section looks at the idea that intellectual work and creative activity can be optimally incentivized in market terms. This model of copyright as providing incentives for cultural production is currently both dominant and easily challenged by both empirical and theoretical work on creativity. The section examines incentives theory as a particular form of neoliberal biopower (one aimed at producing subjects that conform to its demands) and shows how it occludes other understandings of cultural production, even within the copyright regime.

The remaining two sections look in detail at two recent developments at the intersection of copyright and culture. In the first case, litigation surrounding hip hop music sampling, I argue that the neoliberal model of copyright works to nudge music into commercial channels, where all cultural borrowing is mediated through market transactions. On this occasion, copyright makes people by making art. In the second case, I take up the recent expansion of copyright into what scholars have termed "paracopyright:" not copyright as the regulation of cultural production, but copyright as a prohibition on circumventing copyright protection technologies, which generally function as forms of "digital rights management" (DRM). Through a detailed examination of how DRM technologies – such as the regional restrictions on DVDs – function, I show how this addition to the law clearly marks a move of copyright in the direction of into training individuals that they are consumers of the products of culture.

Chapter 2 turns to developments in trademark. The fit between neoliberal models of subjectification and trademark is less precise than in copyright, but by contextualizing the analysis in the context of the development of brand capitalism, I argue that aspects of trademark doctrine are almost uniquely explicable in those terms. Traditional trademark analysis displayed the features of a public biopolitics; developments around branding push it in a neoliberal direction. I emphasize the way that the intersection of law and markets works to make people into brand-focused consumers, who understand themselves in terms of brand loyalties. The best doctrinal example of this process is the emergence of trademark dilution. Nearly inexplicable by an economic analysis grounded in public biopower, dilution doctrine can be better understood as a form of biopower designed to facilitate neoliberal brand loyalties and affective attachments to brands. After an analysis of the emergence of dilution and its departure from more market-based views of trademark, I turn to an extended case study of Victoria's Secret's successful attempt to shut down a sex-toy shop that called itself "Victor's Little Secret."

I then offer a reading of the problem of disparaging trademarks, with particular focus on sports mascots and the recent *Tam* case, in which the Supreme Court ruled that PTO rules against registration of disparaging trademarks violated the First Amendment. The *Tam* decision provides an initial example of juridical resistance to expanding IP, but it also (despite itself) serves to legitimate the push toward branding by removing a mechanism by which the state might attempt to influence this process. I then turn toward the global extension of trademark law into the protection of "traditional" cultural indicia. For a long time, trademark protection has been applied in most countries to food and alcohol; both European farmers and indigenous groups are pursuing the strategy as a way to protect local economies. I argue that this resistance strategy is a dubious one, insofar as it risks entrenching conservative and stereotypical views of cultural groups, often at the expense of dissident forms of cultural affiliation. The strategy thus illustrates an unexpected way that branding can function as a form of subjectification, and the potential limits of using trademarks and branding as strategies of resistance.

The final main chapter (Chapter 5) treats developments in patents. Patent law is where the messy evolution of IP into neoliberal biopower is most contested, substantially because it is here that the Supreme Court has repeatedly pushed back against it. This pushback has understandably been a source of confusion; the chapter here provides a new theoretical framework through which to interpret it. In the opening section, I lay out the emergence of a new model of medicine in genomics and other biotechnologies and show how that model functions as a form of neoliberal subjectification insofar as it conceptualizes health as a form of risk management and human capital development.

I then turn to the difficult question of the patentability of isolated gene fragments. The Supreme Court's decision rejecting such patentability was a surprise to most observers. Looking at the litigation at both the appellate and Supreme Court levels, I examine how judicial understandings of patentability intersect with the test for the BRCA1/2 mutation. Because gene fragments were routinely considered as patentable for nearly a generation before the Supreme Court's decision, the litigation and the research around cancer-causing genes offer a nearly ideal case study of the stakes in how one models the form of power underlying subject-matter patentability, and how patentability encourages the development of neoliberal agents who model their health in terms borrowed from financial risk.

I then turn to other areas where the Supreme Court appears to be pushing back against an expansive, biopolitical notion of patentability. Specifically, I show how the Supreme Court's recent revival of patent exhaustion doctrine as well as several decisions on subject-matter patentability all represent a juridically based effort to limit patent protections. In the final section of the chapter, I make explicit a question which has been underlying the analysis throughout, the extent to which IP functions as a form of "property." Specifically, nearly all theories of biopower note the rise of the administrative state, often at the expense of judicial law, as central to the emergence and functioning of biopower. The chapter concludes by studying the Court's ruling upholding the PTO's *inter partes* review process. The administrative state is a key feature of public biopolitics, and the opinion, concurrence, and dissent clearly illustrate what is at stake in the intersection of differing understandings of power and IP law.

In the brief concluding Chapter 6, I both provide a condensed case for why the analysis of IP through differing regimes of power is a fruitful one, and detail a couple of its implications. One is that we need to be attentive to the way IP law creates certain kinds of subjects, and to be willing to critique it on those lines. The other takes the form of a brief discussion of alternatives proposed to IP, in such areas as "low IP" zones and in creative commons-style proposals. I will conclude that the degree to which those fundamentally challenge the neoliberalization of IP, and its move away from public biopower, is essential in assessing the extent to which they actually are alternative. The goal is not to be strongly prescriptive, but, in the manner of Foucault, to help figure out what are the right questions to ask.

Theorizing Intellectual Property

In what follows, I develop the theoretical lens of this book. In brief, I will argue that the question of what IP does can be approached through an analysis of how power operates socially. That, in turn, requires an understanding of what we are talking about when we talk about "power." I will argue that there are three competing ways of understanding power that are relevant in the present context. One is the power of law in the traditional, "juridical" sense: Repressive and coercive, "law" tells you what to do and prescribes penalties for not doing it. The second, emergent in classical liberalism – around the same time as the first IP policies – I will call "public biopolitics." Power in this sense is less a matter of repressing than it is of generating, of harnessing the life energies of a population toward some sort of end, usually cashed out in terms of public/social welfare. The third, currently ascendant, is that of neoliberal biopolitics. Neoliberal biopolitics takes from its public predecessor a concern with generation and optimization, but drops the focus on the public sphere: Neoliberalism is a regime of intense privatization.[1]

The central theoretical claim I will make is that intellectual property (IP) evidences a move away from both juridical law and public biopower, and toward neoliberalism. This process is uneven, incomplete, and contested, but the trend is

[1] As Phillip Mirowski notes, neoliberalism is not a monolithic entity; it does "not impart a dose of that Old Time Religion. Not only is there no ur-text of neoliberalism; the neoliberals have not themselves opted to retreat into obscurantism ... you won't often catch them wondering, 'What Would Hayek Do?'" (2013, p. 51). Mirowski identifies thirteen overlapping theoretical features of what he calls the "Neoliberal Thought Collective," many but not all of them recognizably adapted from neoclassical economics. These include the need to construct markets; the market as information processor for social needs by way of the price mechanism; a rejection of neoclassical accounts of market failure and externalities; the need to convince people to endorse a neoliberal theory they would probably reject if asked; a redefinition of the human subject as economic; and a redefinition of "freedom" as economic. Two features are common to all of these, both of which are foci here: the spread of economic thinking into all aspects of life, and an effort to convince individuals that they are in fact agents in the sense that neoliberalism says they are or should be.

nonetheless evident in a number of doctrinal areas. In so doing, IP has begun to adopt two of the key techniques of neoliberal biopower. The first is the production of a specific "truth" about what it means to be a person. All ways of life of course encourage an understanding of what it really means to be human; in the case of neoliberal biopolitics what it means to be human is to be a rationalizing economic agent: The human is *homo economicus*. The second technique, consequent upon the first, is that neoliberalism deploys an intense strategy of "subjectification," which is to say that neoliberalism deploys a number of strategies for making people into exemplars of *homo economicus*. I will develop specific examples of how IP has adopted these strategies of subjectification in subsequent chapters, and suggest that they help to explain otherwise puzzling departures from the traditional goals of IP.

The present chapter examines the ways that IP is traditionally theorized, in particular the arguments that are typically taken to justify it. There has been a marked shift in the language used to study IP. The original framing was along the lines of classical liberalism. Current theory draws much more from the law and economics movement that has gained steady ascendency since its rise at the University of Chicago in the 1950s and 1960s. It is important to attend to this theoretical shift because not only does it track the changes in policy fairly closely, but it also provides a clue as to how we understand IP. In other words, if we take as a premise that IP is about making people, an important part of how it does so is found in how we talk about IP. Tracing the sorts of arguments that find academic traction, the ones that do not, and the ones that are deemed unintelligible provides an important, initial clue to understanding how IP policy is made, and what it does.

The chapter is organized into two primary parts. The first part develops the understanding of power articulated earlier, with primary reference to Foucault and more recent work on neoliberalism. The second part uses this analysis to look at theoretical justifications of IP. In particular, I track the emergence and subsequent occlusion of IP as a form of public biopolitics, and study in detail the primary neoliberal narrative currently at the core of IP theory and policy. I include a brief proof of concept about subjectification using recent work on the construction of university science and the kind of person that university researchers are encouraged to become. The discussion in the second section, which focuses on the work of Harold Demsetz, sets the broader framework for understanding the doctrinal developments studied in subsequent chapters and illustrates the extent to which academic discussion of IP is now heavily dominated by neoliberal biopolitics.

2.1 THEORIZING POWER

2.1.1 *Models of Power*

Power is not some sort of abstract essence sitting in the ether. Power only exists as it is exercised and practiced in and by institutions, social norms, individuals, and so on. That said, power tends to act in specifiable ways during different historical periods. The boundaries between these periods are necessarily fuzzy, and there is considerable overlap but, drawing on the work of Michel Foucault, I will contend here that there are three different models or kinds of power that are most relevant in understanding contemporary developments in IP. Two of them – juridical and what I call "public biopower" – were central to Foucault's research. The third, neoliberal biopower, has largely emerged institutionally since his death in 1984, although he was able to develop a prescient reading of neoliberal theory in a late 1970s lecture course.

In the mid-to-late 1970s, Foucault distinguished between what he called "juridical power" and "biopower." Juridical power, which is the model that most of us have when we think about power, is characterized as repressive; a sovereign uses it either "to take life or let live." As Foucault explains in his 1976 *History of Sexuality*, "the sovereign exercises his right of life only by exercising his right to kill, or by refraining from killing; he evidenced his power over life only through the death he was capable of requiring" (1988a, p. 136). Foucault opens his *Discipline and Punish* (1975 [1977]) with a graphic example of sovereign power at work, quoting explicit newspaper accounts of an execution in 1714 that involved public burning and dismembering of the convict. The execution functions as a paradigmatic example of sovereign power: The sovereign is at war with the body of the subject, establishing his sovereign power at the expense of that body. As the rest of Foucault's book demonstrates, and as a moment's reflection on how our society handles the death penalty makes clear, we no longer view power and its privileges in the same way.

In a lecture from roughly the same period, Foucault explains the emergence of rights discourse within juridical power. Essentially, kings used rights language to establish their prerogatives over feudal lords; "in this battle between feudal powers and monarchical power, right was always the instrument of monarchical power against the institutions, customs, prescriptions and forms of bond and belonging characteristic of feudal society" (2012). Once the feudal lords had been abolished, the rising bourgeoisie turned rights language against the monarchy, eventually abolishing the monarchy with it. Importantly, both the monarchy and the bourgeoisie used the same understanding of power to ground their arguments; the bourgeoisie "had every interest in developing a system of rights that would permit it to give form to economic exchanges that assured its own social development. The result being that the vocabulary and form of rights was the system of representation of power common to the bourgeoisie and the monarchy" (2012). That is, all sides came to agree on an understanding of politics and power that centered on the coercive and repressive powers of government, which is then limited by the rights of subjects. One important mechanism is the representation of citizens as autonomous agents entering into contractual relationships with one another. Hence "the constitution of political power is therefore constituted by this series, or is modeled on a juridical operation similar to an exchange of contracts" (2003, p. 13).

The burden of Foucault's arguments about power in the late 1970s is to suggest that the juridical model of power is obsolete, or at least of diminishing importance. As he put it in the lecture course, "we must now free ourselves from this juridical conception of power ... if we wish to proceed towards an analysis of the real functioning of power, rather than its mere representation" (2012). Two clarifications need to be made immediately. On the one hand, this does not mean that judicial institutions or legislation go away as sites of power. Rather, they tend to operate differently. It is important to distinguish between the institutions through which power operates and the techniques that characterize it.[2] On the other hand, it is also not to say that we have witnessed a clean break and that juridical power has gone away, but it is to say that a new model of power is increasingly important.[3]

[2] This book offers evidence in support of the point; I make it in a different context in Hull (2017). Foucault's discussion of Bentham in *Birth of Biopolitics* is instructive: there he argues that Bentham's efforts at reforms (which epitomize disciplinary power and panopticism) were attempted through legal institutions and the law as such. Moving beyond the theoretical confines of the law is one of the moves that characterize neoliberal thought on criminality. This different view of the interaction of explanatory frames and institutions then generates different views of human subjectivity. See Foucault (2008, pp. 248–252). As all of this suggests, legal institutions remain essential to biopower, even as the laws they regulate and express change in nature. Law becomes essential to neoliberalism as it moves into the law and economics movement, of which Judge Richard Posner is probably the most famous theorist (on law and economics as an essential part of neoliberalism, see W. Davies (2014) and the detailed discussion below); see also Biebricher (2014) (on the ways that classic neoliberalism theorizes sovereignty, all of which stem from the difficult-to-solve need for the state to adjudicate impartially between private parties); Harcourt (2011) (on the importance of the state in establishing free markets); and Tzouvala (2017) (on the rise of international, legalistic neoliberal institutions, as exemplified by the WTO dispute-resolution system).
    This point has perhaps been more difficult than it should be in the context of Foucault scholarship because of Foucault's own, somewhat inconsistent remarks on the topic. On the one hand, he seems to be resolutely anti-statist. For example, in the early lectures of *Society Must Be Defended*, he famously says that "we have to study power outside the model of Leviathan, outside the field delineated by juridical sovereignty and the institution of the State" (2003, p. 34). Similarly, in the *History of Sexuality I*, he proposes that once power is over not just legal subjects but living beings as such, a "consequence of this development of bio-power was the growing importance assumed by the action of the norm at the expense of the juridical system of the law" (1988a, p. 144). He adds that "I do not mean to say that the law fades into the background or that the institutions of justice tend to disappear, but rather that the law operates more and more as a norm" (1988a, p. 144). These texts are almost exactly contemporary to one another. Two years later, in the *Security, Territory, Population* lectures, he acknowledges that the rise of norms turns out to require a lot of new law: "what is important for our modernity, that is to say, for our present, is not then the state's takeover of society, so much as what I would call the 'governmentalization' of the state" (2007, p. 109). Foucault also emphasizes the "increasingly huge set of legislative measures" and "real inflation of the juridico-legal code" necessary to enable the rise of security as a state administrative tactic (2007, p. 7). Accordingly, an account of the late twentieth-century legal system needs to accommodate the rise of regulatory law and "a general movement towards and expanding legalization and juridification of social life" (Hunt, 1992, p. 17). Or, as François Ewald says, "normalization tends to be accompanied by an astonishing proliferation of legislation" (1990, p. 38).

[3] Foucault initially tended to speak as if one model of power displaced another. He clarifies in 1978 that "there is not a series of successive elements, the appearance of the new causing the

According to Foucault, power today is generative and not repressive, and because of this switch in orientation, it operates directly on life itself, and not, for example, by way of juridical, rights-bearing subjects. This is evident in two aspects. One is disciplinary, and involves the training of the bodies of subjects to perform in certain predictable ways, and to internalize the demands of power, to desire what power needs them to. The other he calls "a biopolitics of the population" which is focused on the "administration of bodies and the calculated management of life" and "problems of birthrate, longevity, public health, housing and migration" (1988a, p. 140).[4]

Foucault's formulation of the terms in his 1975–1976 Collège de France lectures provides further clarification. There, he suggests that one of the "greatest transformations political right underwent in the nineteenth century" was the replacement of the old sovereign power to "take life or let live" with its inversion, the "right to make live and to let die." Starting in the seventeenth century, one can observe that "the problem of life began to be problematized in the field of political thought," and a roughly contemporaneous development saw the "emergence of techniques of power that were essentially centered on the body." These disciplinary techniques had been the focus of his 1975 *Discipline and Punish*. Now, however, he proposes that "we see something new emerging in the second half of the eighteenth century," a technology of power that "does not exclude" disciplinary power "but does dovetail into it, integrate it, modify it to some extent, and above all, use it by sort of infiltrating it, embedding itself in existing disciplinary techniques" (2003, pp. 241–242).

Although embedded in discipline, this "'biopolitics' of the human race" is distinguished by its operation on "a multiplicity of men, not to the extent that they are nothing more than their individual bodies, but to the extent that they form, on the contrary, a global mass that is affected by overall processes characteristic of birth, death, production, illness, and so on" (2003, p. 243). With the emergence of this biopolitics comes the emergence of its key object of analysis, the statistically constructed "population." The late seventeenth century begins to see the rise of statistics and demographics, and of issues that "become pertinent only at the mass

---

earlier ones to disappear ... What above all changes is the dominant characteristic, or more exactly, the system of correlation between juridico-legal mechanisms, disciplinary mechanisms, and mechanisms of security [the term he uses here to designate the techniques of biopower]" (2007, p. 8). For discussion of this point, see Collier (2009).

[4] In what follows, I will not be making much of a possible distinction between "biopower" and "governmentality." The latter term is clearly broader in its potential application. However, insofar as it develops at the same time as biopolitics, it seems fair to me to say, on Foucauldian grounds, that biopolitics is one form of governmentality. As he notes, one might ask why "study this insubstantial and vague domain covered by a notion as problematic and artificial as that of 'governmentality'? My immediate answer will be, of course, in order to tackle the problem of the state and population" (2007, p. 116). I will therefore speak sometimes of biopolitical governmentality and other times of biopolitics; I mean the terms roughly equivalently.

level" (2003, p. 246). Among them are birth and death rates, hygiene, social insurance programs, and the like.

The point to emphasize is that power operates directly on "life," without taking a detour through the juridical subject. As Foucault's usage of the multivalent "population" suggests, "life" in this context needs to be understood broadly, encompassing not just (for example) the biological processes revealed in DNA coding, but also more sociocultural processes. There are very few human life processes that can be understood at a purely biological level. Eating, for example, is mediated by cultural context, as I will discuss at length in Chapter 4 on trademark with a look at geographical source protections for food and other products. Even more basic biological processes like disease rates are heavily mediated by social and cultural variables, as the differential disease burden between rich and poor countries, the rise of "lifestyle diseases" in rich countries, and the differential ways that diseases are researched all attest. In other words, a given human life is always more than the biological processes that undergird it.[5]

One reason I emphasize the broader reading of "life" is that it allows one to underscore the extent to which biopower also needs to be understood as a process of making people, or what Foucault calls "subjectification." That is, biopower works to create certain kinds of people who interact with others in specific kinds of ways.[6] There are various ways that this can happen; some give individuals constrained choices, others attempt to nudge decisions by changing social norms, and still others make resistance very difficult by means of code or other architectural mechanisms.[7] In a late interview, Foucault claims that his research into forms of power is really an aspect of research into subjectification, claiming that his object "has been to create a history of the different modes by which, in our culture, human beings are made subjects" (1982, p. 208). In a much earlier (1974) lecture, he had underscored that social practices can "give rise to totally new forms of subjects and subjects of

---

[5] In making this argument, I am taking a position in the literature on biopolitics, which tends to favor the more reductive reading as biological processes. I briefly defend the broader reading in Hull (2013).

[6] This analysis presupposes that the liberal notion of an autonomous, pre-existing subject who is then cast into a social situation is a theoretical confusion. Subjectivity can only arise through a complex series of social interactions by embodied individuals. For a defense of this view in the context of an information society, see Julie E. Cohen (2012). As will become apparent, it seems to me that both neoliberal and public biopolitics are acutely aware of this point, as many of the policies and regulations studied here make no sense except in the view that subjectivity is endogenous to social relations. The economically rational subject of much neoclassical economics is also a fiction, but (again) it seems to me that neoclassical economics is increasingly aware of this point, as the literature on preference formation and the large body of research in behavioral economics both attest: If the economically rational subject is a fiction, its creation is also aspirational and functions as a regulative ideal. For discussion of the function of stable preferences in Becker, see Vatter (2017).

[7] See Lessig (1998, 2006) for thoughts on how "code" can regulate. For more on how code and machines generate morality, see Latour (1992); for a normative defense, see Cheng (2006). For engineering of norms as policy, see Sunstein (1996).

knowledge" (1994b, p. 2). The relation between power, subjectification, and knowledge is important; as he emphasizes in several places, part of a regime of subjectification is a regime of truth. That is, part of what subjects do is produce and live a
"truth" about themselves.

In short, the kinds of people we are and the forms of knowledge we take to be
valuable do not preexist social and economic processes; they are created by them:

> In actual fact, the political and economic conditions of existence are not a veil or an
> obstacle for the subject of knowledge but the means by which subjects of know-
> ledge are formed, and hence are truth relations. There cannot be particular types of
> subjects of knowledge, orders of truth, or domains of knowledge except on the basis
> of political conditions that are the very ground on which the subject, the domains of
> knowledge, and the relations with truth are formed.
>
> (1994b, p. 15)

To understand subjects, you need to understand them as formed by interaction with
their social, economic, and political contexts. As I will argue later, this is especially
important in understanding the present shift into neoliberalism.

2.1.2 *Two Forms of Biopower*

If biopower is the form of power that is concerned with population management, as
distinct from earlier notions of juridical power and rights-bearing subjects, there are
nonetheless at least two significant variants of biopower. One of them, the earlier, is
much more concerned with public issues, and the later, neoliberal variant, is much
more focused on achieving public goals by way of private individuals.

A good example of this distinction is in health policy. By the end of the eighteenth
century, the catastrophic epidemics of the Middle Ages had retreated, and "something else" was at issue in "what might broadly be called endemics, or in other
words, the form, nature, extension, duration, and intensity of the illnesses prevalent
in a population" (Foucault, 2003, p. 243). The issue is not directly that people would
die of these diseases; it is that they "sapped the populations' strength, shortened the
working week, wasted energy, and cost money, both because they led to a fall in
production and because treating them was expensive" (2003, p. 244). As a result,
"health" emerges as a political issue, as a question of "the disposition of society as a
milieu of physical well-being, health, and optimum longevity" (1984a, p. 277). These
issues are tied to demographic changes in Europe, especially to the development of
cities and the "economico-political effects of the accumulation of men" (1984a,
p. 278). Although they took different forms in different countries, all were tied to the
emergence of capitalism and the need to produce the body "as a factor of productive
force, of labor power" (1994a, p. 137).

One should not oversimplify the complex ways in which the state, science,
population, and health interact from the eighteenth century forward; one important

moment that Foucault (2004) emphasizes is that in the post–World War II era, the rise of national health insurance programs (like the British NHS) marks a shift from a state concern with aggregated population health to a state concern with individual health. These programs also do not need to be the product of a single, centralized state; as Amy Kapczynski (2017) documents, the WHO Influenza Program operates through a complex, decentralized network of institutional actors of various kinds. Other general examples include public works projects, such as the installation of sewage and other sanitation facilities to promote public hygiene. These public health programs have collectively been responsible for a steady rise in life expectancy that one paper suggests "may be the most remarkable regularity of mass endeavor ever observed" (Oeppen & Vaupel, 2002, p. 1029).

There is a substantial difference in approach between these, public-oriented programs and newer, more individualistic ones. Health and the body are still treated as social concerns, but interventions tend much more directly to target individuals and individual behaviors. In this sense it both radicalizes the individualization associated with programs like the NHS, and focuses increasingly on non-state actors. This new version emerges in tandem with the rise of neoliberalism and the emergence of a post-Fordist economic sector centered around services and cognitive or immaterial labor. These larger economic processes are exemplified, as I will show in detail, by the rise of digital communications, brand capitalism, and genomic medicine. Important to all is the integration of intangible assets and mental life into economic processes. As Paolo Virno emphasizes, the post-Fordist economy specifically depends upon the capitalization of communicative processes – of human life, both biological and social. For this reason, "the living body becomes an object to be governed not for its intrinsic value, but because it is the substratum of what really matters: labor-power as the aggregate of the most diverse human faculties (the potential for speaking, for thinking, for remembering, for acting, etc.)" (Virno, 2003, pp. 82–83).[8]

---

[8] The emphasis on the extension of economic calculation is also prominently in Italian autonomism, which developed the argument somewhat independently of Foucault, although autonomists tend to explicitly endorse Foucault on biopolitics. Compare Hardt and Negri: "biopolitical production" involves not just the economic production of material goods, but the production of "all facets of social life, economic, cultural, and political" (2004, p. xvi). Franco Berardi puts it this way: "Putting the soul to work: this is the new form of alienation. Our desiring energy is trapped in the trick of self-enterprise, our libidinal investments are regulated according to economic rules, our attention is captured in the precariousness of virtual networks: every fragment of mental activity must be transformed into capital" (2009, p. 24). Christian Marazzi: "in the New Economy language and communication are structurally and contemporaneously present throughout both the sphere of the production and distribution of goods and services and the sphere of finance, and that it is for *this very reason* that changes in the world of work and modifications in the financial markets must be seen as two sides of the same coin" (2008, p. 14). Outside of autonomism, Phillip Mirowski is partially critical of Foucault's response to neoliberalism, but he also suggests that the extension of the economy is central (see 2013, p. 104). One can worry that this understanding of biopower is too broad to

As Nikolas Rose extensively documents, this new way of looking at health involves viewing risk less as something that happens to a population as a whole and more as both personal and actuarial, and centered around the idea that "some, perhaps all, persons, though existentially healthy are actually asymptomatically or pre-symptomatically ill" (2007, p. 19). Health policy becomes reoriented around this new understanding of risk, and there is an increasing emphasis on personal responsibility:

> This is an ethic in which the maximization of lifestyle, potential, health, and quality of life has become almost obligatory, and where negative judgments are directed towards those who will not, for whatever reason, adopt an active, informed, positive, and prudent relation to the future.
>
> (2007, p. 25)

I will say more about the account of subjectivity and actuarial agency this model develops for medicine in Chapter 5 on patents; I intend it here as indicative of the difference between public and neoliberal biopower.

As suggested earlier, an essential feature of neoliberalism is its extension of economic rationality into all aspects of life. The extension of economic rationality receives its sharpest formulation in the work of Gary Becker. As he puts it in 1976, "the economic approach provides a valuable unified framework for understanding *all* human behavior, although I recognize, of course, that much behavior is not yet understood" (1995, p. 13). Analysis of this extension is essential to Foucault, and its tendency to encroach on areas traditionally deemed social or political is documented extensively by Wendy Brown (2015). As Foucault puts it, the issue is "the identification of the object of economic analysis with any conduct whatsoever entailing an optimal allocation of scarce resources to alternative ends." He adds that:

> Behind this identification ... we find the possibility of a generalization of the economic object to any conduct which employs limited means to one end among others. And we reach the point at which maybe the object of economic analysis should be identified with any purposeful conduct broadly speaking, a strategic choice of means, ways, and instruments: in short, the identification of the object of economic analysis with any rational conduct.
>
> (2008, pp. 268–269)

In the remainder of this section, I will discuss the extension of economic rationality and how that leads to a notion of subjectivity specific to neoliberalism. In the following section, I will trace the development of two aspects of Chicago school neoliberalism that are of central importance to IP's move away from public biopolitics. The first is the development of a tolerance for monopolies and the second is

be useful; even among those who make this caution, however, intellectual property seems to be regarded as of central importance (see, e.g., Rabinow & Rose, 2006, p. 215).

an absolute priority assigned to innovation and dynamic efficiency, at the expense of concerns about static efficiency. In the section after that, I will show how these factors converge in the work of Harold Demsetz, whose theory of property is central to neoliberal notions of IP.

The centrality of economic rationality to neoliberal biopolitics and the need for agents to consistently engage in it generates a set of policy problems around subjectification. The core issue is straightforward: Whether in Hayekian language about prices or Chicago language about efficiency, neoliberal theory requires that individuals behave in economically rational ways, as tokens of the type "*homo economicus.*" Economically rational ways are those that both express stable preferences and correctly align individual welfare and social welfare. This in turn means that individuals must pursue their own satisfaction in ways that enable the stable functioning of markets, since those are supposed to be the best ways to achieve social welfare.

The neoliberal need to create people that satisfy its theoretical and normative sense of how society is best organized stems from the convergence of three factors. First, as noted earlier, neoliberal economics extends its analytic reach to all aspects of society. All problems and opportunities are economic ones, and so there is no sphere outside of economics where noneconomic behaviors can be tolerated. Traditional sociological distinctions between state and civil society, for example, are particularly undermined by the extension of economic analysis into areas like marriage and crime, or by the extension of economic analysis into law.[9]

Second, the neoliberal description of personhood is noticeably thinner than that of classical liberalism. On the one hand, the neoliberal subject arrives divested of the metaphysical baggage of earlier cultural forms. Earlier, substantive understandings of subjectivity, which ratcheted what it meant to be a person to preexisting categories such as "woman" or "noble" or "criminal," disappear and are replaced with a formal description of a person as the bearer of economic rationality.[10] On the other hand, particularly in classical theorists like Adam Smith, there was an assumption that individuals would naturally behave prosocially. It was not just that the "invisible hand" would lead to the coincidence of individual and social good; it was that

---

[9] For example, the criminal is no longer a personality type, but an ordinary, calculating agent for whom (according to Becker) the risks of committing a crime need to be weighed against its possible benefits (Foucault, 2008, pp. 250–260). If one is worried about the theft of IP, says Harold Demsetz in a paper that framed much of the current theoretical climate for IP, one need to increase the penalties for such theft – a statement he supports with a footnote to Becker's work on crime (1969, p. 10 n16).

[10] See also Dilts (2011). The subject as a substantively empty site for economic rationality aligns neoliberalism with the techniques of capitalist accumulation, which rely on the "dispossession" of social ties and other, noncapitalist forms of wealth (Harvey, 2003). The neoliberal subject, then, is the radicalization of the "free laborer" of early capital, with the difference that the neoliberal subject has fully internalized economic rationality as the truth of his existence. In short, *homo economicus* is a historically specific model of subjectivity.

individuals were also motivated by a natural "empathy" or "sympathy" with one another.[11]

Finally, individuals do not naturally behave as economically rational agents. As Michel Callon has emphasized, *homo economicus* "is obviously not to be found in a natural state – this expression has little meaning. He is formatted, framed and equipped with prostheses which help him in his calculations and which are, for the most part, produced by economics" (1998, p. 51). In order for a system based on the satisfaction of individual preferences to operate successfully, then, individuals must develop a meta-preference for behaviors that are translatable into economically rational terms. That is, individuals must have a strong and stable preference for stylizing themselves as *homo economicus*, and they do not come by it naturally.[12]

A good general example of this problematic is in the case of "happiness." As Will Davies (2011) explains, the subject of neoliberal theory can be neither too happy nor too unhappy. If too happy, they will have no preferences left to satisfy. If too unhappy, they will give up on the entire project of satisfying preferences in markets. At the same time, individuals are burdened with the logic of extension of market logic to misfortune – whatever happens to you is allegedly a result of your freely taken decisions. In this context, it is no surprise that depression and its amelioration emerge as central policy problems for the neoliberal theorist. Indeed, if labor is affective and service-oriented, "depression is the hegemonic form of incapacity":

> Depression is just *sheer* incapacity, a distinctly neo-liberal form of psychological deficiency, representing the flipside of an ethos that implores individuals to act, enjoy, perform, create, achieve and maximize. In an economy based in large part on services, enthusiasm, dynamism and optimism are vital workplace resources.
>
> (2011, p. 68)

Or, more succinctly, "unhappiness has become the critical negative externality of contemporary capitalism" (2011, p. 68).

Neoliberal biopolitics has to intervene directly, not just to destigmatize mental health, but to create strategies where individuals are restless enough to want to compete in an increasingly brutal marketplace, but never sufficiently unhappy that they disengage. At the same time, capital will attempt to internalize this externality, creating a market out of unhappiness, with individuals being conditioned to use markets in the effort to stylize themselves as "happy" or at least "resilient" (James, 2015). A substantial apparatus develops to teach individuals to embrace precarity and risk, on the one hand, and to avow their own happiness on the other. Precarity at

---

[11] On this see, e.g., Foucault (2008, p. 301) (on the importance of nonegoistic interests in Ferguson and other theorists of civil society).

[12] The idea that the poor are economically irrational dates at least to Malthus (Tellmann, 2013). For current welfare policy, see Wacquant (2009). See also Merges (2017a) (citing work in experimental philosophy to note that most people do not normally reason as the sorts of utilitarians that neoliberalism requires).

work moves downward, and workers are told to celebrate it as competition (Amoore, 2004). Neoliberal literature celebrates risk-taking individualism with triumphant narratives about mountain climbing (Simon, 2002) and fathers who achieve wealth by risk-taking rather than staying poor and awaiting their pension (Binkley, 2009). Positive psychology teaches that happiness is a desirable and productive state that is achievable with sufficient effort; the unhappy are those who have not tried hard enough to be happy, a process that involves viewing social relationships in econo- mized, instrumental terms (Binkley, 2014). What all of these efforts have in common is that they individualize social and structural issues, substituting judgments of individual performance for more nuanced analyses of the conditions that inhibit or promote those performances. The apparatus carefully sweeps structural problems under the rug.[13]

Subsequent chapters will study examples of the kinds of subjectivity structurally promoted by neoliberal IP regimes in much greater detail. For now, a good example comes from Katherine Strandburg, who argues that the 1980 Bayh–Dole Act, which enabled universities to pursue patent portfolios, works to turn scientific investigators into economic agents – as she puts it, converting *homo scientificus* into *homo economicus*.[14] Using the literature on social norms, Strandburg identifies several features of the classic, curiosity-driven researcher. This structure of social norms serves to benefit basic research:

> Analyzing traditional scientific norms in this way suggests that the norms of inven- tion, independence, and universalism are largely reflective of the individual prefer- ences of basic researchers, while the norms of communalism, disinterestedness, and organized skepticism serve as a means to provide collective goods to the research community that the pursuit of individual preferences may fail to provide. These social norms are important if the basic research community is to continue to provide a socially useful portfolio of curiosity-driven research.

(2005, p. 95)

Homo scientificus is of course an ideal type; even Pierre and Marie Curie, celebrated for their refusal to assert IP rights over the discovery of radium, kept quiet about the fact that Pierre derived significant income from patented instruments (Hemmungs Wirtén, 2015). So too, as has been well documented, the agenda of post–World War II, government-funded science was heavily shaped by Cold War priorities. These caveats do not undermine the general point that the traditional funding mechanisms for basic science, in the form of university structures and grants, serve to support a

---

[13] Such characterizations have immediate resonance with the creative arts. Walt Disney, for example, who foraged extensively through the public domain for his characters and stories, is celebrated as an artistic genius even as his sources tend to be remembered only in critical literature (on this discrepancy, see Hemmungs Wirtén, 2008, pp. 127–128).

[14] Bayh–Dole is often cited in the literature on neoliberalism as a significant moment in its development. See, e.g., Harvey (2005) and Mirowski (2011).

demand for such research by divorcing it from market exigencies. Since it is impossible to predict what sort of basic research will fare well in a future invention brought to market, these state-funding mechanisms are of vital importance in securing a supply of basic research.

What sort of person is a scientist pursuing such basic research? Strandburg suggests:

> One way to model the university scientist is as an individual who, once a certain fairly comfortable level of material prosperity is obtained, derives a very high marginal utility from performing autonomous, curiosity-driven scientific research and from the direct consumption of scientific knowledge.

(2005, pp. 99–100)

In other words, these scientists value autonomy and intellectual challenge more than salary and prestige; they make considerably less money than industry scientists; and they stubbornly report greater satisfaction with their careers than their industry counterparts.

The problem is that the institutional structure favored by the Bayh–Dole Act, which gives universities an incentive to push researchers to pursue patent portfolios, tends to occlude all motives other than those of *homo economicus*. As Strandburg suggests, there are two primary ways this can happen. One is *ex post*, where the costs of pursuing patents distort downstream research. The issue here is not so much one of licensing costs – though that is one issue – as it is opportunity costs (time spent with lawyers is time not spent in the lab), the introduction of incentives for abuse (using patents to control the results of one's research, and to reduce its dissemination), the erosion of norms of communal sharing, and the distorting effects of rewarding patents with further funding or academic promotion. *Ex ante*, the concern is that offering funding for patentable research will divert scientists away from basic research since basic research is not geared toward developing a patentable product.

This is not to say that universities did not pursue patents prior to Bayh–Dole, although they did so less frequently. Prior to Bayh–Dole, universities did not generally pursue patents as a strategy for revenue generation or as a way to internalize the gains of their research. Research into earlier university patents suggests that they were often instead intended to facilitate responsible, public stewardship of the research in question. For example, the University of Toronto's early patent on insulin was justified as a lever to force licensees to exercise adequate quality control and for its ability to force an open, price-competitive market by open licensing. At a time when there were no regulatory agencies to control production quality and in view of concerns that individual corporations would monopolize the drug and raise prices, UT attempted to address these concerns with a patent; "the idea here was not to use the power of the patent to create a commercial monopoly or to extract a rent, but to make it the instrument of a drug biopolicy inspired by the public good"

(Cassier & Sinding, 2008, p. 166). Similar justifications were offered in defense of patents on a scarlet fever antitoxin and on research related to vitamins D and A. The vitamin patents were quite lucrative, and there was considerable debate over whether the way the proceeds were allocated to future research was appropriate (Weiner, 1987).

Indeed, despite strong norms against patenting, public good arguments made it possible to criticize a decision not to patent. When Harvard decided not to pursue patents on liver extracts to treat anemia, the goal was again to promote public access. But the university had second thoughts because quality-control was more difficult to ensure without a licensing scheme to enforce it (Weiner, 1987). Similarly, Marie Curie was criticized on analogous grounds for not patenting uranium. As T. Swann Harding complained in 1941, she gave "her discovery over to every quack and commercial faker who chose to exploit the public by means of it" and "her inverted and distorted sense of probity turned radium over to rascals" (qt. in Hemmungs Wirtén, 2015, p. 604). These debates on biomedical patents evidence the public biopolitical rationale in operation: The debate is not over who gets to internalize the gains of an invention, but how its public benefits are best managed.

The two models of research neatly represent the two forms of biopower outlined earlier. Strandburg argues that the continued availability of public funding for research balances concerns about a shift away from basic research, even perhaps serving a useful function in guiding *homo scientificus* to basic science and *homo economicus* to industry. So too, basic science forms an important input into commercialization. NIH grant-funded research was involved in every single drug approved between 2010 and 2016, and the vast majority of that funding was for basic research (Galkina Cleary, Beierlein, Khanuja, McNamee, & Ledley, 2018). The problem is that public funding (except at the NIH) is in decline, and this decline is partly justified by the availability of patents as a way to recuperate research costs; the funding model for scientific research is increasingly corporate and generated by a demand for return on investment. Accordingly, there is potential for the move to patents to undermine basic research by recalibrating scientists and their reward structures in market terms.

In defending the university's value as a constructed commons, Strandburg, along with Michael Madison and Brett Frischmann, worries that this encroachment or market is an example of where legal developments push "the university toward a less open and more market-oriented model" and accordingly "indirectly undermine[] the distinctively scholarly character of university-based research" (2009, pp. 393–394). Although they freely admit that the relative gains of the cultural commons versus neoliberal version of the university are difficult to assess, they sound a cautionary tone with the example of the Internet:

> For every example of a technology that might have been exploited earlier and more profitably had universities been permitted to patent it, one can cite a grand

counterexample: the Internet, the basic technologies of which were developed mostly in university settings, largely with federal research support. It is impossible to know the trajectory of the Internet had a Bayh–Dole statute been in place before 1980, when much of the basic architecture of the Internet was being standardized, but there is reason to worry that open, common standards would have been more difficult to establish in the shadow of patenting, and that the explosion of Internet-related innovation and creativity in the years since 1990 in particular might not have benefited so many individuals and firms worldwide.

(p. 399)

2.2 POWER IN IP: FROM LIBERALISM TO NEOLIBERAL BIOPOWER

Why might one need IP? The most common narrative is broadly welfarist, insofar as, other things being equal, having more goods like inventions and art in a society increases overall social welfare. The general argument is that production of intellectual goods requires effort (or presents opportunity costs), and so most people will not do so without some sort of compensating incentive and reward structure. One obvious incentive is the ability to sell one's product. However, it is very difficult to prevent others from free riding on the good, since intangible goods are usually (and increasingly) cheap to copy, and since no one will pay more for something they can get for less. Worse, the relevant goods are generally nonrivalrous, such that indefinitely many people can use them at once without depleting them (compare *Romeo and Juliet* with pizza). In such an environment, it is difficult to see how an even minimally self-interested person would not free ride. Thus, it becomes impossible to recover one's costs in producing a good. In different terms, it is very difficult to establish a market in something which is not fundamentally scarce. In such a world, we will see very few intellectual goods produced.

IP uses law to stop the free riding: By making it illegal to use the good without the owner's permission, IP awards an artificial monopoly to the rights holder, who is then able to set a price that enables them to recover their costs. In short, the law enables a market by establishing scarcity. For example, suppose someone develops the proverbial cure for cancer. If he or she were to then sell the drug on the open market, competitors would quickly reverse-engineer it. Since the costs of reverse-engineering will be much lower than the original development costs, copies will sell for less than the original, and the original investors will quickly find themselves out of business. As a result, fewer desirable medicines will be developed. If the original inventor is awarded the exclusive right to sell the medicine, however, he or she can recover expenses and secure a profit.

Nearly every point of this narrative is of course contested, as a quick survey of recent scholarship will evidence. In what follows, I want to look specifically at different ways of interpreting the basic story, using the models of power outlined earlier. The initial and long-dominant way of understanding IP and incentives was broadly on the model of public biopolitics; current trends in both theory and practice evidence a move to the neoliberal version. Although they, in many ways, use similar language and argument structures, the two models present very different versions of both what IP is trying to do – what the nature of the good to be achieved is, how to measure it, the costs and relative importance of free riding, and the economics of the central artificial monopoly – and of the sorts of people who might engage it. I start with a constellation of nineteenth-century liberalism and the Constitutional development of the IP clause as representative of public biopolitics, and then turn to the emergence of Chicago School neoliberalism in the 1950s. I then look specifically at the theoretical structure of the currently dominant understanding of IP, which centers around the work of Harold Demsetz. Subsequent chapters will explore in detail how individual IP regimes like copyright express the incentives narrative and how different doctrinal developments evidence different models of power.

The story of IP's move from liberalism to neoliberalism can be set against the background of the classical, juridical notion of property more generally. The juridical definition tends to cite, somewhat out of context, William Blackstone's quip that property provides its owner "despotic dominion" over something; more contemporary variations focus on the right to exclude others as central. If something is my property, then at the very least I can stop others from accessing it.[15] This exclusion right is central to popular imaginings of property, and remains important to its contemporary theorization. Especially in the case of IP, it is necessary to see beyond this popular image of property to understand how IP functions as a form of regulation, and the kind of power it presents. It is there that we see the biopolitical aspects of the story.

---

[15] As Carol Rose (1999) points out, this is somewhat of a caricature of Blackstone. Nevertheless, the right to exclude remains central to contemporary conceptions of property. For a defense of this centrality, one that relies substantially on historical and legal precedent, see Merrill (1998). For the argument that contemporary governmental strategies of property – extensions of the Hohfeldian "bundle of rights" by theorists such as Coase and Calabresi and Melamed – are fundamental departures from earlier theories of property, see Merrill and Smith (2001). Merrill and Smith suggest that contemporary understandings of property are actually modeled on *in personam* contract rights, and not *in rem* property rights. One issue where this is particularly apparent in the case of IP is the complexity of the regime and the novelty of many of its rules. This complexity is both more characteristic of contracts than property, and serves (among other things) to make it function less successfully as property, insofar as property requires clear rules that the public can understand at a relatively low information cost (on this, see also Merrill & Smith, 2007). It seems to me that Merrill and Smith provide a useful model of a public biopolitical understanding of property: they assess the basis for, and concept of, property in terms of its utility in reducing information costs to indefinitely many members of the public, and contrast their approach to models that emphasize efficiency in facilitating transfer of resources.

As the preceding analysis indicated, at least in rough outline, biopower undergoes a fundamental change in the move from classical liberalism to neoliberalism. Both fundamentally concern themselves with fostering the productivity of the population. As noted earlier, Foucault remarks that, once politics becomes concerned with life, the political system is "no longer commanded by the immediate problem of surviving and not dying, but is now commanded by the problem of living and doing a bit better than just living" (2007, p. 326). Scientific knowledge is seen as important to that process, as are markets. The sense that knowledge is somehow different from traditional market goods and requires government intervention is noted clearly, for example, by John Stuart Mill. The last part of his *Principles of Political Economy* (1848) is dedicated to the proposition that *"laisser-faire* ... should be the general practice: every departure from it, unless required by some great good, is a certain evil" (p. 945). However, he follows with a number of exceptions to this noninterference rule: education (where those who need it will be poor judges of its value), instances where an individual "may be incapable of judging or acting for himself" (p. 951), and so forth. He concludes with the provision of knowledge, which he clearly perceives as a public good, citing public funding for "a voyage of geographical or scientific exploration," from which "the information sought may be of great public value" even as no one party would derive enough benefit from it to defray its cost. After adding other examples of public infrastructure such as lighthouses for navigation, Mill underlines the importance of encouraging scientific research:

> There are many scientific researches, of great value to a nation and to mankind, requiring assiduous devotion of time and labour, and not unfrequently great expense, by persons who can obtain a high price for their services in other ways. If the government had no power to grant indemnity for expense, and remuneration for time and labour thus employed, such researches could only be undertaken by the very few persons who, with an independent fortune, unite technical knowledge, laborious habits, and either great public spirit, or an ardent desire of scientific celebrity.
>
> (p. 968)

The section concludes with the importance of state provision of university professorships.

Mill does not consistently advocate public provision of all research; he also explicitly says that patents should be an exception to a ban on artificial monopolies, proposing that "this is not making the commodity dear for [the inventor's] benefit, but merely postponing a part of the increased cheapness which the public owe to the inventor, in order to compensate and reward him for the service" (p. 928).[16] In other

---

[16] Mill's defense of patents over direct public subsidies is that markets will ensure that public resources are efficiently spent (pp. 928–929). This partial privatization is tempered by the short duration allowed for patents, and by his willingness to publicly subsidize knowledge production in the more abstract instances of university professorships.

words, even in the case of patents, Mill conceives of the production of knowledge as the production of something that benefits the public generally, and which the application of *laissez-faire* will not supply. This sense of knowledge as a public good is specific to modern liberalism, and is part of what disappears in the move to neoliberalism, with its emphasis on privatization.

The initial language justifying IP in the US context expresses precisely this ambivalence about markets and knowledge: Congress is vested with the power "to promote the Progress of Science and useful Arts, by securing for limited Times to Authors and Inventors the exclusive Right to their respective Writings and Discoveries" (US Const. Art I. §8). The IP clause asserts a biopolitical objective, and then adduces juridical means – property rights – to attain it. As numerous scholars have noted, the structure of this clause is unique among the enumerated powers of Article I §8 more generally in that it appears to contain various limitations: exclusive rights are to be granted for the sake of progress and for limited times only.

The first draft of the Constitution, of August 6, 1787, did not mention IP at all. The IP clause appears to have originated in a proposal by James Madison and Charles Pinckney, on August 17, to vest additional powers in the federal legislature. Among these were patent, copyright, education, and encouragements (Oliar, 2006, p. 1789). The education power, for both Madison and Pinckney, involved establishing federally supported educational institutions. The encouragements power involved public subsidies and rewards to promote science.[17] They thus presage the theoretical account in Mill. All four powers are also involved in seeing to it that, reverting to Foucault's language, everything in the people's "activity that may go beyond this pure and simple subsistence will in fact be produced, distributed, divided up, and put in circulation in such a way that the state really can draw its strength from it" (2007, p. 326).

One of the main factors behind the only partial success of these powers was the fear of monopolies, a strong aversion to which suffused the political climate of both the state governments and the constitutional convention (Oliar, 2006, p. 1800). That the IP clause survived this fear was no doubt in part due to the limitations placed on it. In other words, concern with monopolies was enough to cabin, but not eliminate, an IP power. The jurist James Kent's letter to Nathaniel Lawrence of the New York ratifying convention can be seen as typical: "I have just been reading Smith on the Wealth of Nations & he has taught me to look with an unfavorable eye on monopolies—But a monopoly of the mental kind I take to be laudable & an exception to the Rule" (qt. in Oliar, 2006, p. 1803 n1164). Even this carefully cabined enthusiasm was not universal. When Jefferson wrote to Madison in 1788 to

---

[17] For Madison, the goal was to "encourage, by proper præmiums and provisions, the advancement of useful knowledge and discoveries"; for Pinckney, it was "To establish public institutions, rewards and immunities for the promotion of agriculture, commerce, trades, and manufactures" (qt. in Oliar, 2006, p. 1789).

"sincerely rejoice at the acceptance of our new constitution by nine states," he added that one of the areas needing "retouching" by a Bill of Rights was that of monopolies, at the same level of importance as guarantees of free press and religious expression. Of IP, Jefferson concludes that, although "the saying there shall be no monopolies lessens the incitements to ingenuity, which is spurred on by the hope of a monopoly for a limited time," nonetheless "the benefit even of limited monopolies is too doubtful to be opposed to that of their general suppression" (1956, pp. 442–443). At ratification, several states recommended explicit language against monopolies be added (Walterscheid, 1994, pp. 55–56).

This wariness about monopolies, driven by the value placed on markets, was a hallmark in liberal thought about IP.[18] Locke's opposition to the licensing act (which was later replaced by the Statute of Anne, the first Copyright statute) was premised on the evils of monopoly and price discrimination (Hull, 2009a). When the House of Lords issued its final ruling that Copyright would be limited, unlike perpetual common law property rights, opposition to effective monopolies by the printing house to which authors sold their rights was probably the key to its decision (M. Rose, 1993, pp. 85–91, 102–103). A few years before Mill's *Political Economy* appeared, Lord Macaulay (1841) famously argued in Parliament:

> We must betake ourselves to copyright, be the inconveniences of copyright what they may. Those inconveniences, in truth, are neither few nor small. Copyright is monopoly, and produces all the effects which the general voice of mankind attributes to monopoly ... That monopoly makes things dear is certainly a theory, as all the great truths which have been established by the experience of all ages and nations, and which are taken for granted in all reasonings, may be said to be theories. It is a theory in the same sense in which it is a theory that day and night follow each other, that lead is heavier than water, that bread nourishes, that arsenic poisons, that alcohol intoxicates ... Thus, then, stands the case. It is good that authors should be remunerated; and the least exceptionable way of remunerating them is by a monopoly. Yet monopoly is an evil. For the sake of the good we must submit to the evil; but the evil ought not to last a day longer than is necessary for the purpose of securing the good.

As all of this evidence indicates, the general concern was with the promotion of social welfare, with little effort to compartmentalize the public into individual agents. Incentivized individual agents were at most instrumental to the ends of the public. The free function of markets was a primary objective, coupled with an

---

[18] *Cf.* Foucault: "for liberal theory, there must be freedom of the internal market, of course, but again, for there to be a market there must be buyers as well as sellers. Consequently, if necessary, the market must be supported and buyers created by mechanisms of assistance. For freedom of the internal market to exist, the effects of monopolies must be prevented, and so anti-monopoly legislation is needed" (2008, p. 64). When economic theory switches in emphasis from exchange to competition, monopolies again become problematic insofar as they tend to both arise in competitive markets and erode competition (p. 119).

awareness that scientific progress was unlikely to be fully incentivized in a purely market-driven system. The result was a grudging acceptance of carefully limited IP rights.

To situate the origins of IP within classical liberalism is also to situate it within colonialism, which is to say that the concern with benefitting the public was often articulated without any concern about whether realizing that benefit involved dispossessing others. Locke's involvement in colonialism has been well established, and he argued that indigenous agricultural practices wasted the land they were on, leaving them available for enclosure.[19] More recently, a critique of neocolonialism forms the background of critiques of biopiracy found in authors like James Boyle and Vandana Shiva, and neoliberalism has been thoroughly implicated by contemporary critiques of economic colonialism.[20] Resistance to the expropriation of indigenous and non-Western forms of knowledge by IP regimes forms the core of such strategies as efforts to protect indigenous cultural products with geographic indicators. As I indicate in the discussion of geographic indicators in Chapter 4 on trademark, these strategies are important both in what they can achieve and in their limitations. In addition, as I indicate in the conclusion, problems with expropriation mean that simply romanticizing earlier IP regimes is not a viable political strategy.

In the West, the Mill and Macaulay aversion to patents as a form of monopoly extended into American liberalism of the twentieth century, where it was hegemonic until roughly 1950 and the development of Chicago school law and economics.[21] Courts had vigorously enforced antitrust laws in the early twentieth century, and they tended to view IP through that lens. As one district court wrote in 1923:

[19] Locke was also actively involved in writing the Carolina constitution. For the difficulties in Locke's theory, see, e.g., Tully (1993). As Eva Hemmungs Wirten points out, this particular strategy was specific to the English among the European colonial powers, as "the English . . . were the only ones who drew on the passive-aggressive rhetoric of gardening and cultivation of land to justify their colonial project" (2008, p. 23). As a result, "one of the more drastic results of the English penchant for agricultural labor of the Lockean kind was that among the colonial powers of the time, only the English had relatively little incentive to protect indigenous populations, since they were obviously an impediment to further land procurement" (p. 87). Other recent work shows in detail how British assumptions about the superiority of their enclosure-based farming practices destroyed a viable land use regime among the Maasai (Blewett, 1995).

[20] The literature on this point is substantial, even within the context of IP, as the work of scholars such as Madhavi Sunder (2012, 2000) indicates. For a sustained critique of how the development of the neoliberal pharmaceutical industry has relied on the exploitation of workers displaced by the movement of deregulated transnational capital, see Sunder Rajan (2006). For a more general narrative, drawing an unbroken line from early liberalism to now, see Venn (2009). Cf. also Hemmungs Wirtén: "[B]eginning in the Victorian era and ending up at Disney's headquarters in the twenty-first century, the interpretation of what constitutes use and waste depends largely on the tensions brought about by the matrix of imperialism" (2008, p. 143).

[21] On the distrust of monopolies in the context of IP, see e.g., Wilf (2008). Law and economics are not given sufficient prominence in general histories of neoliberalism; one important exception is W. Davies (2014). For a corrective, see (in addition to Davies) Van Horn and Mirowski (2009).

Patents, copyrights, and trade marks excite two deeply seated feelings. One is the feeling of any one who has originated anything of his right to claim an exclusive property in it and to the trade growing out of it. The other is a hatred of monopoly. The latter feeling gives way to the former so far as to grant limited monopolies through patents and copyrights. This is a concession made for the general good aptly expressed in the constitutional phrase. The purchasing public regards this as the concession of a privilege; inventors and authors look upon it as a right limited only as the price exacted for the aid of the law in enforcing it. Mere dealers in commodities are prone to think themselves entitled to a like monopoly unlimited in time. This is a mistake. The only right they have is their right to sell their goods as such as to protection against the goods of another being palmed off upon their customers as theirs. To aid them in the assertion of this right they are permitted to mark their goods so as to identify and designate them and to name them as their own.

(Loughran (District), p. 697)

The opinion was on trademark, and as I will indicate in Chapter 4 on trademark, the assumption that trademarks protected against palming off was central to earlier trademark doctrine, and it was one of the doctrines that the early development of what became neoliberal protection against dilution pushed back against. On appeal, the Third Circuit affirmed, ruling that "Quaker Maid" and "Quaker City" were not sufficiently similar to bar registration of the former, even though both were marks for candy. Indeed, the Court explained that "the registration of a trade-mark does not give the registrant a monopoly of every word in the trade-mark howsoever disposed and used." *(Loughran (3rd Cir.), p. 827)*

The concern about monopoly was held even among some theorists traditionally associated with neoliberalism. For example, Henry Simons' pamphlet "A Positive Program for *Laissez Faire*" not only rehearses standard neoliberal talking points about the importance of competition and the dangers of planning and labor organization, but also emphasizes that "*the great enemy of democracy is monopoly, in all its forms*: gigantic corporations, trade associations and other agencies for price control, trade-unions – or, in general, organization and concentration of power within functional classes." Such organized groups "possess tremendous power for exploiting the community at large and even for sabotaging the system" (1948, p. 43, emphasis original). If state policy favors monopoly and thereby encourages "the petty warfare of competition within [small] groups" to somehow become "warfare among organized economic groups," then "only ruthless dictatorship can maintain the degree of order necessary to survival of the population in an economy of intricate division of labor" (pp. 44–45). Simons is opposed to trade unionism, wage and price controls, and strong IP alike.[22]

[22] On these and comparable passages, see Van Horn and Klaes (2013, p. 188) and Van Horn and Mirowski (2009, pp. 142–143). Foucault says the pamphlet is "the first, fundamental text of this American neo-liberalism" (2008, p. 216). Not surprisingly, Simons is most bothered by

Simons was not alone; Aaron Director claimed in 1947 that "a study of the American antitrust cases discloses the crucial importance which patents on inventions have played in creating and maintaining industrial monopoly" (qt. in Van Horn, 2009, p. 212). For his part, Hayek had this to say in 1948:

> The problem of the prevention of monopoly and the preservation of competition is raised much more acutely in certain other fields to which the concept of property has been extended only in recent times. I am thinking here of the extension of the concept of property to such rights and privileges as patents for invention, copyright, trade-marks, and the like. It seems to me beyond a doubt that in these fields a slavish application of the concept of property as it has been developed for material things has done a great deal to foster the growth of monopoly and that here drastic reforms may be required if competition is to be made to work. In the field of industrial patents in particular we shall have seriously to examine whether the award of a monopoly privilege is really the most appropriate and effective form of reward for the kind of risk-bearing which investment in scientific research involves.

> (1948, pp. 113–114)

He follows with a critical discussion of trademarks, and their tendency to be used "as a description of the kind of commodity" rather than the commodity itself (p. 115).[23]

Following Simons' unexpected death in 1948, the "triumvirate" of Director, Milton Friedman, and Edward Levi began to develop the beginnings of the Chicago theory of antitrust. The Chicago theory presented a complete reversal of the skepticism about monopolies, beginning with an initial argument that "monopoly, in all its forms, was almost always undone by the forces of competition." This argument authorized a "relatively sanguine attitude ... toward both monopoly and large corporations" (Van Horn, 2009, p. 208). For example, by 1950, Director had

---

organized labor: "it is shameful to have permitted ... the gross abuse of patent privilege for extortion, exclusion and output restriction," even if he regarded the remedy as both less bad and easier to fix than "labor monopolies" with their "access to violence which is unparalleled in other monopolies" (p. 130).

[23] Van Horn and Klaes (2013) point out that Hayek maintained his view on patents even after the Chicago developments; this underscores the specificity of the Chicago program. Hayek underscores in *Road to Serfdom* that he is not advocating strict *laissez-faire*: "The liberal argument is in favor of making the best possible use of the forces of competition as a means of co-ordinating human efforts, not an argument for leaving things just as they are. It is based on the conviction that, where effective competition can be created, it is a better way of guiding individual efforts than any other" (1944, p. 36). He then defends everything from safety requirements to a strong legal contract system. He adds that "serious shortcomings" in the study of legal institutions, "particularly with regard to the law of corporations and of patents, not only have made competition work much less effectively than it might have done but have even led to the destruction of competition in many spheres" (p. 38). He then explicitly rejects the conflation of social and consumer welfare in the provision of public goods: "in all these instances there is a divergence between the items which enter into private calculation and those which affect social welfare; and, whenever this divergence becomes important, some method other than competition may have to be found to supply the services in question" (pp. 38–39).

changed his mind, arguing that the "corroding influence of competition" has the "effective tendency" to "destroy types of monopoly" (qt. in Van Horn, 2009, p. 217). As Van Horn notes (2009, p. 220), this proposition, and its confident extension by Friedman, were advanced without supporting empirical evidence. There is, however, evidence that it was in the service of a political objective; much of the early Chicago work was funded by the conservative Volker Fund, which advocated "freedom" in the sense of "the freedom of corporations to conduct their affairs as they wished" and which "was not interested in bankrolling a classical liberal economic position resembling that of Henry Simons" (Van Horn & Mirowski, 2009, p. 157). The position meshed readily with Cold War concerns; even a cursory reading of Hayek's *Road to Serfdom* underscores its embeddedness in a Cold War context. That emphasis is still present in Robert Bork's antitrust work, where he complains that pre-Chicago antitrust had been "a farrago of amorphous and leftist political and sociological propositions" (1993, p. x).

The Chicago revision of antitrust theory provided a lens that legitimated increased deference to patent and other IP rights and a reduction in concerns about them as monopolies. As Steven Wilf (2008) underscores, as late as the New Deal, IP policy was structured by concern about the risks that IP would entrench monopoly power, a concern that particularly troubled patent policy.[24] But things were changing. Coase's "Nature of the Firm" had already argued that autonomous firms would maximize their value by vertical integration, if it were more cost effective to obtain a needed input by producing it than obtaining it on the market. Furthermore, if the negative effects on competition would be only temporary, then any problems they might cause in the short term could be downplayed or reinterpreted in benign ways. Patent tying schemes, for example, could be described as beneficent price discrimination. Price discrimination charges consumers a price based on their desire for a good, and so can be said both to be efficient and to increase consumer welfare.[25] Patent-tying should accordingly not be regulated by the courts. As I will argue in the case of patent exhaustion, recent Court jurisprudence – even when it pushes back against analogous schemes, as it did in the recent *Lexmark* decision – takes this framing largely into account. So too, trademark dilution essentially

---

[24] There is a complex story to be told – well beyond the scope of this book – about the interaction between New Deal reforms aimed at stabilizing markets (and putting a lid on excessive competition), the import of Austrian arguments about the self-regulating character of markets via the price mechanism, and the subsequent turn in neoliberal theory toward an embrace of monopolies. Although much of the rhetoric of neoliberal theorists like Bork is framed as a Cold War struggle against Soviet state planning, it is equally clear that the actual target of much neoliberal writing is the Keynesian welfare state inaugurated, in the United States, by the New Deal. As Wilf argues, IP served New Deal reformers as a mechanism for ensuring stable markets, an instrument of national economic policy, and as a governance strategy for promoting an economic understanding of consumer-oriented citizenship.

[25] For a critical demonstration of how a monopolist using perfect price discrimination can be said to mirror a perfect market, see Boyle (2000).

endorses what Hayek originally took to be problematic, the strong connection of names and products. And copyright anti-circumvention rules allow owners to bundle block access to unprotected materials by way of encryption and other access-control technologies.

The fully developed Chicago theory of antitrust makes two moves.[26] One is to apply the neoliberal extension of markets into all social relations, discussed earlier and exemplified by Becker, by reducing social welfare to consumer welfare. The other is to insist on interpreting matters according to its own economic analysis, which consistently downplays any negative effects of monopolies by arguing that in open markets, competition always arises to erode monopolies.[27] Together, these meant that the sorts of problems in pricing and distribution that troubled classical liberals receded in importance. Rather than competition, policy should promote "efficiency." Judge Posner puts it this way:

> To the extent that efficiency is the goal of antitrust enforcement, there is no justification for carrying enforcement into areas where competition is less efficient than monopoly because the costs of monopoly pricing are outweighed by the economies of centralizing production in one or a very few firms.
>
> (qt. in W. Davies, 2014, p. 94)

For his part, Friedman had argued that patents could not be monopolies because they were part of the definition of property rights (Van Horn & Mirowski, 2009, p. 167). As Davies notes, all of this amounts to a "wholesale reappraisal of monopoly, resulting in a model of applied neoliberal policy and law in which large concentrations of corporate power and high profitability were typically justified on efficiency grounds" (W. Davies, 2014, p. 94).

It also serves to make traditionally "political" questions invisible to antitrust analysis, since they fall outside of the purview of consumer welfare. The theory provides a good example of Wendy Brown's (2015) thesis that the neoliberal extension of economic categories into all social spheres tends to make democracy impossible. As Lina Khan puts it, the move is "away from understanding concentrated private power as a problem of domination, implicating our ability to self-govern"

---

[26] The canonical statement is Robert Bork's 1978 *Antitrust Paradox*. Bork summarizes the view: "The primary characteristics of the Chicago School of antitrust are two. The first is the insistence that the exclusive goal of antitrust adjudication, the sole consideration the judge must bear in mind, is the maximization of consumer welfare. The judge must not weigh against consumer welfare any other goal, such as the supposed social benefits of preserving small businesses against superior efficiency. Second, the Chicagoans applied economic analysis more rigorously than was common at the time to test the propositions of the law and to understand the impact of business behavior on consumer welfare" (1993, p. xi).

[27] Wu (2013) suggests that recent policy has been colored by a residual juridical, rights-based origin that generates a deference to rights-holders; the introduction of economic analysis has only been partial. One burden of the argument here is to suggest that the issue is less about the penetration of economic analysis into IP and more about the kind of economic analysis deployed.

(2018a, p. 970). Current efforts to resist Chicago antitrust doctrine emphasizes precisely this point; as Khan summarizes, "the fixation on efficiency ... has largely blinded enforcers to many of the harms caused by undue market power, including on workers, suppliers, innovators, and independent entrepreneurs" (2018b, p. 132).

For example, by offering high rewards to the inventors of medicines for diseases that trouble the affluent, the structure of the patent system encourages the development of "me-too" drugs as competitors to pharmaceutical blockbusters like Viagra. As long as these products are sufficiently different from Viagra to avoid patent infringement, they should enhance consumer welfare by introducing competition into the erectile-dysfunction drug market. Even on the assumption that this theory is correct, one should note that it makes it impossible to consider the degree to which the money spent developing competitors to Viagra is money not spent on developing treatments for diseases like malaria. The consumer welfare gain might very well turn out to be a loss in terms of social welfare. Additionally, the focus on consumer welfare makes it difficult to understand welfare in noneconomic terms, as measured by such terms as human capabilities. As I will discuss in the context of geographical indicators in Chapter 4 on trademark, capabilities are central to efforts to repurpose IP for indigenous peoples: One argument advanced for protecting geographic indicators is that they contribute to the viability of rural areas. More generally, as I will argue in the context of Demsetz's work, the focus on consumer welfare makes the sort of public biopolitics that would focus on broad but nebulous benefits to "the public" impossible to account for.

As Khan (2018a) notes, the Chicago school version of antitrust presents a very different view of power from what she characterizes as the republican version. Enforcement of the older version relied on bright-line rules and structural presumptions; Chicago school analysis substitutes an effects-based economic analysis that focuses only on consumer welfare and not on social welfare more generally. For the purposes of the argument here, we can note that the shift represents a slide away from both juridical power and public biopower toward a more purely neoliberal biopower. Traditional antitrust analysis clearly fits the public biopolitics model, aiming to achieve the social good of competition, as defended by classic liberalism. In the case of antitrust enforcement, the enforcement standards were juridical. The Chicago school then makes two departures: first, it moves to a biopolitical enforcement standard by prioritizing economic effects; second, it makes the neoliberal move of treating all welfare as consumer welfare, thereby entrenching universalization of market analysis.

A second general development in early neoliberalism, central to IP, is largely due to the adoption of two theories from Joseph Schumpeter. The first theory, which has reached the status of a popular meme, is expressed as the "creative destruction" inherent to capitalism. In this argument, the primary goal of economic policy and the driver of social welfare is "innovation." Innovation is good, the argument goes, because the social benefits of innovation exceed the private returns to innovators.

A good example of this thesis applied to copyright can be found in R. Pope Wagner's (2003) argument that a given copyrighted work always generates nonappropriable ideas: *Survivor* necessarily generated the immensely profitable idea of "reality TV." One should note here the tension between this thesis and the Demsetzian thesis (discussed in detail later) that privatization is about internalizing gains; at the very least, the tension implies that there is a point above which further strengthening IP generates a loss in social welfare.[28] It also implies that innovation could occur outside of IP rights, with incentives (and disincentives) provided, for example, by social norms (Bair & Pedraza-Fariña, 2018; Raustiala & Sprigman, 2012). I will return to this point both in discussing the incentives theory behind copyright, and in the conclusion.

The adoption of this view also generates a disposition to favor long-term results that are said to be innovative over short-term distributional problems. That is, it generates a disposition to prioritize dynamic efficiency over static efficiency. This disposition is nearly universally held today; as Tim Wu introduces a brief literature review, "there is very little continuing debate among economists as to whether static or dynamic efficiency is more important over the long run" (2012, p. 313). As he cites Joseph Brodley, economic research says that "innovation efficiency or technological progress is the single most important factor in the growth of real output in ... the industrialized world" (qt. in Wu, 2012, p. 313). The effects of this preference are widespread; I will discuss them in detail in the analysis of Demsetz in the context of market-pricing and his conceptualization of externalities.

The second theory, equally consequential but less discussed, is that large firms are more innovative than smaller, distributed ones. There is a sharply contested debate as to whether this theory, or its rebuttal by Kenneth Arrow, is superior either empirically or theoretically. Neither seems to be generally true, with much depending on the precise nature of the markets and firms involved, and the specific kinds of antitrust enforcement in question (Baker, 2007). The only point I wish to make here is that it interacts with the neoliberal preference for monopoly in two ways. On the one hand, if one assumes that monopolistic environments are better for innovation, then that becomes a further reason to suppose that strong IP rights are better than weak ones, because strong IP rights create more monopolistic conditions. This framing can be contrasted with a public goods one that characterizes antitrust as a targeted strategy for securing the supply of public goods, including innovation (Baker, 2007, p. 589 n536).

On the other hand, the general thesis that anticompetitive environments foster innovation licenses the extension of IP rights in ways that solidify their monopolies by creating entry barriers for competitors. As Wu (2012) suggests, the issue of entry

---

[28] One version of this argument is that excessive IP allows content owners to set up inefficient roadblocks to resource development in such forms as high licensing fees and other transaction costs. On this "anticommons," see, e.g., Heller (1998).

barriers may be a more significant factor for innovation than pricing, even as neoliberal antitrust regulation concerns itself with price as the correct index of consumer welfare, and consumer welfare as the correct index of social welfare. The issue here is not the quantity of IP rights, but their nature and how they affect industry structures. From this point of view, the extension of copyright term discussed earlier is unlikely to make much difference in levels of innovation because it does not change how competitive the environment is. On the other hand, if entry barriers are important, then areas like trademark dilution, digital rights management, and trademarks on brands are likely to be significant barriers to innovation.

I will develop detailed discussions in the following chapters, but let me indicate three sorts of neoliberal developments in IP that are supported by the Schumpeterian thesis. First, the combination of DRM and contract licensing provisions enable content owners to restrict activities that would otherwise be "fair use." By making such activities impossible, this sort of code-based regulation both increases monopoly rents by restricting interaction with the product that the content owner cannot internalize and raises entry barriers by making it more difficult to appropriate parts of the protected material as input into new products. Second, licensing requirements imposed on hip-hop sampling raise entry barriers to new music by raising the cost of creative appropriation of existing materials in an art form heavily based on homage and appropriation. Third, trademark dilution doctrine increases monopoly rents by extending protection to even noncompeting uses of a mark and to cases where consumers would not be confused; it simultaneously extends those rents to unrelated markets.

2.3 THEORIZATIONS OF IP

2.3.1 IP Theory Is (Mostly) Biopolitical

The hegemonic view of IP in the legal academy is biopolitical. Discussion based on other considerations, such as moral or cultural theory, is marginal. Initial evidence of this dominance is the way Mark Lemley, one of the most influential and prolific of IP scholars, treats these alternatives in his "Faith-Based Intellectual Property" (2015), a manifesto against what he characterizes as nonutilitarian or nonempirical theories of IP. Lemley laments that "participants on both sides of the IP debates are increasingly staking out positions that simply do not depend on evidence at all" (2015, p. 1336). He adds, "I call this retreat from evidence faith-based IP, both because adherents are taking the validity of the IP system on faith, and because the rationale for doing so is a form of religious belief" (2015, p. 1337). He treats Robert Merges' *Justifying Intellectual Property* (2011), a book-length argument for the relevance of moral theory to IP, as the paradigmatic example of this phenomenon. Work such as Merges' book, Lemley proposes, is unintelligible.[29]

Lemley's view is largely legible as an example of public biopolitics, reminiscent of classical liberalism. Accordingly, his first presupposition is that the Market is Good: "almost all of the debate" in economics these days "takes place at the margins of the fundamental discovery that market mechanisms supplemented with some infrastructure investment and health and safety regulation generally work better than anything else in providing most goods and services" (2015, p. 1330). His second presupposition is that IP is a "form of government regulation of the free market designed to serve a useful social end – encouraging innovation and creation" (2015, p. 1330). He then makes the central claim of the biopolitical state:

> The fact that IP is government regulation of the marketplace doesn't mean it is a bad thing. Many regulations are desirable, and I think IP rights of some form are among them. But it does mean that it is not an inherently good thing. In a market-based economy, regulation requires some cost-benefit justification before we accept it.
>
> (2015, p. 1331)

He then cites a number of recent studies that present an empirical debate about the merits of IP, noting that they don't support either the status quo or, more to the point, the continuing upward ratcheting of IP rights. However, "when you are spending a lot of time and money every year in a government-sponsored departure from the free market, even maintaining the status quo ought to require some evidentiary support. And doubling down on that policy certainly should" (2015, p. 1335).

At the same time, Lemley sharply disputes the dominant neoliberal version of IP. For example, in an early paper rejecting James Boyle's argument that IP has been (misfortunately) governed by the mythology of romantic authorship, Lemley (1997) argues that overreliance on proprietization is the actual problem; in a later paper

---

[29] His other principal targets are Madhavi Sunder's *From Goods to a Good Life*, which argues from Amartya Sen's capabilities approach that basing policy on welfare maximization along neoclassical lines occludes consideration of much of what is important about human flourishing; and Amy Kapczynski's "Cost of Price" (2012), which critiques neoliberal reliance on the price mechanism. Kapczynski also underscores the significance (detailed later) of a move away from the consideration of deadweight loss as central to IP.

Lemley's characterization of these other theories as antiempirical seems unfair to me. (He also critiques Lockean theories on that ground; I want to leave that more juridical discussion aside here.) seems unfair to me. Merges' integration of economic evidence is apparent not just in his book, but in, e.g., Merges (2017b); for Merges' reply to Lemley, see Merges (2017a). Although it treats privacy loss as a moral problem generated by price discrimination, Kapczynski's argument is primarily based on a survey of the field of information economics. Sunder rejects law and economics for its misallocation of incentives, and Sen's work on capabilities of course begins with the observation that the reported preferences of Bengali women during a famine were economically irrational.

(2012) he suggests that patent law is too heavily motivated by a myth of the solitary inventor. A paper coauthored with Brett Frischmann argues not only that externalities can be positive ("spillovers"), but also that the neoliberal framing of IP can be called deeply into question by a proper accounting of positive externalities, and in particular by not internalizing them – by leaving them as public benefits. As I will argue in the next section, following Frischmann's lead, a focus on internalizing externalities is central to the neoliberal understanding of property and to its formulation of IP. For now, note that Frischmann and Lemley propose that allowing these positive externalities to remain external benefits any number of third parties, and even drives innovation, a point for which they adduce considerable empirical support.[30]

At the same time, it is worth noting that Lemley's distancing from neoliberalism is not a distancing from an economizing view of the public good. One might compare Lemley's dismissal of "faith-based" IP with Felix Cohen's (1935) famous dismissal of "transcendental nonsense." Arguing against "transcendental" theories that look at questions such as what law "is," Cohen argues, on pragmatist grounds, that it would be better to look at what law does – what he calls a "functionalist" approach. Lemley follows Cohen in dismissing out of hand legal theory that is not empirically grounded.[31] However, Cohen argues that the "chief service of the functional approach [is] that in cleansing legal rules, concepts, and institutions of the compulsive flavors of legal logic or metaphysics, room is made for conscious ethical criticism of law" (1935, p. 847). For Lemley, normative concerns such as capabilities or privacy – even when explicitly raised as separate from economic ones, as in the work of Merges, Sunder, and Kapczynski that he criticizes – are simply unintelligible. In other words, Lemley's vision of social welfare is squarely economic.

---

[30] Lemley also presents a version of the argument that the externalities of IP are positive (as against theory that treats property as a remedy for negative externalities) in Lemley (2005). For the argument that Friscshmann and Lemley inadvertently endorse neoliberal principles even though they discount IP maximalism, see Barron (2010).

[31] He also cites Cohen in his critique of Locke. Lemley writes: IP "intervenes in the market to interfere with the freedom of others to do what they want in hopes of achieving the end of encouraging creativity. If we take that purpose out of the equation, we are left with a belief system that says the government should restrict your speech and freedom of action in favor of mine, not because doing so will improve the world, but simply because I spoke first." He then cites Dreyfuss' "Expressive Genericity" and Cohen's "Transcendental Nonsense" (2015, p. 1339 n1342). Cohen is referring to the circularity inherent in the idea that legal protection is based on economic value, when the economic value in question – the scarcity attached to a trademark – is itself the result of its legal protection. Cohen cites Schechter's (now) famous development of dilution theory as exemplary of such work (1935, pp. 814–815). One need not endorse Cohen's forays into ethics to notice that he thinks there is something to the study of ethics that does not reduce to economics (or emotivism, as his citations in "Transcendental Nonsense" might lead one to suspect); he concludes his "Subject Matter of Ethical Science" by suggesting that the logician must give way to the "poet or artist who discovers intrinsic goodness in realms of life and nature where its existence had not been suspected" (1932, p. 418).

2.3.2 *Demsetzian Theory: The Neoliberalization of IP*

If Mark Lemley's attack on "faith-based" IP shows that dominant IP theory is biopolitical, it also shows that, even in contemporary discussions of IP, there is both a public and a neoliberal variant. One way of marking the difference is in the way the former is solicitous of the public interest in the form of positive externalities and the creation of a semicommons that incorporates aspects of both private property and commons-based regimes. Another was noted by Kapczynski (2012) as one between the efficiency of market-based incentives (advocated by Harold Demsetz) and a concern about deadweight loss (advanced by Kenneth Arrow). As Kapczynski noted, the Demsetzian version won, and in a real sense, that moment is central to the neoliberalization of IP. The result is what Brett Frischmann (2007) calls a "Demsetzian trend" in copyright, and, I will argue, in IP more broadly.

The initial question is the extent to which market analysis is appropriate to the domain in question. As noted earlier, for theorists like Becker, the answer is almost always an unqualified "yes." In a recent essay, Demsetz suggests that:

> Extensive decentralization, characterized by independently acting private owners of resources, describes the core of the spontaneous order problem. The market place, in turn, is the dominant arena in which independently acting persons interact with each other in deciding how the resources they own are to be used. The virtue of the economic model of man is that it is well suited to the task of exploring behavior in this area, *whether it is located in a solidly capitalistic economy or in a solidly socialistic economy.*
>
> (2008, pp. 10–11, emphasis original)

As the Hayekian language about spontaneous order indicates, Demsetz views market analysis – and the view of humans as *homo economicus* – as the best way to understand social interaction when actors are supposedly independent of one another. He is careful to distinguish "conditions in the marketplace" from "those within the family, neighborhood, and political bureaucracy" and within a firm. These are situations with hierarchies and where "personalized interactions, borne of durable associations" dominate, and where "emotionalizing and strategizing are much more likely ... than in the marketplace" (2008, p. 11).

Broadly speaking, then, Demsetz seems to envision two basic types of interactions, one economic and the other sociopolitical. The sociopolitical situations that Demsetz notes are much more likely to be characterized by juridical concepts such as repressive rules and declarations of rights as limits of those rules. Although Demsetz does leave space for such political relations, their sphere is sharply limited: Any time subjects can be viewed as operating separately from one another, market logic applies. The neoliberal view of subjectivity occludes the role of social forces and norms in shaping these actors; in other words, it overstates the independence of economic actors. This means that in the absence of overt hierarchical, institutional structure, individuals are going to be treated as economic agents. It turns out that this is most of the time.

Demsetz is best known for his theory about the emergence of property rights. As a given resource becomes more valuable, he argues, the benefits of a property rights regime come to exceed the costs in creating and enforcing it; at that point, one can expect a property rights regime to emerge. One of the central benefits of property rights for Demsetz is that they internalize externalities. If externalities are negative, property rights ensure that those who cause the negative externalities bear the costs of dealing with them, rather than being able to diffuse them into society. If they are positive, they become additional incentives to develop. As Demsetz argues, property rights "convey the right to benefit or harm oneself or others" within socially prescribed limits, as for example "harming a competitor by producing superior products." Accordingly:

> It is clear, then, that property rights specify how persons may be benefited and harmed, and, therefore, who must pay whom to modify the actions taken by persons. The recognition of this leads easily to the close relationship between property rights and externalities.
>
> (1967, p. 347)

The fundamental Demsetzian theory, then, is that "property rights develop to internalize externalities when the gains of internalization become larger than the cost of internalization" (1967, p. 350). From the point of view of the argument being developed here, two initial points about this narrative are particularly important.

First, given that the theory is subtended by a view of subjectivity that tends to discount structural and social factors that determine individual autonomy, and although it relies on a distinction between economic and political actions, the framework has a very difficult time in distinguishing the two. As Saul Levmore (2002) has shown, in the case of empirical examples like the English enclosure movement, it is very difficult to separate economic from interest group, political, or other motivations, an argument that he specifically applies to IP. The work of scholars such as Susan Sell (2003) has amply demonstrated the viability of his intuition: If there is an economic story to be told about the emergence of IP in the 1980s, there is an equally plausible interest group story about regulatory capture by the pharmaceutical industry, which presented IP as an issue of trade policy. Similarly, Jessica Litman (2006) has argued that the current copyright regime is a morass of interest group politics, an argument that is easily exemplified by legislation such as the Copyright Term Extension Act, for which Disney heavily lobbied and which conveniently extended protection for Mickey Mouse. In such a context, Demsetz's insistence on both the separation of economic and political narratives, as well as the primacy of economic narratives in market relations, indicate what one might better call a normative theoretical preference, and not an empirically superior theoretical framework.[32]

Second, although Demsetz's narrative suggests that property rights will grow and common-access regimes will decline with rising resource costs, Henry Smith (2002) has shown that the empirical evidence of English grazing suggests a more complicated narrative, with a back and forth between property and regulated commons ("governance") strategies. This complication of the Demsetzian narrative allows one to make two important points here. On the one hand, Smith suggests that vacillation between the two will be related more to the relative costs of governance and dividing a resource into smaller parcels than it will be to the value of the resource itself. As regulatory strategies, property rules are cheap but also coarse; governance strategies are costly but much more granular.[33] It is a commonplace that technology has made enforcement of increasingly granular restrictions on use radically cheaper, and so we confront a situation where a reliance on property rhetoric can hide study of the emergence of the specific regulatory techniques involved in IP; we should not expect those to necessarily track property rules. On the other hand, Smith points to the need to understand regulatory strategies on a continuum, with the pure despotic dominion of an (imaginary) property regime on one end, and a purely governance-based commons regime on the other. Thus, "exclusion and governance are alternative methods of preventing dissipation, but they do differ in their costs and benefits at different levels of precision" (2002, p. S474). Recognizing this continuum is important because it shows that, once one understands property biopolitically, as IP does, there can be more than one way of interpreting property and the overlapping aims of governance strategies.

Not only that, the Demsetzian conceptualization of the problem property rights solve is very different from its framing by public biopolitcs. Recall that for theorists such as Mill, information is a "public" good, where "public" indicates that it should be considered as outside of the market, and not amenable to market logic. Even in the case of patents, Mill conceptualizes the patent as the public paying in advance for the social benefit the patent accrues. In other words, the move to internalizing externalities is a substantial shift in how property is framed, and it does so precisely by extending economic logic outside its original sphere. Indeed, as Frischmann suggests, the focus on internalizing externalities means that "arguments in favor of a leaky" system – one that leaves positive externalities in place as public goods – "are often viewed as non-economic or as (re)distributive" (2007, p. 662).

---

[32] Cf. Frischmann (2007), indicating slippage between normative and descriptive aspects of Demsetz, and underlining the explanatory superiority of public choice theory to economic theory in explaining the rise in IP protections.

[33] As Smith puts it, "exclusion is a low-cost method of defending a broad cluster of attributes: using a crude proxy that simultaneously controls access to a wide range of uses saves on the costs of delineating the rights, monitoring for compliance, and processing by duty holders" (2002, p. S474).

The Demsetzian logic makes public biopolitics unintelligible. For example, there are good welfarist reasons to think that, in many cases, the poor will benefit disproportionately from increased access to IP such as textbooks or patented drugs. However, this is unlikely to generate patent-based investment in drugs for the poor, since the poor are unable to pay. Similarly, certain goods such as education or healthcare might be sufficiently valuable that they should be publicly provided, whether or not the recipients of them would be willing to pay.[34] In the context of her discussion of the global influenza network, Kapczynski (2017) suggests that IP incentives may be subject to a bell curve: goods with too little market value won't be incentivized; those with too high a market value (such as a vaccine during a pandemic) will be appropriated by states. In short, the Demsetzian view poorly models the production of information goods whose market value is difficult to express.

More generally, and even for market goods, the account seems to over-emphasize the effects of legal rules on innovation at the expense of other economic factors such as industry norms, first-mover advantages, and trade secrecy. At the same time, the emphasis on innovation hides the way IP affects things like the organization of firms (Merges, 2017b; Silbey, 2014). It also renders either invisible or incomprehensible highly innovative industries like fashion that do not depend on IP (Raustiala & Sprigman, 2012; Rosenblatt, 2011). In all such instances, the public disappears from view, blocked by a theoretical preference for markets understood through the price mechanism.

In short, Demsetz's move to externalities is not logically entailed by characterizing property as social, even in a market-based framework. Indeed, the view that a regime of well-defined understanding of property is social, and designed to optimize population-wide resource allocations, is a common one. To cite just two examples: first, Carol Rose suggests that "property is one of the most sociable institutions that human beings have created, depending as it does on mutual forbearance and on the recognition of and respect for the claims of others" (2005, p. 1019). Second, Abraham Bell and Gideon Parchomovsky (2005) suggest that the core of property rights is allowing for the benefits of stability of ownership insofar as value is created and preserved when owners know that their possessions will durably remain theirs.

The transaction costs argument about externalities allows Demsetz to rely on market pricing and questions of dynamic efficiency. He is able to frame the question as one of static versus dynamic efficiency, and then to downplay concerns about the

---

[34] As noted above, even J. S. Mill thought that education should be an exception to *laissez-faire*, as those who lack it will not correctly value it. On these points, see Chon (2006) and Kapczynski (2012, pp. 998–1006). Both Chon and Kapczynski situate their argument in terms of Amartya Sen and Martha Nussbaum's "capabilities" approach. The capabilities approach, in turn, originates with Sen's observation of "adaptive preferences" on the part of female victims of a Bengali famine: unlike men, they preferred less medical attention than their condition indicated.

static inefficiency of deadweight loss.[35] Deadweight loss is a necessary consequence of above-market (i.e., monopoly) pricing: When something is priced at more than marginal cost, there will be some number of people who desire access to the good but will be prevented from getting it purely by the presence of the higher price. This lost social value is "deadweight loss"; not only are the potential consumers relatively worse off because they do not have the good, but so is the producer, who fails to realize the revenue that would have accrued had they sold the product at a price between the monopoly price and marginal cost.

Recall that Kenneth Arrow had objected that IP regimes created sufficient deadweight loss that other means of encouraging the production of immaterial goods was appropriate. As Arrow put it, "in a free enterprise economy, inventive activity is supported by using the invention to create property rights; precisely to the extent that it is successful, there is an underutilization of the information." This is because "(1) since the price is positive and not at its optimal value of zero, the demand is bound to be below the optimal; (2) as seen before, at any given price, the very nature of information will lead to a lower demand than would be optimal" (1962, p. 617). The first point is that there will be deadweight loss; the second is that purchasers of information do not know its value until after a purchase, and possibly not even then. Demand for information is subject to complicated calculations of risk. Arrow concludes:

> We expect a free enterprise economy to underinvest in invention and research (as compared with an ideal) because it is risky, because the product can be appropriated only to a limited extent, and because of increasing returns in use. This underinvestment will be greater for more basic research. Further, to the extent that a firm succeeds in engrossing the economic value of its inventive activity, there will be an underutilization of that information as compared with an ideal allocation.
>
> (1962, p. 619)

Demsetz responds with two moves. One is to repeat the assertion that markets are more efficient than government in making decisions about economic risk. IP regimes will therefore be *ipso facto* more efficient than forms of government procurement. Demsetz's interlocutor (like Hayek's before him) is clearly an imagined Soviet state planner, and there is no evidence that this is more than a

---

[35] For a thorough treatment of this trade-off, framed as one of the relative – and often technologically dependent – benefits of coordination in resource development versus foregone uses of a resource, see H. E. Smith (2007). As Smith puts it, "in regular property, the right to exclude indirectly protects use privileges, but the presence of positive transaction costs does prevent some beneficial, nonharmful—and in that sense nonrival—uses. The analogous rights in intellectual property likewise benefit from their indirectness but at the price of forgone use. The right to exclude is both the greatest strength and the greatest weakness of intellectual property rights, as it is in regular property" (2007, p. 1785). Smith's framing then allows him to treat changes in information costs (like technological developments) as an independent variable which then alters the trade-off.

straw position today. In any case, the markets argument encounters its own difficulties. For example, the financial crisis provides specific evidence that markets judge risk very poorly due to the pervasive influence of group narratives on the thinking of supposedly epistemically independent market actors (Bronk, 2013). Additionally, market actors deciding whether to invest in a given project are unlikely to know one another's cost estimates. The result can be either overinvestment in a given project (if too many actors invest such that the total investment exceeds the value of the project) or an inverse underinvestment (Kapczynski, 2012, pp. 984–985).

Demsetz's second move is to claim that property rights are much better at spurring innovation, and that this matters more than Arrow's concerns about underutilization: "it is hardly useful to say that there is 'underutilization' of information if the method recommended to avoid 'underutilization' discourages the research required to produce the information" (1969, p. 11). He concludes that "the practice of creating property rights in information and allowing its sale is not clearly inefficient in comparison with these real alternatives" (1969, p. 12).[36] He then argues, against Arrow, that IP monopoly rights provide better incentives to innovate than the alternatives: "if it is thought desirable to encourage invention by granting monopoly power through the patent or through secrecy ... at least in the linear model of two industries of equal output size, the more monopolistic will give the greatest encouragement to invention" (1969, p. 19).

There are several things to note here. First, Demsetz's argument depends on the neoliberal tolerance of monopolies. Indeed, in the paper against Arrow, he cites Director for his "revealing insights into the problem" of monopolies, which Demsetz, following Chicago antitrust theory, says can actually encourage innovation under the right conditions (1969, p. 14 n26). In an economic framework in which monopolies were presumptively bad, such as the one presupposed by Mill or Macaulay, his claim about innovation would fail. Indeed, the last pages of Arrow's paper sound much more like Macaulay or Mill than Demsetz. Arrow talks about the financing of inventive work in universities or comparable settings, worries about the need for society to have access to basic research in particular, and analogizes the situation to that of public infrastructure. In this sense, one might characterize Arrow's invocation of static inefficiencies as a version of the classical liberal critique of monopoly. Demsetz, in contrast, is adopting the thesis that dynamic efficiency will happen not just in spite of but because of monopoly. Following Schumpeter, "innovation" is the primary driver of welfare.

Second, the Demsetzian strategy depends on price discrimination (charging differential rates for access). In principle, a regime of perfect price discrimination

---

[36] I will not pursue the point here, but it seems to me that Arrow makes more of an argument about dynamic inefficiency than Demsetz credits him with: For Arrow, for example, one of the peculiar properties of information is the dependence of downstream information production on information now. Underutilization of information now thereby negatively impacts downstream innovation.

would, in efficiency terms, mirror a well-functioning market. At the same time, there are disadvantages to price discrimination. First, it is very informationally intensive and so presents serious privacy concerns for consumers.[37] In addition, gathering information carries considerable transaction costs which then have to be set as limits to price discrimination. Not only that, monopoly rights in information, even with price discrimination, will disproportionally impact uses with a high social but low market value, such as academic research, basic science, and so forth.[38] These are uses where willingness (or ability) to pay functions poorly as a proxy for value, or where market and social value tend to diverge. In other words, the argument about monopolies presupposes the market framework, in which information is treated exclusively as a market good, that it is meant to justify. The social welfare costs of price discrimination disappear from view.

Third, Demsetz relies on an argument about excludability that is arguably made obsolete by technological developments. He claims that "it is true that all 'theft' of information cannot be eliminated at reasonable cost. But knowledge is not unique in this respect, since the same can be said of any valuable asset" (1969, p. 10). However, this implies that if copying – "theft" – becomes very cheap, making excludability very costly, a property regime becomes less efficient, and deadweight loss more serious, even on his own terms. Elsewhere, while defending the possibility of a market in "public" goods that are nonrivalrous but excludable, Demsetz (1970) concedes that "collective goods" – nonrivalrous and nonexcludable – will be poorly provided by markets, though he tries to hedge the conclusion by suggesting that the collective good might be financed by market-oriented goods: Radio broadcasts can be paid for by advertisers, for example.

Fourth, and perhaps most importantly, as Kapczynski (2012) notes, contemporary information economics tells a much more nuanced story about other kinds of incentives to creation, which are not obviously inferior to markets. When Demsetz says property rights are not clearly inefficient, he is comparing them to the "socialist ideal," which stacks the deck in favor of neoliberal property rights by mischaracter-izing the alternatives. It is here that one can clearly see the production of a social truth: Based on a Hayekian claim about the efficiency of markets, the neoliberal account of IP ignores serious challenges to its central claims about efficiency, producing a discourse about the production of information that presupposes the

---

[37] This point is emphasized in Kapczynski (2012), and it is the precise point where Lemley (2015) accuses her of irrationality.

[38] For a critique of price discrimination, as well as privacy concerns, see Boyle (2000). For granularity, deadweight loss, and social versus market value, see Benkler (2000). Arrow also makes the argument: "basic research, the output of which is only used as an informational input into other inventive activities, is especially unlikely to be rewarded. In fact, it is likely to be of commercial value to the firm undertaking it only if other firms are prevented from using the information obtained. But such restriction on the transmittal of information will reduce the efficiency of inventive activity in general and will therefore reduce its quantity also" (1962, p. 618).

merits of proprietization. Ignoring the potential benefits of positive externalities and structurally downplaying the risks of negative externalities makes a public biopolitics unintelligible. Not only that, this supposed truth about the necessity of IP then generates the need to create both a regulatory infrastructure and individual market actors that subscribe to its basic framework.

Those actors do not just think economically; they accept a very specific narrative about epistemically independent market actors making investment decisions based on the price mechanism. They believe that the best way to deal with information is through proprietary exclusion mechanisms, and not as a public good. Indeed, they think that being too solicitous of a nebulous public interest poses an unacceptable risk to future innovation. This framing then makes it difficult for them to articulate distributive or other concerns, because they always live in a theoretical world where access is in conflict with creation. In this way, neoliberal reliance on prices, its tolerance of monopoly, and the radical extension of market mechanisms into all of life becomes the truth through which the production of information is understood.

Because people are not necessarily born with the beliefs and dispositions necessary to support the Demsetzian account of property, they will have to be created. The theory, in other words, encourages a process of subjectification. How such a process is to happen emerges as a question even in the basic articulation of the theory. As Carol Rose notes, the Demsetzian account basically takes a before and an after snapshot, and proposes that "people figured it out" in between. However, one needs immediately to ask where the norms on which the property regime relies came from, and how they became generally accepted (2006, p. 10). The only plausible answer to this question is that these governing norms had to be created, which is to say that the property regime has to make people who follow these norms and that the presence of a mass of people who follow the norms is central to making the property regime.[39] As the following chapters will argue, making people who assent to the basic Demsetzian narrative about IP is a central task of current IP regimes.

The specificity of the neoliberal, Demsetzian model can be seen in one of the most prominent critiques of it – efforts to defend the creation and maintenance of commons-based governance strategies, or to argue that IP should facilitate the development of a commons. The literature on intellectual and cultural commons is large and diverse, but I want to single out two aspects of it which are salient here.

---

[39] As Rose notes elsewhere, the narrative covers over the fact that the sorts of utility maximizers the theory presupposes would have difficulty in cooperating enough to create a property regime: "a property regime, in short, presupposes a kind of character who is not predicted in the standard story about property. And that, I suggest, is why the classic theories of property turned to narrative at crucial moments, particularly in explaining the origin of property regimes, where the need for cooperation is most obvious: Their narrative stories allowed them to slide smoothly over the cooperative gap in their systematic analyses of self-interest" (1990, p. 51).

First, a substantial percentage of this literature is dedicated to articulating benefits of cultural production that cannot be successfully realized through strategies of internalization. Either these benefits cannot be incentivized through the Demsetzian model or they become unintelligible as benefits through it. For example, Frischmann and Lemley (2006) argue that positive externalities – "spillovers" – are important for infrastructural and intellectual goods because the social value of their use might exceed the private value to users, especially because the use might itself be productive and not just consumptive. In earlier work, Yochai Benkler (2000) had argued that uses with particularly high social value, such as transformative uses, basic science, and academic research, were particularly vulnerable to this mismatch between private willingness (or ability) to pay and the social value generated by the work.

Frischmann and Lemley conclude that "there is good economic evidence that greater innovation spillovers are associated with more, not less, innovation," an empirical fact which is unintelligible within a Demsetzian framework (2006, p. 127). They argue that IP regimes need to be conceptualized as advancing a "semicommons," where the ability of property owners to internalize the gains of their work deliberately be limited so as to promote these externalities. After all, if the goal is to incentivize innovation, internalization beyond that necessary to incentivize is socially wasteful. Similarly, Madison, Frischmann, and Strandburg (2010) and Strandburg, Frischmann, and Madison (2017) emphasize that a commons is a governance strategy constructed through policy, and can be strengthened and weakened in a more public facing or more neoliberal direction.

Second, prominent work defending commons-based production is not only oriented around making it economically intelligible, but also doing so on normative grounds that highlight the kinds of subjectivity it fosters.[40] This is central to Yochai Benkler's earliest work on the matter (2002), and it is the central focus of later work by others as well (Kapczynski, 2012). Benkler takes peer-production projects as a given and asks how they can be understood. His answer is essentially that, for some kinds of goods, they solve a series of problems better than either markets or firms. One is that individuals are able to self-identify for given projects, which is an efficient way to match productivity to task; individuals know their own talents more efficiently than managers do, especially given that managers are constrained by the boundaries of their firms. Another is that commons-based production can be more efficient in allocating tasks to individuals best able to complete them, because it makes a broader pool of individuals and resources available to each other at a lower cost than markets or firms, which both accrue significant transaction costs in the

---

[40] Conversely, and with reference to Foucault and Habermas, Lessig underscores that a full view of a regulatory apparatus committed to rational-choice-based manipulation of markets shows it to be normatively problematic: "the regulation of this school is totalizing. It is the effort to make culture serve power, a 'colonization of the lifeworld.' Every space is subject to a wide range of control; the potential to control every space is the aim of the school" (1998, p. 691).

form of contracts and property. Additionally, commons-based production accommodates a different set of incentive structures from those of markets or firms. For
example, individuals who desire to contribute for something other than money are
able to do so easily. In addition to the focus on economic factors, Benkler's
argument is significant in that it envisions human subjectivity outside the bounds
of *homo economicus*. Indeed, Benkler and Helen Nissenbaum (2006) suggest that
participation in commons-based projects can help to develop virtue, and his normative defense of commons-based production in *Wealth of Networks* (2006) emphasizes the values of classic liberalism.[41] In short, the core of the commons-based
critique of the Demsetzian model is focused on shifting the economic model in a
way that is more accommodating to the idea of non-privately owned intellectual
goods, and along with it, shifting the underlying vision of human subjectivity
undergirding it.

The point here is not to condemn the Demsetzian turn in IP law, although I will
argue in Chapter 3 on copyright that it very poorly understands incentives and will
express skepticism about its outcomes throughout. The point here is to note that the
Demsetzian turn is unmistakably a neoliberal turn. It not only tolerates but
embraces monopolies. It suppresses the possibility of viewing information in terms
of a public biopolitics by way of condemnation of consideration of deadweight loss.
It both presupposes and creates a situation in which individuals approach information and cultural artifacts more broadly as autonomous market actors. And it
nearly inexorably extends market logic into cultural arenas in which it formerly had
no purchase.

---

[41] In his review of the book, Hetcher (2009) suggests that one can model large-scale social
production best with a "Humean" model of rationality that assumes that individuals can act
for non-self-interested reasons. In other words, the argument accommodates the classical liberal
view of rationality as potentially prosocial.

3

Copyright

As noted in Chapter 2, intellectual property (IP) helps to make us who we are. Nowhere is this more directly evident than in the case of copyright, which directly regulates the structure of our information environment. Changes to copyright can therefore produce, directly or indirectly, changes to ourselves. Early copyright law exhibited the concerns of public biopolitics. It has been also moving steadily away from public biopolitics toward its neoliberal variant for some time, increasingly codifying the view that authors are entitled to appropriate all the potential gains of their creative activities. When John Locke wrote to complain about the British Licensing Act that the first copyright law, the 1710 Statute of Anne, replaced, he registered a complaint about the damaging effects of monopoly on the literary public.[1] The original US Copyright Act of 1790 protected only maps, charts, and books. It provided for a fourteen-year term, renewable once if the author was still alive at the end of it. It also required that the work in question be officially registered. After this, or in the absence of registration, or if the work did not originate in the United States, it could be freely published by anyone. By 1976, the term was being extended to the length of the author's life plus fifty years; in 2003, the Supreme Court upheld the addition of twenty years on top of that (*Eldred*). Although it codified fair use defenses for the first time, the 1976 Act also dropped the registration requirement (although it heavily rewarded creators who were sophisticated enough to register their works) and provided explicit protection for so-called derivative works, like sequels, allowing authors to control much of what the public could creatively do with their works, other than consume them passively.

The aggregate result has been a substantial shift in how copyright approaches artistic and literary expression. Of course, more such expression is covered by copyright, and it is covered longer. But the experience itself changes as well. Nineteenth-century practice involved the widespread remixing and reinterpretation

---

[1] Locke (1997, pp. 332–333). See the following discussion.

of popular works (Tehranian, 2012); such practices today are limited. So too, historically, much of the experience of reading was under the reader's control; they did not have to read a book in any particular order, and were free to skip the copyright notice. Today, DVDs force users to view not just copyright notices, but often advertising as well. This expansion of copyright is typically the lead example in complaints about what James Boyle (2008) calls the "enclosure of the commons of the mind." Not only that, this process has largely been accepted by the Supreme Court; the Court's defense of parody as fair use stands out as anomalous, and even that is limited in ways that I will discuss.[2]

To understand this shift in copyright, I begin first with an outline of its initial articulation as a form of public biopower. I then turn to the theory of incentives at the core of current copyright theory, as this model of production offers a clear window into the contours of a neoliberal view according to which everyone involved in copyright is primarily or even exclusively a market actor, operating according to the rules of *homo economicus*. I then look at two kinds of consequence of this view. One is the difficult relation between copyright and hip hop sampling, which illustrates why the ability to internalize all possible externalities of a work is impossible to reconcile with public biopolitics, including as it has tended to evolve in related areas of fair use. Fair use that protects public interests, including not just participants and listeners, but also those not recognized as "authors" by the dominant narrative of creation, is the exception, not the rule. The second is a ban on circumventing "digital rights management" (DRM) technologies in 1998. By banning the circumvention of DRM, the Digital Millennium Copyright Act (DMCA) enabled content owners to force much of the public's interaction with their products into a consumer model, facilitating the subjectification of individuals as consumers by changing the experience of interacting with content. Embodying the view that externalities are to be internalized (taking a limited range of fair uses as exceptions), that all of society should be understood in market terms, and that monopolies are an efficient way to generate consumer welfare, current copyright increasingly expresses a neoliberal understanding of power. In so doing, the legal regime itself works to create certain kinds of subjects – those whose incentive structures map more accurately onto the economic model used to describe them.

3.1 COPYRIGHT AS PUBLIC BIOPOLITICS

There was a time, not too long ago, when those who used media – books, radio, television, newspapers, etc. – did not have to think about copyright very much, if at

---

[2] The other obvious example of the Court not using neoclassical economics when it had the opportunity was the decision against the Grokster file-sharing service, in which the Court based its decision on internal emails in which the company essentially bragged about facilitating infringement. See Gordon (2008).

all. Copyright was an industrial policy, in the sense that it primarily regulated large corporations. This was because it was expensive to make a copy of something, and only companies with considerable capital investment could produce copies of sufficient quality fast enough to cause the owners of copyrighted works any serious concern. A certain amount of noncompliance, of course, was to be expected, but it would also remain at the margins of society, where it would remain sufficiently marginal that it could be safely ignored.

The original copyright regime in England was also designed to allow publishers to base publication decisions on market factors, rather than on royally controlled licensing guilds, opening entire new areas for safe literary and other exploration. Critics of licensing, such as John Locke, were convinced that the move to markets would improve the quality and quantity of works available, and were even able to point to the Netherlands as an example of how doing things differently might be better:

> For the Company of Stationers have obtained from the crown a patent to print all or at least the greatest part of the classic authors, upon pretence, as I hear, that they should be well and truly printed, whereas they are by them scandalously ill printed, both for letter, paper and correctness, and scarce one tolerable edition made by them of any one of them ... This certain[ly] is very absurd at first sight that any person or company should now have a title to the printing of the works of Tully's, Caesar's or Livy's, who lived so many ages since, exclusive of any other, nor can there be any reason in nature why I might not print them as well as the Company of Stationers if I thought fit. This liberty of printing them is certainly the way to have them the cheaper and the better and 'tis this which in Holland has produced so many fair and excellent editions of them, whilst the printers all strive to outdo one another which has also brought in great sums to the trade of Holland.

(Locke, 1997, pp. 332–333)

As with later theorists like Mill and Macaulay, copyright emerges here in the context of modern liberalism at the boundary of juridical and biopower, and as a way to generate public benefits such as access to quality literary works, as well as education and scientific progress more broadly.[3] Early twentieth-century copyright tended toward narrow protections balanced against concern about monopolies. In a 1908 case, the Supreme Court declared the view that "a mechanical instrument which reproduces a tune copies it" is a "strained and artificial meaning" of the word "copy"; Congress had to revise the statute to cover piano rolls.[4] Much discussion

---

[3] Locke also tends to think price discrimination is immoral: see his "Venditio" essay (1997, pp. 339–343). Whether it is possible to get a theory of intellectual property out of Locke is a matter of considerable debate. I have argued that it is, but that it would be a limited one. See Hull (2009a) and the citations there. For Mill and Macaulay, see Chapter 2.

[4] *White-Smith* (1908, p. 17). In a concurring opinion, Justice Holmes expressed his surprise at this result: "one would expect that" a copyrighted object "would be protected according to what was its essence. One would expect the protection to be coextensive not only with the invention ...

around copyright through the New Deal was oriented around concern about ASCAP's monopoly on performance rights for music, and whether provisions like compulsory licensing were adequate protections for the public (Wilf, 2008, pp. 176–183). By the end of the New Deal, "copyright's new-found purpose was to promote the aggregate economic interests of an emerging industrial economy" (Wilf, 2008, p. 190).

According to a story that has been told numerous times, digitization changed all of this, and the last major piece of copyright legislation, the Digital Millennium Copyright Act of 1998, emerged at the end of a conscious effort to update copyright for the information age. As I will argue, the DMCA marks a significant moment in the neoliberalization of copyright. The central issue with digitization is that copyright affects nearly all aspects of a digital culture, because nearly all engagement in a digital culture involves making a copy of something, even if only to display it on a screen to read it. This is radically different from the world of print, where reading and rereading (and loaning or reselling, etc.) a single book entailed no further copying beyond its initial printing. At the same time, information as an immaterial good is increasingly economically important, fueling demands for the legal regime to control its dissemination.[5] The move from print to digital culture, then, has turned copyright policy into cultural policy at a very granular level, and relatively small changes in copyright can have tremendous cultural implications. As Tarleton Gillespie suggests:

> Copyright is at the heart of cultural policy – those rules that help to govern what is said, by whom, and with what effect. If we are at all concerned about the power of communication, the dynamics of democracy, the politics of culture, or freedom of expression, copyright must be a fundamental part of our inquiry. Shifts in the design and application of copyright law must be recognized as having consequences in all of these domains as they migrate to the digital realm.
>
> (Gillespie, 2007, p. 10)

Copyright law has responded by neoliberalizing.

For example, consider the extension of the copyright term, as this sort of extension is only comprehensible in a world where monopoly rights are no longer perceived as

but with the possibility of reproducing the result which gives to the invention its meaning and worth" (*White-Smith*, 1908, p. 19). For the history of the piano roll case and subsequent legislation, see Litman (2006, pp. 35–69, esp. 38–40). I discuss *White-Smith* in the context of the original/copy distinction and digitization in Hull (2003a).

5   As Mark Poster only somewhat hyperbolically put it several years ago, copyright law has become "nothing less than the general law of property. Wealth increasingly is defined as information and copyright is its police force. Crimes against property are less and less the appropriation of or damage to a physical object than the illicit copying of text, image, and sound" (2001, p. 91). Compare Tehranian: "copyright law represents a key battleground in power relations, especially in the twenty-first century, as various societal actors struggle for the rights to control, regulate, or manipulate cultural content" (2012, p. 1248).

the evil that Macaulay took them to be, or where price discrimination is no longer perceived as the evil that Locke took it to be. Consider Richard Posner's defense of lengthy copyright terms. On the one hand, he says they can prevent congestion externalities (the analogy is to excess traffic on non-toll roads). If Mickey Mouse were to revert to the public domain, "the resulting surfeit of copies might produce a net reduction in the market value of the character if overexposure induced a degree of boredom or even disgust that caused, via a downward shift in the demand curve, a decline in total utility" (2005, p. 61). In other words, fewer copies of Mickey Mouse at a higher price might be worth more in the aggregate (measured in terms of money to Disney, of course) than more copies at a lower price. On the other hand, the marginal costs of maintaining the Mickey character might be higher than it would initially seem: Disney spends considerable sums on "advertising and promotion and continual minor modifications in the character itself designed to maintain the character's appeal in the face of changing tastes" (2005, p. 61). Presumably, these resources would not be spent on a character Disney did not own. For Posner, the idea of a public benefit is interpreted in economic terms that focus on Disney itself.

Other examples are more subtle. Consider, for example, the so-called safe harbor provision in §230 of the Communications Decency Act (47 USC §230, 1996), which provides substantial protection from liability for sites that host content on the Internet, even if that content is infringing. In a basic sense, §230 enables the business model of sites like YouTube. These sites both make a lot of material available to the public – much of it user-generated, independently of large media companies – and encourage the monetization of that availability. On the other hand, §230 also requires content providers to remove allegedly infringing material, at the request of content owners. Content providers that refuse to do so lose protection for contributory infringement, and so have been eager to comply with takedown notices. However, individual users are given almost no protection from these notices, and almost no opportunity to contest them. There is a mechanism to dispute takedowns, but material must first be taken down, and it is at the site's discretion whether to reinstate it. Needless to say, sites have no incentive to do so. For all the good it has done, then, §230 has also enabled a privatized enforcement regime for a public law, a regime that has profound impacts on what users are able to share and see online, especially as content providers have taken to using auto-mated processes to detect content they view as infringing, and then to order its removal. The implications of this regime extend beyond pop culture. As Wendy Seltzer (2010) documents, both the Obama and McCain campaigns had YouTube ads deleted with a week to go before the 2008 election. This was too close to the election for even the weak appeal process to function, and in any case, YouTube never looked at the validity of the complaints, even though the takedown mechan-ism enabled a commercial third party to silence what should have been core, First Amendment-protected speech.

Behind these developments, copyright as a legal regime faces a number of problems beyond those directly induced by cheap copying. Most people do not understand it, do not think that much of the activity it forbids either is or should be forbidden, and resent what they take to be the lavish lifestyles of content industry executives. Industry efforts at enforcement are hampered by both the scale of copying and the difficulty in targeting the individuals doing it. Even for those who try to understand copyright, the law is extremely complex and difficult to follow in all but the most obvious cases (Litman, 2006). This complexity and its dissonance with cultural norms about sharing erode copyright's moral authority further, which in turn lowers its viability as a property regime (Merrill and Smith, 2007). Producers increasingly turn to code-based enforcement strategies like DRM, the equivalent to dealing with speeding by installing speed bumps, rather than increasing police patrols (for a defense, see Cheng, 2006). Consumers bitterly resent DRM, both because producers use it to do a lot more than stop copying (Elkin-Koren, 2002; Hull, 2012), and because it appears to take control of devices that they own away from them (Gillespie, 2007). In such an environment it is perhaps not surprising that, when copying became easy, users stopped paying. This problem has been particularly intractable for the music industry, though the industry's own responses have often been perceived as inappropriate or as blaming consumers for problems in its own business model (Knopper, 2009).

There are of course many ways to tell the story of the preceding paragraph, and the story by itself says nothing about how much protection is enough. Nor does it say which of the many possible interventions are the correct ones to use in an effort to shore up copyright as a legal regime.

3.2 INCENTIVES THEORY: IMAGINING NEOLIBERAL CREATIVE SUBJECTS

As I argued in Chapter 2, IP doctrine has historically promoted the public good by way of an effort to incentivize the private production of immaterial goods. These goods, the narrative goes, will be underproduced without some way of ensuring that their producers can recuperate their costs and generate enough revenue to make creation worth the time. Since the late 1970s, the general rise of neoliberal biopower has been accompanied by a neoliberalization of IP, particularly in the form of an increasingly myopic consideration of the supposed benefits of internalizing externalities. If the New Deal marked the emergence of copyright as an industrial policy and the retreat of what Steven Wilf characterizes as a "romantic image of authorship" (2008, p. 190), the last decades have seen a rehabilitation of precisely this vision of authorship, newly packaged under a revised theory of incentives.[6]

---

[6] Mark Rose (1993) shows in detail how a more utilitarian view of copyright as limited, and perhaps akin to patents, versus one that promoted the interests of a romantic author with

By focusing on internalization, the Demsetzian narrative not only tends to ignore political and public choice explanations for the rise of copyright, it also tends to occlude consideration of anything like a public good.

In what follows, I want to look more concretely at the kind of social actor that this theory imagines as the creator of intellectual works. As the discussion in Chapter 2 of the shift from *homo scientificus* to *homo economicus* in patenting suggests, my general claim will be that current copyright doctrine assumes that creators are *homo economicus*; in so doing, it encourages creators who understand themselves as rational economic actors, discourages those that do not, and nudges the undecided toward economic rationality. This construction is both myopic and coercively deployed. First, public benefits and spaces lose significance except as whatever can be internalized, as does creative work that does not conform to the model. Additionally, copyright is using increasingly coercive structures to get people to behave as market actors. The present section assesses the theoretical construction of creators as "authors" as imagined by neoliberal theory. The following section looks in detail at how the legal treatment of hip-hop sampling nudges creators in that direction. The final section looks at DRM as a coercive means to ensure that "authors" have well-behaved consumers for their work. In all these cases, copyright functions as neoliberal biopower by way of strategies of subjectification.

Copyright's protection of authorship interacts with deeply held social convictions of originality and personhood. As Mark Rose concludes his study of the emergence of copyright in eighteenth-century Britain:

> Copyright is not a transcendent moral idea, but a specifically modern formation produced by printing technology, marketplace economics, and the classical liberal culture of possessive individualism. It is also an institution built on intellectual quicksand: the essentially religious concept of originality, the notion that certain extraordinary beings called authors conjure works out of thin air ... The institution of copyright is of course deeply rooted in our economic system ... But, no less important, copyright is deeply rooted in our conception of ourselves as individuals with at least a modest degree of singularity, some degree of personality.
>
> (1993, p. 142)

What is perhaps most striking about modern incentives theory is how reductive of this complexity it is.

When applied to copyright, Demsetzian theory is essentially a dressed-up version of James Boswell's quip that "no man but a blockhead ever wrote, except for money." No doubt many people create purely with the expectation of financial

---

perpetual copyright was central to debates around copyright in eighteenth-century England. Of course, it was booksellers and printers that were the primary beneficiaries of extended copyrights, since authors generally transferred their rights to them. Promotion of romanticized views of authorship helped to distract from this state of affairs in a way that "elides the real means of cultural production" (p. 135).

remuneration (though it is worth pointing out that many of those are not recognized by copyright law as rights holders, since their output is strictly "for hire"), and Robert Merges (2011) makes the strong case that copyright enables creative industries where many people can be employed. That said, the theory also completely fails to square with the creative experience of many, many individuals, including children, prisoners, authors of fan fiction, creators of YouTube videos, bloggers, Anne Frank, academics, open source authors, and others.[7] As I noted in the introduction, religious groups have used copyright authorship to exert control over texts they claim are divinely inspired; notions of authorship have also caused difficulties for recovered religious texts like the Dead Sea Scrolls (Nimmer, 2001). Not only that, as will become apparent in the discussion of music sampling, the theory also fails to recognize political motivations as such, attempting to reduce them to disguised attempts at economic gain, especially when the material in question works through reappropriation of existing material. At the same time, it authorizes uncompensated appropriation of material not created according to Western understandings of authorship.[8]

These occlusions enact the theoretical reduction of social welfare into consumer welfare in Chicago antitrust theory. That is, it is able to understand social interactions only as market transactions between producers and consumers. What is one to make of a theory of incentives to create that is unable to model the creative process of so many? To assert that these individuals nonetheless have an incentive structure amenable to economic analysis requires asserting that what they experience as their desires does not in fact model or represent accurately their felt desires, because the only desires that matter are expressible as economic preferences.

The core insight of a substantial body of recent literature is that the incentives model radically underemphasizes both nonpecuniary extrinsic rewards like prestige, and the intrinsic reasons people create. It also fails to account for the potential social benefits of fostering creativity in these broader ways.[9] As such, it is profoundly procrustean. In advocating a more complex view, Julie Cohen argues:

7   For the Boswell, see Tushnet (2009, p. 517). Tushnet offers a particularly forceful critique of this assumption, as does Julie E. Cohen (2007) (arguing that most IP scholarship requires strange theoretical precommitments: to rights or economics, to progress or relativism, and to abstraction over materiality. It thus fails to understand the cultural contexts in which creativity occurs). Some of my examples are also from Kwall (2006). For a critique of the incentives model as failing to understand IP as a site of cultural struggle, see Sunder (2006, 2012). For Web 2.0 creativity, see Balkin (2004).
8   This point is a mainstay in critiques of the ways that IP fails to protect indigenous, non-Western cultural artifacts. See, e.g., Riley (2000). It analogously fails to model collaborative work in the case of patents (Dreyfuss, 2002).
9   Part of the interest of this literature here is that it allows one to emphasize, by way of contrast, the neoliberal nature of current incentives theory. That is, this literature does not abandon either biopolitics or even economics; rather, it emphasizes public biopolitics against its neoliberal reduction.

Methodologically, the distinction is one between a social theory of creativity that embraces an eclectic range of methods, including economic methods, and an economic model of creativity that has room only for its own methods and that consequently distorts in predictable and predictably damaging ways. Substantively the distinction is one between deploying known cost-benefit calculations in an attempt to generate predictable results and deliberately leaving room for unpredictable results to emerge. Creativity requires breathing room and thrives on play in the system of culture.

(2012, p. 103)

The specific case studies that follow will illustrate this point concretely, and show the extent to which the neoliberal model of creativity precludes all nonmarket logics. Here, I want to focus on the theory itself.

As Yochai Benkler summarizes a significant body of research, "for any given culture, there will be some acts that a person would prefer to perform not for money, but for social standing, recognition, and probably, ultimately, instrumental value obtainable only if that person has performed the action through a social, rather than a market, transaction" (2006, p. 96). In other words, the value of some of this material to its creators depends on it *not* being readily explainable in market terms. The Internet has facilitated both individual creative works, like blogs and mash-ups, and collective ones, like Wikipedia. For individual works, it solves a problem of distribution by making it possible to publish to a potentially indefinitely large audience, nearly for free. (Whether anyone reads that material is a separate consideration.) For example, the Internet has revolutionized how people find music, with artists posting videos on SoundCloud or YouTube and then trying to generate social media buzz to drive views (Levy, 2018). For collective works, the Internet solves a problem of scalability. Historically, non-market-based forms of production have been limited to small, tightly knit social communities because it was very difficult to coordinate larger groups of people. For projects that are sufficiently modular (divisible into discrete tasks) and granular (those tasks that can be performed by individuals, often in their spare time), the Internet not only allows collaborators to self-select from an enormous number of individuals, who contribute to the extent they want or are able to, but also to efficiently distribute those contributions. The result is "the emergence of information production that is not based on exclusive proprietary claims, not aimed toward sales in a market for either motivation or information, and not organized around property and contract claims to form firms or market exchanges" (Benkler, 2006, p. 105).

Benkler's formulation is not without difficulties. First, as he notes, not all kinds of work are easily modular or granular. Encyclopedias make sense in this model; novels do not. Second, as Lior Strahilevitz notes, one of the main advantages of social production is the ability to efficiently recruit individuals to work on projects. This also poses a problem of resilience to malicious users, as recent concerns with

Facebook and election meddling amply demonstrate. Wikipedia's difficulties in dealing with malicious edits and sock puppetry are further examples, as is the violent harassment faced by women who attempt to participate online (for Wikipedia, see Strahilevitz, 2007, pp. 1485, 1493; for harassment, see Citron, 2014). Third, large corporations like Facebook and Google will always emerge to capture market value from users' creative outputs (1497–1503). However these larger issues play out, it seems to be the case that social production lets one understand the incentives of producing copyrightable material without invoking copyright. Although there is debate about how much of this material exists, it is substantial, and supported by a coherent economic model. This research into the role of social norms and even law suggests that there are many non-market-based reasons why people create, none of which are captured by the standard incentives narrative.

Scholars such as Roberta Kwall and Rebecca Tushnet have pointed to fundamental difficulties caused by the incentives argument's reliance on a reductive, behaviorist account of the reasons people do things: As Tushnet puts it, it is as if "the scientist might have been a journalist, if only her internal utility calculus and/or the relative rewards from the two fields differed enough." The problem is that "the actors in this story are unrecognizable as people. Creativity, as lived, is more than a response to incentives, working from fixed and random preferences" (2009, p. 521). Tushnet cites several published accounts by authors about their own motivations, which often do not seem susceptible to economic explanation. Kwall (2006) highlights the importance that authors assign to "inspiration" and the intrinsic value they find in expressing themselves in their works; these values are also deeply embedded in religious accounts of divine and human creation. Feminist scholarship has looked particularly at fan fiction. Produced largely by women, and often exploring issues of sexuality that are difficult to explore in more commercial contexts, fan fiction is a form of expression that seems largely indifferent to the legal modeling of creativity in copyright (Katyal, 2006a; Tushnet, 2009).

The research cited earlier speaks primarily to the motivations of individual creators. In the case of corporate creators or media companies, the blockhead model works much better, as companies have to pay whomever they hire to do creative work, and they expect that the work will contribute in some way to corporate profitability. However, recent work by Jessica Silbey (2014) complicates even this story considerably. On the one hand, she adds further evidence that individual creators are not monolithically motivated by the incentive structures of copyright. On the other hand, pointing out that it is often a mistake to treat large corporate entities as univocal actors, she reports on a series of interviews with corporate agents, whose "descriptions of corporate culture and management choices reject the monolithic identity of a corporation whose only goal is to make money," and "even for the companies that may exist to make money ... the progress of science and art requires passion for the work, which does not appear to be incentivized by IP's investment function." When IP law does intervene, it often "serves goals relating ... to

relationship building and business flexibility" (2014, pp. 13–14). In sum, the economic incentives model is important. However, such incentives seem to be neither
necessary nor sufficient to explain more broadly why people create.

The gap between creative processes and the neoliberal incentives model suggests
that the model is doing a different kind of work. By treating agents and their desires
as fundamental, this approach also tends to occlude the extent to which agents can
be viewed not just as entry points into a regulatory environment, the parameters of
which then structure that agent's desires, but as themselves the products of the
regulatory environment that they inhabit. That is to say, one can view the current
incentive narrative as attempting to create a certain kind of subject, incentivizing not
just creative work, but work by people who understands themselves as "authors" with
a proprietary relation to the work they create. As Foucault suggests in an early
lecture responding to literary theory about authorship, it is important to recognize
that authorship does important political work, whatever one thinks of it as a way to
approach textual interpretation.[10] In particular, we are prone to organize texts
according to "authors" in part as a strategy for managing meanings and assigning
them to creators. Foucault's language is difficult, but striking:

> The author is the principle of thrift in the proliferation of meaning. As a result, we
> must entirely reverse the traditional idea of the author. We are accustomed … to
> saying that the author is the genial creator of a work in which he deposits, with
> infinite wealth and generosity, an inexhaustible world of significations … The truth
> is quite the contrary … the author does not precede the works; he is a certain
> functional principle by which, in our culture, one limits, excludes, and chooses; in
> short, by which one impedes the free circulation, the free manipulation, the free
> composition, decomposition, and recomposition of fiction.
>
> (1984b, pp. 118–119)

What does it mean to view authorship as a reductive rather than a generative
function?

Note first that incentives theory maps this customary view of authorship nearly
perfectly: An author is one who creates something "original" and in so doing adds to
the amount of meaning in the world.[11] What is important in this context is that
authors do not precede the works they create. Authorship as imagined by the
incentives theory of copyright is a functional role that content creators can occupy,

---

[10] Foucault's essay is specifically applied to IP in Heymann (2005), which notes that authorship
serves an identifying function similar to trademarking. Of course, the author function is also
central in viewing work as the product of a juridical, rights-bearing subject, and so it also finds
resonance in earlier views of creativity that melded juridical subjectivity and literary romanticism. On this, see Boyle (1997) and Peeler (1999). Both views of subjectivity overstate the initial
autonomy of social actors, a point strongly emphasized in Julie E. Cohen (2012).

[11] "Original" here serves as a marker for legitimacy and as a template for separating legitimate
from illegitimate copies. See my Hull (2003a) (discussing what, following Deleuze, I call a
"Platonism" in copyright).

and the effort to attach financial incentive to that role is an effort to nudge creators into occupying the role of authors in that sense. They become legible as well-disciplined, market-oriented actors who serve as origin points for discrete works; if they used others' material in those works, it too should come from authors who can be easily identified and paid. One immediate consequence is discouraging other modes of production, whether the production of basic science with little immediate financial reward, or the production of hip hop that borrows explicitly and heavily from wide ranges of previous material. A central component of authorship is the author's proprietary relation to their work; this is a consequence of adopting the internalizing narrative of property.

Incentives theory thereby combines what have been presented as its competing interpretations. On the one hand, it depends on what James Boyle (1997) has characterized as the core myth of literary romanticism, that of a solitary creator who generates work whole-cloth in isolation. On the other hand, it also depends on proprietization, a point that Mark Lemley (1997) advances as a critique of Boyle. The incentives narrative does both, by creating a subject position that creates in isolation with the expectation of internalizing, as financial reward, all of the benefits of that creation.

If authors have a proprietary relation to their material, then that relation creates the parallel need for those who access the work to do so as consumers, which is to say that they need to treat the material as offering them something original that they will then access only by way of financial compensation. Two variables that matter here are the cost of copying the material, and the costs of ignoring legal prohibitions on copying. As noted earlier, digitization has fundamentally changed the material condition for the reproduction of works covered by copyright by radically reducing copying costs. These decreased costs have led to demands for increased protections, since the effect of reducing copying costs is to remove a barrier to making illegitimate copies. It turns out that in the absence of copying costs, consumers tend to copy promiscuously. The response has not just been to transfer an increasing enforcement burden on the law as a technique for sorting legitimate and illegitimate copies (Hull, 2003a), but the development of a moral panic around excessive copying (see, e.g., Patry (2009)). The rapid rise in copying suggests that individuals do not naturally approach creative expression as consumers; in the same way that creators have to be nudged by copyright into occupying the author function, so too will copyright have to nudge individuals into the position of consumers.

The inflation of copyright as a form of IP, then, is not just because technology has changed. Technological change by itself would not explain the current situation. The real issue is that changes in technology have made evident a relatively poor fit between the kind of neoliberal subjectivity assumed by the dominant narrative of copyright and the actual ways that people tend to encounter creative expression covered by copyright.

3.3 MUSIC SAMPLING AND THE AMBIGUOUS BIOPOLITICS OF FAIR USE

3.3.1 *Fair Use as Cultural Optimization*

There are at least two prominent ways to conceptualize fair use. Economically, it can be said to address market failure: it emerges when it would be too costly or too difficult for downstream users to obtain licenses for their socially valuable uses of a work. Fair use emerges as the most efficient way to deal with the problem. This explanation is readily recognizable as an application of Demsetzian theory. When externalities are too costly to internalize, i.e., when licensing regimes involve too many transaction costs, it is efficient to declare an exemption for certain kinds of reuse. For example, compulsory cover licenses allow artists to cover songs according to a set royalty scale without negotiating with the copyright owner(s) individually. The dependence of such a system on the Demsetzian model is readily apparent in its conceptualization of when fair use would go away. On the one hand, if the value of a work rises sufficiently, we would expect to see the emergence of a licensing regime, despite its costs. On the other hand, if technological developments make it much cheaper to police reuse and to establish licensing, then we would also expect licensing regimes to emerge. In both cases, fair use would disappear, as the product of a time when it was a stopgap measure on the way to better-functioning markets (see the explanation in Lessig (2006)).

This neoliberal version of fair use contrasts sharply with one oriented toward public biopolitics. The public view finds social value in certain kinds of unauthorized use of copyrighted material; fair use rights that protect these uses are good for the public. For example, reproducing parts of a work as part of a critical essay on it is generally considered fair use, because the social interest in having critical essays outweighs the author's interest in not having their work quoted. As the litigation around the Worldwide Church of God discussed in the introduction suggests, the application of fair use can be complicated. These difficulties emerge most clearly in the application of derivative works doctrine. Granted that simply copying material violates copyright, when is a work sufficiently "derivative" that it should be enjoined, and when is it sufficiently valuable to the public that it should be allowed? If one puts the question this way, the difference between a neoliberal (in the former case) and a public (in the latter) logic of fair use becomes clear. The neoliberal version is concerned, above all, with markets. The alternative logic is concerned about public benefit. Current fair use doctrine sits uneasily between the two.

Recall from the introduction that fair use defenses are to be judged on a case-by-case basis, with reference to four statutory factors.[12] Of these, the most important in

---

[12] "In determining whether the use made of a work in any particular case is a fair use, the factors to be considered shall include – (1) The purpose and character of the use, including whether

case law is generally whether the use in question is "transformative" of the original work into something else. A good example of how this thinking works is found in a case in which the commercial pornography site "Perfect 10" sued Google and others for linking to infringing repostings of its pictures, by way of complete thumbnail images of the works in question. In other words, individuals had illegally reposted images from the porn site onto their personal pages. Google's search engine found those pictures, cached them as thumbnails, and presented the thumbnails in search results. The pornography site reasoned that this was infringement on Google's part, since it profited from using illegally reproduced images (the thumbnails) to then direct traffic to illegally reproduced images (the pirated copies of the pictures).

Some of the fair use factors pointed heavily against Google: They were profiting off the images, using the entire images, and caching them on their servers. Not only that, by linking to pirated versions of the images, they were probably hurting the market for the legitimate versions. All of that said, the Ninth Circuit reasoned that none of these outweighed the transformative value of what Google was doing:

> Google's use of thumbnails is highly transformative ... Although an image may have been created originally to serve an entertainment, aesthetic, or informative function, a search engine transforms the image into a pointer directing a user to a source of information ... A search engine provides social benefit by incorporating an original work into a new work, namely, an electronic reference tool.
>
> (*Perfect 10*, p. 1165)

In this line of thinking, fair use serves an entirely public function, insofar as it directly limits the ability of content owners to internalize the full gains of their work, for the sake of a socially desirable end.

Subsequent litigation affirmed the distinctly biopolitical nature of this argument. In that case, the Ninth Circuit explicitly abandoned a juridical rule about presumed harm, and replaced it with a case-by-case analysis. Perfect 10 argued that Google's practices – including sending URL's that were the objects of takedown notices the website chillingeffects.org, where they would still technically be available for an intrepid surfer – would likely cause Perfect 10 irreparable harm. The Ninth Circuit cited the Supreme Court's recent patent decision in *eBay* v. *MercExchange*, which held that the principles involved in a summary judgment finding in IP law were equitable, and "warned against reliance on presumptions or categorical rules."[13] Thus, the Supreme Court's reasoning required the court to abandon its own rule that "[a] showing of a reasonable likelihood of success on the merits in a copyright

---

such use is of a commercial nature or is for nonprofit educational purposes; (2) The nature of the copyrighted work; (3) The amount and substantiality of the portion used in relation to the copyrighted work as a whole; and (4) The effect of the use upon the potential market for or value of the copyrighted work" (17 U.S.C. 107). Whether a coherent body of doctrine has or can emerge from such guidelines has been a matter of dispute; for doubts, see Nimmer (2003).

[13] For equitable relief as a juridical technique for enacting biopolitics, see Hull (2017).

infringement claim raises a presumption of irreparable harm." Instead, "irreparable harm" was to be found on a case-by-case basis. In this case, the Court ruled that, although Perfect 10 established that it was near bankruptcy, "Perfect 10 has not established that the requested injunction would forestall that fate," noting that "to begin with, Perfect 10 has not alleged that it was ever in sound financial shape," citing testimony from the company's president that it had been a money loser from the start (*Perfect 10 v. Google*, pp. 981–982). In other words, instead of a juridical rule establishing irreparable harm, the court argued the harm was inevitable, and the causal link with Google's actions was not established.

Parody functions similarly, and even reached the Supreme Court, which in 1994 carved out an exception for parody as fair use, citing concerns such as the need for critique. In the 1994 case, *Campbell v. Acuff Rose* (1994), the estate of Roy Orbison sued 2 Live Crew for its vulgar appropriation of "Pretty Woman." The 2 Live Crew version makes the song into an explicit discussion of sex and female bodies, and the Supreme Court agreed that this usage was fair, since it was parody. Culture requires, in other words, the ability to make fun of a copyrighted work, even if the owner would not and did not like the parody. This reasoning serves to protect uses of works that have cultural value, even at the expense of their commercial success.

The parody defense articulated in *Acuff Rose* has been the object of considerable attention. First, critical work has noted that certain kinds of work are much more likely to succeed in a fair use defense than others. As Rebecca Tushnet (2007) notes, there is an apparent gender politics at work, as vulgar sex, such as in the 2 Live Crew "Pretty Woman," is more likely to be protected than other kinds of transformative work. As she puts it, "by favoring sexualization over other types of critique, fair use doctrine systematically treats sex as especially oppositional and liberating, when in fact it has no monopoly on critique and no necessarily disruptive effect on a copyright owner's message" (2007, p. 275).[14] So too, John Tehranian argues that parody decisions often reflect the social status of the text being parodied more than anything else. The successful application of a parody fair-use defense on behalf of Alice Randall's *The Wind Done Gone*, a parody of *Gone with the Wind*, should be contrasted with its failure to protect John David California's arguably more-protectable use of *Catcher in the Rye*. Tehranian concludes that contrast mainly shows that *Gone with the Wind* has lost its status as a sacralized cultural artifact, a status still enjoyed by *Catcher* (2012, pp. 1281–1291).

More generally, the definition of parody in question seems rather limited in its ability to protect culture: the defense is limited to cases where the parody is of the

---

[14] In the context of a discussion of Foucault, it should be noted that the tendency to favor sexualization underscores Foucault's (1988a) point that our current regime of sexuality requires that we talk a lot about sex in order to congratulate ourselves on being liberated. For more on the complex interplay of depictions of sexuality in neoliberal IP, see the following chapter's discussion of the Victor's Little Secret litigation.

work being parodied. What one is not allowed to do is use the work to parody a cultural norm or a cultural configuration of which that work is representative. The most famous example of this is the litigation against the Air Pirates, which used Mickey Mouse and other Disney characters to poke fun at 1950s values. More recently, a Court ruled, on the same grounds, against a parody of OJ Simpson called "The Cat *Not* in the Hat," which included such lines as:

> Did you take this person's life?
> Did you do it with a knife?

> I did not do it with a knife.
> I did not, could not, kill my wife.
> I did not do this awful crime.
> I could not, would not, anytime.

Not only did the book confuse *Green Eggs and Ham* with *The Cat in the Hat*, of greater import legally, the book used Dr. Seuss as a vehicle to pursue something else.[15]

Culturally, this would seem to be misdirected. As Sonia Katyal notes, citing Robert Merges (1993), this approach would appear to be exactly backwards, or at least seriously underinclusive: "using a copyrighted work as a vehicular tool rather than as a target for commentary and criticism is even more deserving of fair use protections because it serves the goal of promoting more commentary on larger social issues" (2006b, p. 540). Indeed, Julie Cohen has suggested that fair use needs a general rethinking, along these lines. As she writes, "instead of looking for necessary and sufficient conditions for labeling a use 'transformative,'" we should "consider a more open-ended set of questions about the role of retellings in the process of working through culture" (2007, p. 1202). As she later puts it, "a regime of copyright recalibrated to facilitate play should sharply limit copyright owners' rights to control adaptations and remixes by third parties" by explicitly naming "the [limited] list of adaptations to which copyright-holder control is permitted to extend" (2012, p. 247). These sorts of biopolitical priorities in the form of attention to social welfare and social goods seem implicit in any discussion of fair use; what Tushnet and Tehranian's arguments show is the importance of being honest about them.

There are also gray areas of fair use, where reuse has been tolerated, but is also not clearly protected, again reflecting the ambivalent status of derivative works. Among these is noncommercial fan fiction. The owners of Star Trek ordinarily get to decide what stories, films, and other works may be produced using Star Trek characters, storylines, and so forth. This right is justified on the grounds that it incentivizes production when authors are able to internalize economic value of their immediate work, but of subsequent work based on it. Rights to derivative works are culturally anomalous, and carnivalesque incorporation and reworking of supposedly sacred

---

[15] *Dr. Seuss Enters v. Penguin Books, USA, Inc.*, 109 F.3d 1394 (9th Cir., 1997).

cultural artifacts dates at least to Rabelais, as the Russian literary theorist Mikhail Bakhtin famously argued. Tehranian emphasizes that the nineteenth century was full of popular appropriations of Shakespeare and opera; protection against derivative works would prohibit most such activity, at least for works not already in the public domain (2012, pp. 1249–1257). Contemporary fan fiction is a current example of such carnivalesque incorporation, and it has largely been tolerated by copyright owners.[16] This tolerance has been extended to the more controversial case of "slash" fiction, which retells aspects of culturally significant stories – like *Star Trek* – by emphasizing homoerotic themes, and staging, for example, a love affair between Kirk and Spock. That said, "tolerate" does not mean "condone:" As Wendy Brown (2006) points out, "tolerate" implies an obstacle that a system puts up with or is able to function in spite of.

What I would emphasize here is that there is a distinct line of theory that understands fair use rights for fan fiction and other ostensibly derivative cultural works as important precisely because they are good for the public. They extend and generalize the logic of protecting parody. In considering fan fiction, Katyal (2006a) notes that fair use does not just carve out an exception or a limit to the law's reach, but it also highlights a different notion of what a text is – not just the work as an expression of the author, but as a mediation among author, performer, and audience. Parody is exemplary, insofar as "through the law's protection of parody, property becomes a dialogue, instead of a one-way transmission of meaning" (2006a, p. 479). The legally gray status of slash creates unprotected speech, which is valuable precisely insofar as it challenges cultural heteronormativity. That this occupies a legally grey area "is part of a larger tale of how intellectual proprietization affects different groups. Copyright law's requirements of originality, tangibility, and fixation tend to minimize the contributions of non-market, amateur participants and often penalize them in the process" (2006a, p. 499). Following a similar line of argument, Julie Cohen (2007) suggests that fan fiction should be protected because of the importance of individual dialogues with collective culture and the way this interaction "enables broader collective dialogues to take shape" (2007, p. 1202). All of these cases are directly political insofar as they represent the "resistances, imaginative strategies, and creative reappropriations enacted by subjects alienated from networks of public expression and representation" (Coombe, 1998, p. 298)

Fair use in music presents an area where the difficulties surrounding the author function in copyright are particularly evident. In this, the intersection of dominant forms of social stratification and the model of authorship favored by copyright leads to difficult results. On the one hand, the model of authorship tends to occlude

---

[16] Tushnet suggests that this tolerance has become standard; "essentially no one sends cease and desist letters over fan fiction. Copyright owners recognize, at the very least, that it's not worth it to go after fan fiction in court." The current frontier for analogous questions is video (Goodrich et al., 2013, p. 608).

sources. This has been of particular concern for appropriation of "indigenous" music. For example, the rock group Enigma's "Return to Innocence," which made millions of dollars for the band and which was used in television ads for the 1996 Summer Olympics, turns out to have been lifted from the indigenous Ami people of Taiwan, who saw their sacred music exploited and who received nothing in return (Riley, 2000). As Sunder emphasizes, such cross-cultural exchanges often exhibit a colonialist structuring. Asian cinema is portrayed as derivative, while Western works from *E.T.* to *The Lion King* with uncomfortable similarities to unacknowledged Asian predecessors are celebrated for their originality. As she puts it, "in all three cases – *The Alien*, *The Lion King* and 'The Lion Sleeps Tonight' – new works in the United States appear to have been derived not from the work of unknown foreign artists, but from the artistic expressions of great masters." That is, in such cases "copyright law implicates mutual recognition as misrecognition of others" (2012, pp. 156, 171).[17] Indigenous people are not "owners," so their consent is not required.[18]

Even within Western societies, however, the model functions awkwardly because authorship can be – often deliberately – difficult to measure in discrete quanta. Different recording tracks can be separated and combined in mashups like "The Grey Album" (Sunder, 2006, p. 303). Music can be combined with video to create social commentary, as in Sloane's "Star Trek Dance Floor," which combined footage from the *Star Trek: Reboot* movie with the song "Too Many Dicks on the Dance Floor" to critique the machismo (and lack of women) in the movie. Artworks are often in communication – implicit or explicit – with other art forms, and almost any work will contain a lot of borrowing, conscious or otherwise. For example, when Kanye West stood on national TV and, gazing at the ruins of immediate post-Katrina New Orleans, proclaimed that "George Bush doesn't care about black people," New Orleans-based The Legendary K.O. produced a song of the same name, borrowing liberally from West's "Gold Digger." West's song, in turn, refers to and borrows from Ray Charles' "I Got a Woman." Charles took liberally from the gospel standard "I've Got a Savior." The legal status of "I've Got a Savior" was unclear, and nobody asked. Under the different and more expansive copyright laws of today, however, Boyle notes, "one thing is clear. Much of what Charles and [Renald] Richard did in creating their song would be illegal" (2008, p. 137). More generally, as Tushnet (2004) argues, verbatim copying can sometimes be key to original expression, especially for political speech. As I will indicate in the next section, this is precisely the case in hip-hop sampling.

---

[17] Disney also takes advantage of other public domain sources, such as Rudyard Kipling's problematic *The Jungle Book*: see Hemmungs Wirtén (2008, pp. 109–140).
[18] This tradition dates at least to Locke, who went to great lengths to explain why the indigenous people of North America had no cognizable property claims to the land they lived on and used. On this, see, e.g., Hemmungs Wirtén (2008), Hull (2009a), Tully (1993).

3.3.2 NWA *and the Neoliberal Policing of Unauthorized Use*

If understanding fair use on a model of public biopolitics can undermine procrustean models of production and consumption by allowing greater scope to creative freedom, its neoliberal variant in particular can also be used to chill expression in the name of the police function of the state. As noted earlier, questions surrounding derivative works and fair use indicate the contours of the issue. The tension between public biopolitical and neoliberal understandings of fair use, or, rather, the complexity of the ways that fair use functions biopolitically, can be found in music sampling cases. These cases center around the late 1980s and early 1990s hip hop and "wall of sound" rap in the United States, and its practice of widely incorporating snippets of other material into its own work. As I will show, this is a practice that was radically changed by an interpretation of copyright law; the change is one that undermined the aesthetic of sampling of the period and pushed hip hop in a neoliberal direction.

In 1991, a district court ruled that it was not fair use to take the guitar riff from one song, and simply reproduce it in another. In the case in question, Biz Markie's "Alone Again" (1981) appropriated several measures of the background guitar in Gilbert O'Sullivan's "Alone Again (Naturally)" (1972). In finding against the defendants, the court began with a Biblical invocation:

> "Thou shalt not steal" has been an admonition followed since the dawn of civilization. Unfortunately, in the modern world of business this admonition is not always followed. Indeed, the defendants in this action for copyright infringement would have this court believe that stealing is rampant in the music business and, for that reason, their conduct here should be excused. The conduct of the defendants herein, however, violates not only the Seventh Commandment, but also the copyright laws of this country.
>
> (*Grand Upright*, p. 183)

Read purely on its own terms, *Grand Upright* makes sense. Samples take and reuse parts of copyrighted material for other purposes, and so they trespass on the owner's property.

Read in the context of models of power, things are more complicated. The Court's Biblical rhetoric seems designed to invoke a juridical model of power, with its focus on law and transgression. The social context is important, especially when one considers how the decision constructs the sampler. On its own terms, sampling is not theft; theft happens when nothing new is created: "within hip-hop, piracy or biting another's style – not sampling – constitutes theft because it does not add anything to the original. If a new perspective, beat, or take on something old is created, then it is sampling" (Schur, 2011, p. 48). Not only that, as noted earlier, art is generally in communication with other art, and usually borrows, either explicitly or implicitly. Some of this borrowing is protected as fair use, and other

borrowing – especially from indigenous sources or those where authorship is not
legible in Western legal terms – is allowed to proceed with apparent impunity.
Sampling arguably represents an emergent aesthetic that crosses a number of literary
genres, and often presents social commentary (Schur, 2011). Not only that, there is
no reason to think sampling damages the market for sales of the work sampled. If
anything, when it operates as homage, it should draw renewed attention to the
original. In short, if one abandons the formal logic of juridical power, the real
question is why sampling is not protected.[19]

I will say more about sampling as an aesthetic later, but for now, note that the
juridical language in *Grand Upright* serves as part of a strategy of subjectification,
one that explicitly attempts to construct sampling as an act of pure consumption (or
as an act of consumption that can be separated from subsequent production).[20] At
the same time, it constructs the appropriate form of aesthetic subjectivity as
authorship as understood by the incentives model. Treating the creative work of
African Americans as noncreative (generally by making it free for appropriation by
white artists) of course has a long tradition in American music, and, as I will suggest
in Chapter 4 on trademark, it has analogues internationally in the context of, for
example, Disney movies like *The Lion King*.

The decision also pushed hip hop toward a neoliberal model of authorship, one
governed by the notion that single authors produce works, and that they are entitled
to internalize all the benefits that their work provides for others. *Grand Upright*
established the principle that sampling required a license and payment. Its effects
were profound; nearly twenty years later, the *Washington Post*'s Chris Richards
(2012) declared that "no court decision has changed the sound of pop music as
much as this, before or since." After *Grand Upright*, sampling happened in one of
three ways. The first is covertly. This of course requires hiding the activity, depriving

[19] Sampling is of course commercial, and hip-hop artists are happy to be paid. But as the *Perfect
10* litigation shows, being commercial is not sufficient to defeat a fair use claim. On this tension
in hip hop, see Schur, who notes that "intellectual property law enables texts created by hip-
hop aesthetes to circulate within popular culture and threatens the vitality of hip-hop aesthetics
as an ongoing cultural paradigm for textual production," and "as its practitioners and critics
alike note, hip-hop aesthetics is concerned with 'keepin' it real' and authenticity claims as
much as it is concerned with monetary rewards – although its practitioners willingly take the
money. Even if hip-hop music has frequently concerned itself with the legality of sampling,
hip-hop artists nonetheless assert their ownership rights over their songs and their styles" (2011,
pp. 64–65). Of course "real" refers to an aesthetic, not the erroneous idea that hip hop
constitutes some sort of journalistic documentation.
[20] Again, compare Schur: Sampling "bridges the acts of consumption and production. It requires
cultural workers to rearrange the symbols, phrases, rhythms, and melodies circulating within
American culture into something completely new. Sampling is part active listening and part
production" (2011, p. 46).

it of its ability to accessibly generate social commentary or even appropriate cit-ation.[21] Covert activity also runs the risk of detection. The second possibility is one of industry forbearance. This strategy requires a fairly high level of risk tolerance, and relegates sampling to the same sort of fair-use gray zone occupied by fan fiction.

The final possibility is to pay licensing fees; sampling is to be subject to the rules of a "permissions culture." The problem is that producing hip-hop music in its original form becomes like producing laboratory science: extravagantly expensive, because it would be necessary to obtain a license for virtually everything, perhaps hundreds of snippets per song. Systems with so many potential veto-points and high transaction costs risk devolution into an anticommons, an underproduction of the resource because its production becomes artificially and prohibitively expensive (Heller, 1998).[22] Not surprisingly, *Grand Upright* led to a precipitous drop in sampling as a form of homage or social commentary. Instead, as Richards notes, the decision turned overt sampling into a marker of wealth, a strategy deliberately deployed by artists such as Kanye West and Jay-Z: "once hip-hop's foundation, the sample has become a trophy." In this regard, turning sampling into an act of consumption enables it to function as a sumptuary code in a way analogous to the way the consumption of trademarked brands does.[23] These points are evident in a consideration of a follow-up case and the musical context of the late 1980s.

In *Bridgeport Music* v. *Dimension Films* (2005), the Sixth Circuit was confronted with a more subtle example of sampling. In it, NWA had taken a few seconds from a guitar riff originally in George Clinton's "Get off Your Ass and Jam," looped it to the point it was unrecognizable, and made it part of the wall of sound in "100 Miles and Runnin'" (1990).[24] The appropriation could not have been accidental. Clinton, as

---

[21] Although it was not a sampling case, consider in this context the recent copyright suit lost by Robin Thicke and Pharrell Williams for "Blurred Lines." As the appellate court noted, Thicke's free admission that he had access to Marvin Gaye's "Got to Give It Up" meant that the bar for how much similarity was needed to prove infringement was low, and made it easier for a jury to resolve competing expert testimony on the similarity in Gaye's favor. See *Williams* v. *Gaye* (2018). Thicke said in an interview with GQ: "[O]ne of my favorite songs of all time was Marvin Gaye's 'Got to Give It Up.' I was like, 'Damn, we should make something like that, something with that groove' . . . Then [Pharrell] started playing a little something and we literally wrote the song in about a half hour and recorded it. The whole thing was done in a couple hours" (Phili, 2013). Copyright thus directly regulates music as a form of homage.

[22] Empirical research in the visual arts suggests that permissions culture has a substantial and negative effect on cultural production: see Aufderheide, Milosevic, and Bello (2016). One could of course reduce transaction costs by reproducing the sounds on one's own and going through ASCAP's compulsory licensing regime, but not only does that change the nature of the material produced, it still entails licensing costs.

[23] On this, see the discussion of luxury goods in the Victoria's Secret section of Chapter 4; the specific reference for trademark as sumptuary code is Beebe (2010).

[24] As the Court explained the appropriation: "'Get Off' opens with a three-note combination solo guitar 'riff' that lasts four seconds . . . A two-second sample from the guitar solo was copied, the pitch was lowered, and the copied piece was 'looped' and extended to 16 beats. This sample appears in the sound recording '100 Miles' in five places; specifically, at 0:49, 1:52, 2:29, 3:20

the godfather of P-Funk, was a major figure in the history of hip hop, and NWA's Dr. Dre's creation of West-Coast rap – which relies heavily on sampling – was heavily influenced by Clinton's Parliament (Keyes, 1996, pp. 226, 239). NWA's inclusion of "Get Off" both pays homage to Clinton as a forerunner and reimagines it for a hip-hop format. In this way, NWA is incorporating the history of Black music into its own work.

Sampling, as the successor to live mixing of records, and as distinct from studio reproduction of the desired sounds, is aesthetically important as a bearer of cultural memory. As one producer put it, "we've done it real grimy and dirty and it works better ... the popping on the record is the essence of the music ... After a while, you listen to some old record, hear that popping, it takes you back. That's really the aesthetic value to it" (qt. in Keyes, 1996, p. 240). As suggested earlier, sampling is also key to the political aesthetics of hip hop; as such, it deliberately attempts to recast ownership in cultural terms, against the market norms of IP. Richard Schur suggests that its importance lies in the effort to finally realize the otherwise thwarted goals of the Civil Rights movement:

> Hip-hop aesthetics, rather than constituting a break from the Civil Rights Movement, may be its culmination, because perhaps the only way to realize the movement's social and political goals is through a cultural transformation that necessitates a reconstruction of the property concept.
>
> (2011, pp. 97–98)

In this sense, sampling is a thoroughly political act.

From the point of view of the argument being developed here, it is noteworthy that hip-hop aesthetics generally, and sampling more specifically, reject the market internalization theory assumed by neoliberal IP, casting it instead as an act of cultural dispossession. As I will argue in the following chapter, this rejection, and how to contest it, is also central to aspects of trademark law surrounding culturally significant symbols and products. In short, practices like sampling can be a form of resistance to the loss of public and political spaces and values, specifically against the erasures of a copyright system that renders such political questions invisible by reducing cultural production to a question of markets and consumer preferences. Schur even goes as far as to argue that "such borrowings ... are fundamental to African American vernacular practices" (2011, p. 35).

From the point of view of the neoliberal economist, on the other hand, the only question is whether the borrowings can be efficiently licensed. *Bridgeport Music* is important in this regard because NWA rendered the original Clinton sample essentially unrecognizable, and so the result indicates less any actual economic effects than it does a theoretical preference for how cases should be analyzed and

and 3:46. By the district court's estimation, each looped segment lasted approximately 7 seconds" (*Bridgeport Music*, p. 796).

what sorts of conduct the law should discourage, regardless of its immediate effects. In other words, *Bridgeport Music* takes a view as to the appropriate form of aesthetic subjectivity. It prefers "authors" and markets, arguing that "if you cannot pirate the whole sound recording, can you 'lift' or 'sample' something less than the whole[?] Our answer to that question is in the negative" (*Bridgeport Music*, p. 800).

The case's construal of sampling as theft was embedded in and expressive of deeply racialized cultural currents specific to the late 1980s and early 1990s. The neoliberal demand for licensing in this context enforces disciplined market behavior at the explicit expense of hip hop as a vehicle for cultural memory and political expression. The 1980s in general had seen an explosion of adult concern over music, particularly directed to heavy metal and hip hop. 1987 saw the publication of Tipper Gore's *Raising PG Kids in an X-Rated Society*, which was a jeremiad about the corruption of the youth, coupled with a call for censorship and warning labels. Metal, as represented in the cultural imaginary by bands like Iron Maiden, Judas Priest, and Motley Crüe, was accused of promoting Satanism.[25]

This concern, however, was heavily raced. If metal victimized white youth, rap became the expression or marker of unruly Black youth. As Tricia Rose notes, with a nod to a 1989 Public Enemy album, "the social construction of rap and rap-related violence is fundamentally linked to the social discourse on Black containment and fears of a Black planet." Hence:

> [This] ideological position ... separates resistance to rap from attacks sustained by rock-and-roll artists ... The terms of the assaults on rap music, for example, are part of a long-standing sociologically based discourse that positions Black influences as a cultural threat to American society. Consequently, rappers, their fans, and Black youth in general are constructed as co-conspirators in the spread of Black aesthetic and discursive influence ... Unlike heavy metal's victims, the majority of rap's fans are the youngest representatives of a Black presence whose cultural difference is an ongoing internal threat to America's cultural development.
>
> (1991, p. 280)

Rose documents how these inflated, racialized fears were used to justify refusal to book rap acts in urban arenas because of the "violence" they supposedly fostered, while violence by white concert-goers was ignored.

Hip hop emerged in the Bronx in the aftermath not only of the hopes and disillusionment associated with the Civil Rights movement, but also of the destruction of urban Bronx by the construction of a highway through its middle. Rose writes:

[25] As a child, I was told by peers that "AC/DC" stood for "Against Christ, Devil's Children," for example, and that playing Led Zeppelin's "Stairway to Heaven" backwards produced an audible utterance of "The Lord is Satan."

In the 1950s, the Bronx was the embodiment of the American Dream for second generation immigrants from the impoverished lower east side of Manhattan. The densely populated stable neighborhoods of the Bronx, comprising mostly working and lower-middle class Jews, also contained solid Italian, German, Irish and Black communities.

(1989, p. 36)

The Robert Moses highway, portrayed as urban renewal, resulted in the razing of the homes of 60,000 people, rapid white flight, the relegation of apartment buildings to slum lords, and the consequent relegation of the remaining Black community to ever-deepening poverty. At the same time, Disco became increasingly technologically dependent and white; what was left was the P-Funk movement and the need for communities in the South Bronx to "build[] their own cultural networks ... Hip Hop developed as part of a collective voice for those who had been condemned to silence" (1989, p. 39).

Hip hop drew from earlier American Black music, Afro-Caribbean music, and more traditional African music (Keyes, 1996). It represented both a deliberate response to perceived limitations of the Civil Rights movement and a re-imagination of urban spaces against invisible encroachment by white music, as evidenced by such work as A Tribe Called Quest's parody of Lou Reed (Schur, 2011, pp. 32–33). This music – already foreign to more mainstream forms – was then presented as unruly and violent. The fact was not lost on Black artists, who "have re-articulated a long-standing awareness among African Americans that crimes against Blacks (especially Black-on-Black crimes) do not carry equal moral weight or political imperative" (T. Rose, 1991, p. 284). In sum, as Rose puts it, "the institutional policing of rap music is a complex and interactive process that has had a significant impact on rap's content, image, and reception" (1991, p. 288).

The preceding narrative presents hip hop in its oppositional aspects; as many scholars have noted, it can also reproduce or even intensify hegemonic social norms, especially patriarchal and emerging neoliberal ones.[26] That is, hip hop cannot be

[26] In particular, gangsta rap often exhibits a blatant misogyny, treating women as disposable objects for sexual gratification whose presence indicates wealth. (For available women as an image cultivated in the luxury economy, see (Bartow, 2015) and the discussion of the Victoria's Secret brand in the following chapter.) One problem with the narrative is that it strategically overgeneralizes. First, as Elizabeth Wheeler puts it, "it does not take a feminist critic from outside hip hop to identify these problems: the critique of misogyny starts within rap dialogue itself" by both male and female rappers and producers (1991, p. 202). Second, the critique often comes from white critics, and is suspiciously convenient for cultural conservatives like Robert Bork to appropriate as a cudgel with which to attack all hip hop, misogynist or not. Third, it blurs the boundaries between art and advocacy. If hip hop is a form of protest – and undoubtedly much of it is – then songs like NWA's "Fuck the Police" and Body Count's "Cop Killer" protest police violence against black communities, both by calling it out and spinning out revenge fantasies. But these are clearly fantasies. "Fuck the Police" is based on an imaginary juridical process, and "Cop Killer" trades in caricature in that the Body Count album begins by white police refusing to help a stranded black motorist on the grounds that "right now, my job

separated from its social context. As Lester Spence puts it, "even as black artists used hip-hop and rap to create a vibrant alternative to the status quo, they reproduced neoliberalism in their lyrics, in their music videos, and in some of their attempts to create political organizations" (2011, p. 17). Celebrating entrepreneurial hustle and overt symbols of wealth are all well-established neoliberal tropes, as is the presentation of non-white urban areas as unruly and violent. If rap "expose[s] the exception" that the urban core poses to neoliberal narratives of upward mobility, it tends simultaneously to express a "crack governmentality" that celebrates subjectivity as human capital (built through violence and hustle) and ignores structural inequalities (pp. 27–28).[27] Spence suggests that genuinely critical lyrics are much less common than those that describe or celebrate, and many of the critical songs deflect away from structural problems. *Grand Upright* and its progeny like *Bridgeport Music* need to be read in this context, as they show intellectual property as an apparatus of neoliberal biopolitics. Characterizing wall of sound as theft is a moment in domesticating cultural practices that not only potentially respond to racial injustice, but also resist reduction into consumer market norms. It puts another finger on the neoliberal side of the scale.

Although *Grand Upright* set a broad precedent, it should be noted that not all sampling cases follow the *Bridgeport Music* model. For example, consider *VMG Salsoul, LLC v. Ciccione* (2016).[28] In that case, Madonna and her producer had been sued over her alleged incorporation of a quarter-second snippet of the Salsoul Orchestra song "Love Break" into her 1990 "Vogue." The Ninth Circuit used juridical reasoning to impose a limit to the neoliberal biopolitical logic that drove *Bridgeport Music*: The use was *de minimis*, below whatever legal threshold exists to warrant a copyright infringement claim. In reasoning that could be a mirror of the Sixth Circuit's, the Ninth argued that:

> After listening to the audio recordings submitted by the parties, we conclude that a reasonable juror could not conclude that an average audience would recognize the appropriation of the horn hit. That common-sense conclusion is borne out by dry

is eatin' these donuts." Fourth, hip hop can also call out the hypocrisy of white America's treatment of black women, as happens in Public Enemy's indictment of Hollywood's treatment of black women in "Burn, Holywood Burn" (1990): "for what they play Aunt Jemima is the perfect term / even if now she's got a perm." Finally, the question of sampling is not the question of all hip hop. The question of sampling is simply the question of historical memory and the possibility of fusing oral and technological expression into a new form of resistant literacy. Removing sampling from hip hop would not remove misogyny. Misogyny sells; in this sense the misogyny illustrates Spence's point that hip hop exists within neoliberal culture.

[27] The authentic subject of neoliberal hip hop thus occupies the same space as the heroic climber who summits (and ignores the contributions of his sherpas) (Simon, 2002) or the rich dad who eschews pensions for entrepreneurialism and the stock market (Binkley, 2009).

[28] Given the concern with colonialist and racialized logics in this context, it should perhaps be noted that Madonna is white. "Voguing" refers to dance moves specific to black queer club culture in New York; Madonna's invocation of voguing has been seen as exploitative. For a history and discussion, see Lawrence (2011).

analysis. The horn hit is very short – less than a second. The horn hit occurs only a few times in "Vogue." Without careful attention, the horn hits are easy to miss. Moreover, the horn hits in "Vogue" do not sound identical to the horn hits from "Love Break" .... Even if one grants the dubious proposition that a listener recognized some similarities between the horn hits in the two songs, it is hard to imagine that he or she would conclude that sampling had occurred.

(*VMG Salsoul, LLC* v. *Ciccone*, p. 880)

Although the decision hinges on the *recognizability* of sampling and not sampling itself (and so, in a roundabout way, it affirms the police-function of the Sixth Circuit), it clearly goes against the grain of *Bridgeport Music*.

3.3.3 *Fair Use and Models of Power*

In what ways do sampling cases suggest that one can understand fair use? It should first be noted that, beyond its cultural meaning, sampling itself is inherently oppositional to the neoliberal regime of copyright, for at least two technical, legal reasons. First, this regime requires, among other things, the ability to treat all expression as alienable property. Whatever the normative value of such a proposition, it has a more fundamental problem when applied to sampling. For a property regime to function efficiently, it has to be possible to draw boundaries around discrete objects in order to designate them as properties (Fennell, 2012; H. E. Smith, 2007), and for this boundary-drawing to produce a conceptually simple, morally straightforward schema (Merrill and Smith, 2007). In a word, property presupposes easy modularity. Sampling and mixing precisely undermine this ability to draw boundaries, especially between appropriation and creation. The point of sampling is continuity, not boundaries. Second, the copyright regime heavily emphasizes originality, defined as bringing something new into the world that was not there before. One might think that a complicated pastiche of sound would count as original, but that pastiche is built out of "unoriginal" sounds. Not only that, as I discuss in Chapter 5, longstanding Supreme Court jurisprudence in the case of patents has been very clear that mixing existing things together does not by itself create anything new. For copyright, some level of "originality" must be present, but the case establishing this proposition rejected a decision to arrange existing phone numbers alphabetically as unoriginal and heavily emphasized that the labor of putting those phone numbers together did not suffice for copyright eligibility.[29] In short, sampling tends to run up against a dominant copyright discourse that emphasizes original creation, almost along the lines of literary romanticism (Boyle, 1997; Peeler, 1999).

Applying a *de minimis* rule to sampling sets a limit to the subsumption of society by capital and the internalization of expression by copyright owners in the same way

---

[29] *Feist Publications, Inc.*, v. *Rural Telephone Service Co.*, 499 U.S. 340 (1991).

that other fair use rules do: These are areas where social relations need not be overdetermined as market relations. In particular, hip-hop sampling of the late 1980s and early 1990s is an artistic practice that can enable the creation of a historical memory and cultural form that is alien, and often oppositional to, mainstream neoliberal culture. It supports the sorts of ends favored by public biopolitics in supporting cultural forms with significant positive externalities, externalities that are resistant to internalization by copyright owners. In this regard, decisions to allow sampling align with those allowing parody, or with tolerance of practices like fan fiction. All of these see in fair use a question beyond whether establishing a licensing regime would have too many transaction costs.

As all of this indicates, there are at least three different ways to understand fair use, corresponding to the different kinds of power expressed in this study: one neoliberal (which sees it as permissible only in cases of market failure), one as public biopolitics (where it functions to serve population-oriented ends such as cultural critique), and one juridical (where it preserves the rights of individual creators). As that discussion should indicate, it seems to be the public biopolitical usage that has the most traction in resisting neoliberal efforts to meter access to culture. That said, it is worth noting briefly that the juridical function can also be important, and not just as establishing juridical standards beyond which the copyright standard cannot go, as happened in the Madonna "Vogue" case. As I will argue in Chapter 5 on patents, several recent Supreme Court decisions express an ambivalence over the extent to which IP should be understood biopolitically or juridically. In the latter, which Court has recently favored, longstanding rules from real property law can serve to limit IP. In the case of copyright, this is perhaps most easily illustrated in the case of Solomon Linda.[30]

Linda was an itinerant South African farmer who, in 1939, recorded the hit song "Mbube" ("lion" in Zulu). In 1952, he was persuaded to sign over the copyright to the song to Gallo Studios, who produced the record, for less than $1. The song soon made its way overseas, where, misquoted as "Wimoweh," the song earned millions of dollars as part of "The Lion Sleeps Tonight." When Linda died in 1962, he had less than $25 in his bank account. In 1983, his widow Regina was persuaded by an American music company to sign a renewal of the copyright under American law, also for $1. However, in 2004, after a *Rolling Stone* exposé, surviving members of the Linda family brought suit, arguing that the 1911 British Copyright Act, which would have governed the 1952 transaction (since South Africa was at the time a British colony), included a provision according to which rights to the song would revert to

[30] I draw the following account from O. Dean (2006) and Lafraniere (2006). See also the brief discussion by Sunder, who concludes that the case "tragically illustrates the interrelationship between intellectual property rights and other freedoms. His failure to be recognized – and rewarded – for his contribution to our shared cultures in turn prevented him and his family from having the resources to access medicines first for himself and then for his daughter to live" (2006, p. 265).

the Executor of Linda's estate 25 years after his death, notwithstanding any other transfers of right. Regina was not executor of Linda's estate, and so she had no legal ability to transfer the renewal rights. In 2004, the estate was reopened and an executor appointed, who promptly sued on behalf of Linda's interests. Facing both public condemnation and a *prima facie* case of copyright infringement covering the years from 1987–2004, Disney eventually settled. For Linda and some of his family, of course, this was far too late. But it did finally allow the surviving members of his family a measure of legal justice.

3.4 PARACOPYRIGHT

As I have been arguing, it is important to view law as one of the structural compon-ents of the information environment and of ourselves in our ordinary lives. That is, changes to the legal regimes governing information can in turn produce, directly or indirectly, changes to ourselves. In this section, I will consider an example of a structural regulation that indirectly but deliberately encourages individuals to encounter cultural artifacts as consumers.[31] This regime of "digital rights manage-ment" (DRM), sometimes called "paracopyright" for its uneasy fit with traditional copyright, represents a significant effort to push copyright in a neoliberal direction. By giving legal imprimatur to copy-control regimes, it privatizes access to copy-righted (and, potentially, uncopyrighted) material, increasing the ability of owners to regulate and dictate the terms of access to their work, and undermining such potentially public-facing exemptions as fair use.

3.4.1 *The Legal Development of Digital Rights Management*

The 1998 revision of the Copyright Act, the DMCA, introduced something entirely new: §1201 of the act, variously dubbed "paracopyright" or the "anti-cicrumvention clause" (a) establishes that "no person shall circumvent a technological measure that effectively controls access to a work protected under this title" (17 USC 1201.1) and (b) makes it illegal to "traffic" in products "primarily designed or produced for the purpose of circumventing a technological measure that effectively controls access to a work protected under this title" (17 USC 1201.2). In other words, if somebody encrypts a DVD or ebook such that only his or her own players/readers can access it,

---

[31] The concept of structural regulation in the context of IP dates at least to Lawrence Lessig's description of code as a regulatory strategy (e.g., in Lessig (2006)); for a response, see Cheng (2006). It has since gotten traction in analyzing such areas as search engines (Introna and Nissenbaum, 2000) and platforms (Gillespie, 2010). Tarleton Gillespie (2007) makes extensive use of it in his critique of DRM. The concept has considerably wider play in STS and Philosophy of Technology, as for example Landgon Winner's (1980) famous claim that the bridges on Long Island are deliberately low to deter buses, and the poor who ride them, from easy access to the beaches.

it is illegal to break or otherwise bypass that encryption. The idea is to keep such digital fences useful. Fences only work if one is compelled to respect them; if they're easy to climb, then that compulsion will have to come from something other than the fence itself. Content owners use this legal scaffolding to establish choke points: The movie industry, for example, will only give the decryption key for DVDs to companies that agree to produce players that are designed to stop copying. At that point, the hardware manufacturers, like publishers, have a serious incentive to comply, and only the most determined users will trouble themselves to hack their devices or media. Indeed, copyright has even been used to make it difficult to access information about how to circumvent DRM schemes.[32]

The strategy is possible because digital media arrive in a format that humans cannot access on their own, and so we require the aid of external instantiating devices. External instantiating devices are not new. Early case law dealt with the rolls for player pianos; humans cannot read magnetic media or phonographs, either. Nor are industry efforts to stop the production of such devices new, as the music industry's failed lawsuit to stop the VCR demonstrates.[33] Digitization adds cheap encryption to the mix. Because the instantiating devices are mass-market products, device manufacturers need to produce a product that can legally read the media it plays. Content owners know this, and so encrypt their content, and then release the decryption keys only to device makers who agree to install DRM technologies. Since §1201 makes it illegal to produce a device that reads the material any other way, the device manufacturers have to do what content owners want. As a result, the material is only accessible with DRM strings attached.[34]

Digital media like DVDs are importantly unlike books, which can be accessed without another device. In a sense, the book is its own representing device insofar as it already represents its content in a manner legible to humans. Digitality significantly decouples the information from any specific instantiating device, without

---

[32] See, in general, Gillespie (2007). Gillespie emphasizes that enforceable DRM requires the collaboration of content industries and device makers, and traces the fragility of this cooperation, given that the two industries often have incompatible goals for consumer behavior: The potential success of DRM "will not be a technological feat, but a political project in which the content industries try to bring together allies that can collude to enforce their rules on users" (2007, p. 139).

[33] *Sony v. Universal*, 464 U.S. 417 (1984).

[34] This dependence on instantiating devices gives the lie to one of the great myths of the information age: however much information wants to be free, our experience of it is utterly dependent on devices over which we potentially have no control. For a cultural history of information, see Hobart and Schiffman (1998). Gillespie underscores that this presents a very different cultural norm for interacting with technologies: "It makes quite a difference if you weld a car's hood shut − not only for what users can and cannot do, but for how users will understand themselves as users, around whether having agency with that technology is possible, or even conceivable;" and "when the technology is legally and materially in my possession, it has until now been nearly impossible to prevent me from opening it up and seeing how it works; I can just lift the casing of my VCR to see where the tape meets the head" (2007, pp. 237, 240; see also pp. 247–281 more generally).

thereby decoupling it from dependence on *some* instantiating device. The point is evident enough in the contrast between books and e-books, which often come with DRM strings attached. For example, early users of Amazon's Kindle reader were surprised to discover that their purchased copies of George Orwell's 1984 had been deleted after a copyright claim against Amazon (Stone, 2009). No doubt publishers would like very much to be able to do similar things to people's print books, but there is no choke-point of an additional mediating device with the sophistication to impose this sort of control. Print books can no more be made to disappear than couches. So too, a publisher has no idea how someone reads a book, how many times they do so, whether they pay attention to the copyright notice, or even how many times the book is copied. Paracopyright makes it illegal to stop content owners from trying to learn this information, and then to regulate consumer behavior accordingly.

Although §1201 includes a series of exceptions, as for security research, securing the interoperability of media across different device types, and some other quite specific uses, it is a broad prohibition with a short list of exceptions. The Copyright Office is charged with periodic rulemaking to add requested exemptions to the list. These exemptions must be approved every rulemaking period. The 2018 set includes exemptions for educators to play DVDs in class, for disabled users to use assistive technologies to access e-books, for individuals to "jailbreak" their cellphones (and use them on a different wireless carrier), and to access and repair a range of software products including "voice assistants" like Amazon's Alexa and the software included on tractors (for more on tractors, see later) (37 CFR 201.40(b)). The logic of general ban with specific exception applies to the rules as well; for example, while the current rulemaking allows access to the software inside "lawfully acquired motorized land vehicle such as a personal automobile, commercial vehicle, or mechanized agricultural vehicle . . . when circumvention is a necessary step to allow the diagnosis, repair, or lawful modification of a vehicle function" (37 CFR 201.40(b)(9)), the specification of "land vehicle" means that boats and airplanes (including drones) are still covered by the ban.

The mere prohibition is of course without teeth, since it would be virtually impossible to enforce against people in their homes. Furthermore, the creation of encrypted content that restricted use would create a market in decryption programs. Accordingly, the "anti-trafficking" section provides that "no person shall manufacture, import, offer to the public, provide, or otherwise traffic in any technology, product, service, device, component, or part thereof" that "is primarily designed or produced for the purpose of circumventing a technological measure that effectively controls access to a work protected under this title" (17 USC 1201.2). This anti-trafficking provision pulls the rug out from under some otherwise consumer-friendly rulemaking by the Copyright Office. Although it is legal to pay someone else to jailbreak your phone, it is not legal to distribute software or other tools that allow the less technologically sophisticated to exercise their right.

In the first case to test this provision, *Universal City Studios* v. *Corley* (2001), the motion picture industry successfully sued 2600.com (an online hacker magazine), forcing it to take down links to code that broke CSS, the DRM scheme on DVDs. The 2600.com case is notable not just because it involved litigation against a third party that did not make or even directly host the software in question, but also because the person who did code the software, a Norwegian teenager named Jans Johannsen (he did so in eight lines of C++ code), had a colorable defense: there were no licensed players available to play DVDs on his Linux computer, so he should theoretically have been able to circumvent CSS in order to create one.[35] Of course, it is still fairly easy for the technologically sophisticated to find programs that decrypt DVDs. However, decrypting DVDs is much harder for the rest of us, and is generally impossible to do legally. In short, DRM, backed by the anticircumvention provision, makes it very difficult if not impossible for ordinary users to evade DRM, by making it criminal for those with the technical expertise to design products that help them to do so.

3.4.2 *DRM as Neoliberal Biopolitics*

The anticircumvention protections afforded to DRM techniques are among the most striking examples of IP law's imbrication in the world of cultural meaning and its assimilation of neoliberal governmentality. They serve as a way of producing certain kinds of subjects, those for whom access to culture and the commodities that populate it is primarily understood as a market activity. In so-doing, they also reinforce the norm that culture is itself a market, working to induce individuals to find joy/utility in consumption patterns that are structured by market relations. DRM thus is a technique of subjectification and participates in the neoliberal presumption that all of society can and should be treated economically. With their legal ratification of access control technologies, anticircumvention laws like those in §1201 serve to grant unilateral control over one's experiences with culturally significant sets of meanings to content owners, device makers, or both. In the case of content owners, those owners are able to restrict when and where and how one accesses a work.

Since the anticircumvention regulations function independently of other copyright protections, they can also be used to undermine the sorts of fair use provisions that would otherwise be juridically available. A content owner, for example, could use encryption to restrict access to those who signed a contractually enforceable pledge not to parody the encrypted work. It would then be illegal to access the work without authorization by breaking the encryption scheme, and a breach of contract

---

[35] I leave aside the obvious question of whether this defense was pretextual. For the case, and its failure to stop the general dissemination of the DeCSS code, see Peñalver and Katyal (2010, pp. 71–76).

to parody the work if one had authorized access. Parody of the work would become effectively illegal, despite the Supreme Court's explicit ruling that parody is fair use.

As I noted in Chapter 2, capital's expansion beyond Fordist factories and into immaterial goods entails its extension into communicative and cultural practices more generally. Yochai Benkler makes the general point in a way that resonates with Foucault's discussion of subject formation. He begins with the premise that "the structure of our information environment is constitutive of our autonomy, not only functionally significant to it" (2006, p. 156). He adds:

> All of the components of decision making prior to action, and those actions that are themselves communicative moves or require communication as a precondition to efficacy, are constituted by the information and communications environment we, as agents, occupy. Conditions that cause failures at any of these junctures, which place bottlenecks, failures of communication, or provide opportunities for manipulation by a gatekeeper in the information environment, create threats to the autonomy of individuals in that environment. The shape of the information environment, and the distribution of power within it to control information flows to and from individuals, are, as we have seen, the contingent product of a combination of technology, economic behavior, social patterns, and institutional structure or law.
>
> (2006, p. 157)[36]

In other words, if it is true that we are in the world with others and that we understand ourselves and comport to the world by way of public structures of meaning, then we will need to view ourselves and others as agents in the world whose intentions are composed with and through these public structures of meaning.

As Foucault (1977) notes, disciplinary technologies tend to migrate from their original location to become more diffuse forms of social control, and as the presence of an exemption for land vehicles suggests, one can see a similar pattern here. There is some debate about the extent of the diffusion of DRM. For example, as part of an argument against the possibility of perfect access control, R. Polk Wagner proposes that "there are very good reasons to doubt the meaningful impact of DRM anytime soon" (2003, p. 1015). As he argues, the software industry's failure at copy protection serves as a lesson to future rights-holders. Initial steps toward DRM in music (such as the comically flawed SDMI) have failed; the need to be compatible with current

---

[36] Benkler aligns his work with political liberalism, and it is not clear how deeply it meshes with the Foucauldian argument here. That said, his view that we are ontologically constituted by our information environment is at substantial tension with most of the liberal tradition; he distinguishes his argument by emphasizing the need to understand autonomy as a substantive, not merely formal value (in this, he follows Fallon (1994). I deploy the formal/substantive distinction to critique mandates that libraries install filtering software on their Internet terminals in Hull (2009c)). For a similar critique, one that directly attacks liberalist assumptions about formal autonomy, see Julie E. Cohen (2012). For the cognitive science behind the assertion that the information environment is constitutive of subjectivity, see, e.g., Clark (2003, p. 26).

technology will stop it (as long as I can play the CD, I can always play it into my computer, even if I can't rip it); legal efforts like suing individual downloaders can (and did) fail; and countermeasures are always possible.

I think there is considerable reason to be less sanguine than Wagner. There is compelling evidence that industry has learned from the failures of the 1980s and SDMI; what industry has learned is that it is necessary to keep device makers on board. The combination of encryption and the antitrafficking provisions of para-copyright enable precisely this by criminalizing the distribution of noncompliant devices. As Gillespie (2007) documents in detail, this discovery accounts for the comparative success of the DVD copy protection scheme. Indeed, contrary to Wagner's prediction, the litigation against CSS has been a success in that it has considerably raised the cost, in terms of effort and skill required, to bypass copy protection on DVDs. This sort of expansion is not surprising; one market forecast in 2018 predicted that globally, DRM would be a $9 billion industry by 2026, with an expected annual growth rate of over 15% until then (Bode, 2018).

Consider the history of the right to unlock a smartphone to use it with different carriers, currently covered as Copyright Office exemption. The right only existed because it was initially granted a special exemption to the §1201 rules by the Copyright Office, which future rulemaking then took away. Congress then passed a law and the Federal Trade Commission pressured carriers to voluntarily allow customers to use phones with expired contracts on different carriers, but the fragility of this and other exemptions indicates the scope of DRM (Sasso, 2014). There are numerous other examples. In an effort to shut down the secondary market in toner cartridges for its printers, Lexmark introduced a "prebate" pro-gram, designed to get consumers to return empty containers to Lexmark, rather than let them fall into the hands of third-party manufacturers. As part of this program, Lexmark installed a microchip into the cartridges that would disable them unless Lexmark itself removed them. Lexmark then sued Static Control technologies, which made an imitation chip that it sold to toner remanufacturers. Static Control counter-sued, arguing that Lexmark's statements about the prebate program, which declared among other things that Static Control's chips were illegal, violated trademark law. In 2014, the Supreme Court unanimously affirmed that Static Control had standing to sue (*Lexmark* v. *Static Control* (134 S.Ct. 1377 (2014)).

There is also evidence of the diffusion of DRM well beyond the consumer electronics sector. In 2015, Keurig attempted to use microchips and DRM to restrict consumers to Keurig branded coffee cartridges. After a consumer revolt, the com-pany relented and removed the technology. What is notable in this case is not so much that Keurig ultimately lost, but the effort to extend the diffusion of DRM into even the most fundamental aspects of life. As a writer for *Wired* put it, a "coffee maker limiting your choice of grind seems as out of place as a frying pan dictating your eggs" (Barrett, 2015). The effort was not just to extend market logic to morning coffee, but to force individuals to submit to monopoly behavior by a specific market actor.

Consider another example, the one that generated the right to repair land vehicles. John Deere had all but locked down its tractors, requiring that farmers visit authorized repair centers for authorized repair. The move has a sense of déjà vu to it, as in his warning against DRM, Gillespie (2007) treated the right to tinker with one's automobile metaphorically as the sort of thing that rights management technologies might try to stop. Regardless of the actual diffusion of DRM, farmers were treating the inability to repair their tractors as an emergency, going online to find Ukrainian hacks of the tractors' software. The agreement that John Deere required of farmers contains nearly all the tricks of the DRM playbook:

> A license agreement John Deere required farmers to sign in October forbids nearly all repair and modification to farming equipment, and prevents farmers from suing for "crop loss, lost profits, loss of goodwill, loss of use of equipment . . . arising from the performance or non-performance of any aspect of the software." The agreement applies to anyone who turns the key or otherwise uses a John Deere tractor with embedded software. It means that only John Deere dealerships and "authorized" repair shops can work on newer tractors.
>
> (Koebler, 2017)

That is, the combination of contract and §1201 compelled farmers to have their tractors serviced by authorized dealers or risk suit. Only those contractually authorized by John Deere are allowed to service John Deere tractors.

As Jason Koebler (2017) reported for *Vice*, "the nightmare scenario, and a fear I heard expressed over and over again in talking with farmers, is that John Deere could remotely shut down a tractor and there wouldn't be anything a farmer could do about it." Whether the company would actually do that matters far less than the fact that farmers fear that it might. The current exemption allows farmers to repair their tractors, but it requires that they develop the software to do so themselves, or pay someone who has. It is still not legal to "traffic" in software that allows less technologically savvy farmers to make their own repairs. One should recall the initial example of DRM run amok: In describing the problems with adhesion contracts, Julie Cohen (1998) cited a hypothetical couch that made itself disappear when it decided that too many people were sitting on it at once. Having too many people sit on the couch suggests that the consumer is refusing to buy another piece of furniture that he or she clearly needs.

3.4.3 *Preferencing Immersion: Paracopyright as Subjectification*

Much of the scholarship critical of paracopyright says that "it's all about control" (Elkin-Koren, 2002), perhaps socially legitimated by a moral panic over promiscuous copying (Patry, 2009). In other words, there is a standard interpretation of §1201.

I think that is correct, but I want to add a different emphasis here, one that unpacks the reference to Benkler's discussion of our information environment. Following a distinction drawn in Paul Dourish's work, I propose that we see the shift as an attempt to shift the phenomenological experience of interacting with copyrighted material. Dourish differentiates between two different design strategies for dealing with a user's interaction with a device. One, as represented by immersive virtual reality (think video games, or 3D TV), moves the user into the computer's world. Dourish:

> Interaction takes place in a fictional, computer-generated world; the user moves into that world, either through immersion or, more commonly these days, through a window onto the world on a computer screen. The world of interaction is the world of the computer.

> (2001, p. 38)

The other, "augmented reality," does the opposite. Again, Dourish:

> It moves the computer into the real world. The site of interaction is the world of the user, not that of the system. That world, in the augmented reality vision, may be imbued with computation, but the computer itself takes a back seat.

> (2001, p. 38)

Dourish presents examples drawn from MIT labs, but common examples now might range from developments in wearable computing down to light switches that automatically turn on when someone enters the room. The essential difference from the point of view of the argument here is that the goal of augmented reality is to adapt the technology to the world of the user; the goal of immersion is the reverse.

To see how this distinction matters, note that the vision of interaction with media embedded in traditional copyright basically presents a world of augmented reality. That is, traditional copyright presents interaction in terms of the users and their context, where the technical features of the interface (even if computationally intensive) take a back seat. Even the basic legal prohibition against copying can be defended against by a claim of fair use; the inquiry into whether a particular use is fair is entirely fact-dependent. In this regard, traditional copyright is well-matched to the world of the book, in which the "interface" of the book is relatively undemanding of users who have achieved literacy, and in which literary content is distributed naturally into discrete artifacts that can be used in whatever social context readers desire. Importantly, the meaning of the experience with books and the texts they contain is heavily mediated by those contexts.

Paracopyright, by contrast, follows the strategy of immersive virtual reality by centering the experience on the technology itself. In order to access a text protected by paracopyright, the users must use an authorized machine, and must access the material on the machine's terms. For example, the copy control scheme of DVDs that make it impossible to play a DVD in the wrong geographic location often make it impossible for users to skip copyright notices, company logos, and even advertising for more of that company's products. The comparison with books, which one can take overseas and where one can easily skip the copyright notice or any other undesired material, is striking.[37]

Let us return to Dourish's distinction between virtual and augmented realities. Recall that virtual reality embeds users in the world of the machine. Here, it seems that the point is to remove users from their own social context and to place them into the world of the media devices. The issue is that worlds come with norms, and part of the point of the world of media devices is to inculcate norms of metered (or at least paid) consumption by making noncompliant behavior extremely difficult. Outside the world of these devices, the situation with respect to copyright norms can perhaps best be described as pluralistic. Some users might have strong beliefs about obeying the law, or the need to respect copyright, but it is quite clear that at least a plurality do not. Even among those who in principle think copyright is a good idea, there are large numbers who think the content industries have vastly overstated any just claims to further legal protection. Certainly there is no social consensus that violating copyright is bad in the way there is a social consensus that pedophilia is bad. Not only that, normative language designed to buttress copyright claims can easily be repurposed against such claims. Where industry can demand that copyrights be respected, users can demand that their access rights be respected (Grimmelmann, 2009).

This normative plurality has proven difficult to dislodge, despite extensive advertising and even litigation by content owners. On the one hand, empirical research in developing countries clearly indicates that the effort to use law to establish clear property norms in such a context is unlikely to succeed. Indeed, when there is a large enough disparity between law and local norms, the system tends to move toward open access: the law is sufficient to undermine whatever nonlegal norms existed prior to it, but not sufficient to establish itself as a norm (Fitzpatrick, 2006). On the other hand, the need for property to coordinate the actions of large numbers of people means that the core of property claims must both be simple and perceived as moral (Merrill and Smith, 2007). Copyright fails both standards: the copyright act is staggeringly complex, and the nonrivalrous nature of IP makes it very difficult to convince the average person that making a copy is tantamount to theft. As Jessica Litman truculently put it, "The Digital Millennium Copyright Act is, by any measure, an ugly law. I defy anyone to understand its major provisions on a first (or fifth) careful reading. It takes general principles, like 'fairness,' and translates them into exceptionally long, complicated, wordy, counter-intuitive and internally

---

[37] The resulting user experience is different, and it is important here not to judge one as more authentic than another. For the sorts of normative claim I want to avoid, see e.g., Albert Borgmann's famous complaints about the stereo; see the brief versions in Borgmann (1995, 2010).

inconsistent proscriptions" (2002, pp. 32–33). In this context, one should understand paracopyright not as an effort to enforce copyright, but as an effort to change recalcitrant users into consumers.

In this sense, paracopyright is a logical extension of the antipiracy trailers the MPAA sometimes runs before movies. The difference is that paracopyright attempts the change architecturally. Because users are placed in a space where a different and restricted set of activities is available, the user is compelled to comply with the normative vision enabling those activities. Generally, this is a move from law to code or architecture as a form of regulation, where a police officer would be an example of law and a speed bump one of architecture.[38] Architecture attempts to influence norms in at least two ways. On the one hand, by making offending behavior impossible, it nudges individuals to no longer desire to do it. On the other hand, architecture can attempt to impose its own norms. The most famous example is Bentham's panopticon, which used constant visibility to attempt to get prisoners to internalize norms of compliance with guards, hard work, tidiness, etc. Here, when DVDs force viewers to watch the copyright notice on a DVD that they will find it difficult or impossible to copy anyway, this can only be construed as an effort to shape their norms. Simply making the disc very difficult to copy would suffice to stop most piracy. Similarly, when users are compelled to view advertising, this is an effort both to induce desire for specific products and to normalize the idea that one is to approach media as a consumer. In other words, the immersion into devices enables an immersion into a different normative world. The goal is to get users to adopt the normative grammar of the content industries, where "respect" is owed to producers and "entertainment" is owed to consumers; where "sharing" means "two paying customers watching together;" and where "copying" means "piracy" or "terrorism." The governing logic is that experience with content is to be passive, in the sense that the media sets the range of what one does next.

In addition to moving individuals to a model of passive consumption, DRM works to undermine juridical notions of right and accountability. As I will discuss in the context of what I call "actuarial agency" in the discussion of patents, most people default to juridical notions of responsibility. DRM works against this because it works to absolve anyone of responsibility for access limitations by displacing them onto the supposedly politically neutral terrain of technology. When I have too many authorized devices in iTunes, is the problem with iTunes, the music files, the music publishers, the legal regime enabling all this, or all of the above? In what combination? In other words, these assemblages of code and actors either diffuse responsibility across the assemblage such that no element of it is responsible, or direct focus

---

[38] Cheng suggests that §1201 is an example of the move toward structural law over fiat, and suggests in a footnote that it might be considered an example of a more "regulatory" approach – in other words, an approach that replaces police in the juridical sense with "police" in the biopolitical one (2006, p. 710).

onto the algorithms and technical objects, and, in so doing, tend to obscure precisely the political economy behind them. As Bruno Latour (1992) said, we delegate a lot of our moral work to machines.

At least three factors combine to facilitate this result. First, the system of regulation is complex and dispersed. It is not just that there is an impersonal device instead of a personified authority figure to blame. It is that the regime requires the cooperation of law, device makers, and content owners (which are generally large corporations, not individual authors). As Gillespie points out, "that no single element of this arrangement is solely responsible for its consequences, or for its missteps, helps deflect criticism" (2007, p. 169). Second, the coding of the enforcement into devices encourages us to experience use limitations as politically neutral hardware limitations. In other words, the regulation tends to naturalize itself. Again, Gillespie: the attributes of DVD players are "treated as a natural phenomenon, as if DVD players sprout from the ground without Record buttons. In fact, such characteristics are explicitly mandated in the CSS license at the whim of the movie studios" (2007, p. 186).

Finally, the DRM regime actively works to discourage users from being responsible for themselves. In other words, it actively works to restrict their autonomy and to recreate them as passive, consuming subjects. As Burk and Gillespie argue, "because DRM preempts the discretion of information users, denying them the choice as to how information products are to be used, it treats them as morally immature or incompetent, preempted from, and by implication incapable of, making a moral decision to obey the law" (2006, p. 243). It is in this sense that DRM undermines autonomy in the sense that Benkler uses the term. As Niva Elkin-Koren puts the point:

> When rightsholders govern the format of the work they are able to control what individuals can do with cultural texts. They can determine whether individuals can only passively consume cultural artifacts or whether they could actively use the texts and adopt them to reflect their own agenda. When individuals can use artistic works in a context of their choice, and adopt it to reflect their own agenda, they are able to contest the original meaning attached to it. Copies detached from their original context could be experienced (heard, read, watched) differently and allow individuals to create a new meaning. Information represented digitally, that is disentangled from physical formats, could adapt itself to its surroundings, and facilitate a plurality of voices.
>
> (2002, p. 94)

The law-plus-code enforcement of DRM substantially reduces users' ability to perform an individuating action for which they could then be responsible. One simply does what one must, secure in the knowledge that everyone else experiences media in the same way.

Of course, this description is not entirely correct. There are vibrant communities of hackers online, communities of those sufficiently technically adept to bypass technological barriers to individuating themselves. Others are "judgment proof," willing to flout the law because they have nothing to lose. However, to focus on these individuals is to miss the point about subjectification. Lessig's warning on the point is apt. "Just because perfect control is not possible does not mean that effective control is not possible," he writes, adding that:

> A fundamental principle of bovinity is operating here and elsewhere. Tiny controls, consistently enforced, are enough to direct very large animals ... We are large animals. I think it is as likely that the majority of people would resist these small but efficient regulators of the Net as it is that cows would resist wire fences. This is who we are, and this is why these regulations work.
>
> (2006, p. 73)

Provisions like §1201 do not stop determined hackers, but they do profoundly affect the majority of us by herding us into officially sanctioned media consumption habits, and in so doing, they foreclose possibilities for differentiation from the herd.

There are of course many different videos and commercials to watch; the point is not that DRM creates complete homogeneity. Indeed, as theorists have noted for some time, capital long ago started celebrating diversity, and encouraging niche consumption. As I will argue in Chapter 4, IP in the form of trademark is actively involved in encouraging such consumption. Consumers learn both to assume identities based on their consumption habits and to change their consumption habits frequently to maintain their differentiation from others. The point to underscore here with regard to legal provisions like §1201 is that they nudge identity possibilities toward those sanctioned by capital as it is embodied in copyright owners, and away from individuals' own combinations. In this, they reduce the contingencies associated with our encounters with media, by channeling those encounters down preexisting paths of commodity consumption. In so doing, they shape the forms of life available to us all.

4

Trademark

Trademark law has traditionally been directed at reducing consumer confusion in the marketplace. By giving producers exclusive control over the marks or names they used to designate their products, trademark ensured that when consumers shopped for products bearing those marks, they got what they were looking for and not some other product that was attempting to free ride on the original producer. At the same time, trademark was designed to incentivize product development. Since consumers would know exactly what a given product name or mark would get them, the owners of those marks would have the incentive to improve their products, knowing that consumers would associate the improvements with the owners and their products. However, as capitalism has become increasingly brand-centric, trademark has come to be more protective of marks themselves. This is evident in the growing rights of owners to prohibit use of their mark that might imply product endorsement, for example. This chapter focuses on three brand-oriented developments in trademark that represent the ways that brand capitalism intersects differing models of power.

The first section treats trademark dilution, which is the clearest recent example of neoliberalization of trademark. With a dilution claim, the owner of a mark can seek legal redress against noncompeting, nonconfusing uses of similar marks, if those uses might damage the value of the mark itself. This development in many ways parallels the development of paracopyright, as discussed in Chapter 3. Just as paracopyright extends copyright into new kinds of domain beyond its initial purposes, so dilution extends trademark beyond its initial purposes of avoiding confusion. Another parallel with paracopyright is also readily apparent. The older versions of trademark align with public biopolitics, insofar as they are designed to benefit the consuming public generally, but the advent of dilution seems to move things in a neoliberal direction insofar as it both decouples brands from products and makes consumer affect and feelings part of the direct market value of a brand.[1] In addition, as I will argue, the move to brand-oriented capitalism, aided and abetted by trademark dilution, serves to further the reach of market relations into everyday life as it monetizes the very symbols we use to navigate the world and to constitute us as subjects who live in and through corporate marks. I treat dilution in two parts. The first situates the dilution question into a larger narrative about the development of commodification, and the second analyzes Victoria's Secret's successful litigation against a sex-toy shop that called itself "Victor's Little Secret." By following market research on branding – much of it based on Victoria's Secret – I underscore the extent to which branding and dilution are strategies of neoliberal subjectification.

The second section looks at what can be read as an effort by the Supreme Court to resist a more publicly oriented effort to shape what kinds of brand identities develop. In 2017, the Court ruled that the PTO could not deny formal registration to a mark on the grounds that it was "disparaging," since such efforts at massaging public language use ran afoul of the First Amendment's ban on viewpoint discrimination. The disparagement litigation was immediately followed by litigation against the prohibition on registering "scandalous" marks. The First Amendment decision is, in a way, not difficult. What is more notable about these cases, I argue, is the Court's determination that the issue was a First Amendment one in the first place. Further, the turn to the First Amendment has the perverse effect of enabling the further development of branding culture. Rather than reducing the regulation of speech, the Court effectively hands off regulatory power to the private entities that own the brands in question.

The third section comprises an extended study of efforts by indigenous producers to protect geographically specific local products through geographic indicator protection. Here, the effort is to use the legal tools of branding to protect traditional forms of commodity production. As I argue, these efforts are both promising and difficult, as the invocation of further property rights potentially limits their ability to empower the producers they are designed to protect. I conclude with some remarks on the limits inherent in such a strategy, and what those limits suggest about our understanding of power and property.

[1] Older trademark law is also exemplary of public biopolitics insofar as the emphasis is on reducing information costs to indefinitely many members of the public, rather than treating specific transactions with individual consumers. On this model, see Merrill and Smith (2001) and the discussion in Chapter 2. Merrill and Smith emphasize the *in rem* model of traditional property rights; as the following should indicate, the case of trademark is complicated insofar as the brand-as-commodity is treated as a thing. I discussed this reification of brands in Hull (2003b). Although the discussion here is based on some of the same impulses that motivated that paper, the argument is thoroughly revised.

4.1 DILUTION: THE STRANGE CASE OF VICTOR'S LITTLE SECRET

4.1.1 *Branding and Dilution*

Trademark is classically justified in economic terms as a way to protect consumers from confusing products with one another. By ensuring that a given mark can only be associated with the owner's product(s) (so the Nike swoosh with Nike shoes, etc.), trademark does three primary things to promote the welfare of consumers. First, it lowers consumer "search costs" for finding a specific company's products, since they would be uniquely marked. Second, it stops companies from confusing consumers into buying the wrong products (hence knock-off designer purses violate trademark law). Finally, by letting companies capture the value of their brand, it encourages them to invest resources into improving the products carrying that brand.[2] However, if that economic description was at one time helpful for understanding trademark, it seems less so now. Today, trademark increasingly seems to be about protecting corporate brands and branding strategies, and less about consumer confusion. And, as I will argue, consumers have to be conditioned to invest in brands, rather than in products.[3] Dilution doctrine, which will be my primary focus here, is only the latest in a long string of doctrinal developments that are poorly explained by the consumer confusion model. I will take it as exemplary of an underlying logic, even though it represents a relatively small portion of trademark litigation. This logic allows one to see a move to a neoliberal model of trademark.

The reasons why brands and trademark emerge, and the reasons why trademark is expanding into new areas, can be illuminated by a consideration of the logic of commodification, that is, the conceptual steps involved in understanding how a product comes into the market. Consider first a classic, noncommodified good, such as produce or grain at a bazaar. Here, the consumer and vendor generally meet directly; the consumer has direct access to the good, such that they can inspect it; and the transaction often involves imprecise measurement of or metrics for both quantity and quality. (Consider the vendor who uses an old mug to measure and price his grain.) In addition, consumers will often develop personal relations with vendors, and these personal relations of trust, built on experience with the vendor and his or her goods, become central to the consumer's desire to purchase again

---

[2] For an exposition, see Landes and Posner (1987). For problems with the economic model, particularly as concerns dilution, see, e.g., Beebe (2009), which offers a "semiotic" account of trademark, according to which the signifier (Nike swoosh) is connected to the signified (feeling of athleticism) and the referent (the shoe). Branding culture essentially makes the referent irrelevant to the value of the mark, and companies attempt to exploit the signifier–signified relation as a source of value: hence the need for dilution doctrine.
[3] For general discussion along these lines, see, e.g., Bartow (2015), Desai (2012), and Dreyfuss (2002).

from the same vendor. Nearly every aspect of purchasing goods at a bazaar is concrete and tangible in these ways.

One reason for the emergence of trademark is the breakdown of this personal relation. Literature on the development of trademark in the United States underscores that in the nineteenth century, a period of lower trademark protection, most purchases were local, and made from local vendors. As Devan Desai puts it, this means that "the places of business and goodwill were intertwined" (2015, p. 574). National markets, branding, and advertising developed as railways and large-scale industry made it possible to distribute goods to geographically diverse locations. The early twentieth century also saw companies start to diversify their product lines, offering more than one product, as had previously been the norm.[4] It was that loss of local connection that framed the core of Frank Schechter's initial argument in favor of dilution doctrine. So too, the sense of local *terroir* is what geographical indications (GIs) try to capture in an economy where consumers seem to value a connection, however artificial, between place and goodwill.

The process of commodification can, from this vantage, be seen as one of abstraction. The process of bringing goods to market becomes considerably more complex if they are to be purchased or consumed far away from where they are produced, as the increasing distances and multiplication of intermediaries between producer and consumer work to decrease the ability of consumers to develop an informed opinion of the product before purchase. In other words, the traditional bazaar is relatively rich in relevant consumer information, much of which is lost in the move to commodities. At the same time, the move to commodities involves the introduction of two new axes of consumer information. The first is standardization, whereby the products that will come to bear a particular mark or brand acquire a consistent set of attributes and techniques for their evaluation. The second, familiar from the literature on trademark and branding, is product differentiation: Producers need to have at their disposal an array of strategies that distinguish their goods from those of competitors.

Standardization is necessary in the production process because consumers, particularly nonlocal ones, need to know that products they purchase from a given vendor and with a given designation today will be the same as the supposedly identical product purchased yesterday or tomorrow. The biggest challenge here is that the production process has to be homogenized enough so that its output is consistent. In order for that to happen, there must be some sort of specification as to which of the indefinitely many possible characteristics of the good are to count as its qualities, and standards for how those qualities are to be measured and evaluated (Callon, Méadel, and Rabeharisoa, 2002, pp. 198–199). Some of these qualities, such as weight, are obvious, but others – like "pure" or "traditional methods" – may require extensive specification, and ethnographic research into niche products, such

---

[4]   On this, in addition to Desai (2015), see Bone (2008, pp. 477–480) and Wilf (2008, pp. 161–164).

as canola oil (Busch and Tanaka, 1996), "quality" salmon (Hébert, 2010), Burmese teak (Bryant, 2013), fresh produce (Freidberg, 2004), organic vegetables (Buck, Getz, and Guthman, 1997), and surimi (Mansfield, 2003), attests to the substantial changes and disruption that standardization can bring to producers.

Product differentiation presents a different kind of problem, which is, as Franck Cochoy (2002) memorably notes, that modern consumers frequently find themselves in the position of Buridan's ass, needing to choose between two commodities that are (virtually) indistinguishable. Producers face an unending need for product differentiation strategies as competitors emerge with similar products.[5] In that sense, doctrinal construction of consumers as easily confused can be read as a symptom of increased commodification. Producers have the incentive to imitate successful commodities, and at some point even the most conscientious consumer will either be unable to make a principled distinction between two goods, or will find the effort at distinction more troublesome than it is worth, especially in the absence of heuristics like local "goodwill."

One tool for producers is the brand, which is, following David Aaker, a "distinguishing name and/or symbol (such as a logo, trademark, or package design) intended to identify the goods or services of one seller or a group of sellers, and to differentiate those goods or services from those of competitors." In particular, he adds, brands serve to indicate the "origin" of a product, and to protect both producers and consumers from being confused by competing products (Aaker, 1991, p. 7). The need for trademark is immediately apparent: Brands could not perform their differentiating function if competitors could simply identify their own products with the same mark. At the same time, because they incorporate goodwill, brands as markers themselves become a reason to choose one good over another. In that regard, the process of creating distinction is also one of creating brand value that firms then attempt to internalize.

Producers accordingly use a strategy of various layers of packaging and marks to create identifiable differences between otherwise indistinguishable goods. One step in this process is the introduction of packaging according to brand, so consumers can shop for "wheat x" as opposed to simply "wheat." As Cochoy indicates, the packaging functions as a screen in a double sense: On the one hand, it screens/hides direct access to the good; on the other hand, it serves as a projection screen to indicate features of the good's origin and the qualities the producer wants to associate with it (2002, pp. 61–62). It is at this level that traditional economic justifications of trademark offer the most explanatory value. If a brand marker is to

---

[5] As a matter of commodification, the need for product differentiation occurs whether or not consumers are discerning or rational. That is not to say that there is no interaction between the protection of brands and the tendency to treat consumers as irrational: as consumers are construed as less rational, they require more assistance from distinct branding strategies, which therefore require new protections against infringement. See Desai (2015, pp. 590–591, 595).

successfully differentiate a product, then consumers need to be able to rely on it to direct them to the brand in question, and not somewhere else.

A brand's indication of a product's "origin" serves to occlude any details of the process by which it is actually produced, such as what it is made of, or where it is made (Cochoy, 2002, pp. 61–62). The attribution of origin is mythological in the sense that it presents whatever narrative about the origin of the product the producer wants to communicate. Producers accordingly use a variety of strategies to shape and stabilize consumer associations between a brand and the product(s) bearing its name. Jessica Silbey gestures to the social complexity of this process:

> Branding, the art of trademarks, is as much about market share and consumer identification as it is about personal identity politics in today's twenty-first century. We buy goods for what they are and for what they say about each of us: our hipness, athleticism, politics, or sexual preference. Insofar as trademark law revolves around the consumer construct, the trademark origin myth tells the story of how to be unique and different in today's visually crowded and stimulated society.
>
> (2008, p. 363)

As a result, brands themselves come to have a tremendous value, because consumers come to associate them with products and images that they like, and (hopefully) transfer this positive association to other products of the same brand. As Sonia Katyal summarizes, trademarks function as messengers from a producer to the consuming public about a product. As a result, "the trademark represents both a global visual receptacle and a vehicle for all of the emotive and personality characteristics that advertisers hope to associate with a particular brand" (2015, pp. 316–317).

That said, this set of relationships is potentially fluid in at least two ways. On the one hand, the goodwill it carries is potentially quite fragile, as consumer association between the mark and the concept or affect it signifies can easily be derailed. For example, in the 1990s, Nike and several other producers came to be associated with sweatshops in the minds of many consumers.[6] On the other hand, because the relation between the mark and a given product is also purely conventional, and there is no reason why producers cannot apply their mark to some other product, in an effort to give it the same reputational capital conferred on the original product by its association with the mark in question.

These features interact to produce an incentive for producers to treat successful brands themselves as commodities, independently of any particular product. Indeed, this result can be viewed as the logical extension of the commodification process: If the brand itself has value, and if there is no intrinsic connection between the brand and any particular product, then it makes sense for brand owners to detach the brand

---

[6]   On the use of corporate logos by activist groups advocating for greater corporate responsibility, see, e.g., Katyal (2015). I return to these campaigns in the context of the public/neoliberal biopolitics distinction in the conclusion.

from the product, especially if the greater value is in the brand.[7] Brand attachments encourage consumers to both draw upon their experience with products bearing the same mark and durably differentiate a producer's goods from their competitors. Globalization pushes all of this further, as most consumers have little information about the origin of their products other than as products somehow originating with the trademark holder. In such a context, brands and origin labeling become even more valuable, since they provide some prepurchase guidance to consumers.

Reflecting this growing importance of brands and branding, trademark law now protects against "dilution," diminishing the value or distinctiveness associated with the mark, independent of any association with particular products.[8] There are two principal kinds of dilution: tarnishment and blurring. "Tarnishment" occurs when someone uses a sufficiently similar mark on a product that could be said to damage the owner's reputation (as, for example, on pornography or drugs). "Blurring" is the broader, nonderogatory version of the claim, as, for example, using the name "Tiffany" to refer to a restaurant. In either case, the point is that the signifier's ability to refer exclusively to the producer's chosen signified is diminished by the introduction in consumers' minds of extraneous meaning.[9] As I will argue, enforcement of dilution claims implies an effort at subjectification. That is, in the universe contemplated by dilution doctrine, not only is one to be a consumer, but corporate brand owners have increasing power over the content and manner of that consumption.

The point about detached brands is evident enough in, for example, the ubiquitous presence of "Hello Kitty" logos. Someone who purchases a "Hello Kitty" lunchbox and shirt is making a decision based on logo, and may even be more interested in the logo than whatever product bears it; no contextualized history of the production process is relevant. In the face of proliferating trademarks, the referentiality of the marks becomes more and more difficult for consumers to sustain, and so they default to associations with the mark itself, associations that can therefore be detached from the product to which the mark refers. Although Hello Kitty is a largely a detached signifier – few individuals could associate it with an original product – brand detachment is evident even in corporations central to the industrial economy. For example, a 1999 *Financial Times* article quoted a Ford executive predicting that the "manufacture of cars will be a declining part of Ford's

7   For some literature on this, see Beebe (2009, p. 59), Foster (2007, 2008), and Silbey (2008, p. 367). For a survey of recent such efforts and a discussion on the ability of these branding efforts to subsume even their critique, see Katyal (2010a).
8   Dilution is notoriously difficult to explain in traditional economic terms. This is noted, for example, by Lubochinski (2003), who suggests (with reference to the Victoria's Secret case) that Hegelian personality theory much more adequately captures corporate investment in brands. From that point of view, dilution can be understood as a protection against dilution of brand personality. I will not pursue that line of thought here, as it is reliant on dubious notions of corporate personhood.
9   For dilution more generally, see Beebe (2009, p. 58), Long (2006), and Senftleben (2009).

business," to be supplanted by "design, branding, marketing, sales, and service operations" (qt. in Katyal, 2010a, p. 800).

Dilution is a relatively recent phenomenon. The term (*verwässewrt*) was coined in a German case of 1924, and the concept made it from there to Frank Schechter's famous "The Rational Basis of Trademark Protection" (1927).[10] Schechter argues at length that trademark does not protect the link between a "definite and particular source, the characteristics of which or the personalities connected with which are specifically known to the consumer, but merely [indicates] that the goods in connection with which it is used emanate from the same – possibly anonymous – source" as others bearing the same mark (p. 816). In other words, the trademark is about the brand as the source of a product, where, as noted earlier, the brand serves as a screen or a mythological origin point. In different terms, the willingness to say that the mark itself has value is the conceptual core of the dilution argument.[11]

Having defined the trademark in terms of the symbol and not the product it refers to, Schechter is able to claim that "the true functions of the trademark are, then, to identify a product as satisfactory and thereby to stimulate further purchases by the consuming public" and as something the "most potent aspect" of which is "an agency for the actual creation and perpetuation of good will" (p. 818). Trademark is not about deception, but the capacity of the mark to generate value for its owner. Schechter then claims that the now normal kind of trademark infringement is the use of similar marks on noncompeting goods.[12] The "real injury in such cases" is then properly recognized as:

The gradual whittling away or dispersion of the identity and hold upon the public mind of the mark or name by its use upon non-competing goods. The more distinctive or unique the mark, the deeper is its impress upon the public consciousness, and the greater its need for protection against vitiation or dissociation from the particular product in connection with which it has been used.

(p. 825)

---

[10] For a general history of the article and Schechter, see Bone (2008) and Wilf (2008, pp. 158–171).

[11] It is also central to the Chicago School representation of brands as a mitigating factor in antitrust, as expressed by Bork. In response to the complaint that a set of only four cigarette companies dominate the market, Bork responds that the movement of brands in and out of the market nevertheless ameliorates any concerns one might have about market power: "since cigarettes were a heavily advertised product, the dominance of the four was attributed to the entry-barring effect of advertising. But the crucial aspect of cigarette advertising is that the companies advertise brands rather than company names. Few smokers can tell you which firms make which brands, and even fewer care. Moreover, the industry has been characterized by the introduction of new brands characterized by heavy advertising, as well as by the decline and disappearance of old brands. Advertising was a route of entry for new brands, and it did not save older ones" (1993, p. 316). Bork does not explain why all of the major brands emanated from these four companies.

[12] It is in this sense that Robert Bone (2008) is able to argue that Schechter's account is realist: it is an attempt to reform trademark law to better fit with actual practice.

Schechter then cites the German *Odol* case as supporting precedent for his view. In it, the plaintiff had an established brand of mouthwash bearing the "Odol" name, and the defendant had registered the term on steel products, such as nail clippers. Although the products would not compete, the court argued that the other use would hurt the plaintiff's ability to compete against other brands of mouthwash by diluting the significance of its mark.[13]

Schechter is particularly concerned about displacing any discussion that negatively associates trademarks with illegitimate monopolies. In his *Historical Treatise*, he cites (*Loughran (3rd Cir.)*, p. 158) the "Quaker Maid" case (see Chapter 2) and the District Court's invocation of concern about monopoly as problematic. The appellate decision there is even more illustrative. As I noted in Chapter 2, the Court concluded that "Quaker Maid" and "Quaker City" were not similar marks, even though both applied to candies. In so doing, the Court rejected a more expansive view according to which allowing the Quaker Maid registration would deprive Quaker City of protection of a "valuable good will asset in a business that has grown through the years to very large proportions" (*Loughran (District)*, p. 824). Against the property/monopoly dichotomy, which Schechter claims leads to numerous "subtleties and metaphysics," he cites an article on trademarks and goodwill as providing a sounder basis for property protection (1925, pp. 160–161). Against the concern about monopoly, Schechter then adds that "the dictionary is quite large enough to justify such limited monopolies" (1925, pp. 159–160). In "Rational Basis", he similarly argues that a "groundless obstacle to so broad a protection of marks is that historical fear of monopoly which has possessed the courts ever since in the first trademark case in equity Lord Hardwicke refused injunctive relief on that account." On the contrary: Dilution protects "fair trading," and not only may competing goods and services be sold under different symbols, but there is no limit to the number of symbols available (p. 833).

The hedge against monopoly fears indicates the extent to which dilution doctrine is an awkward fit with the reasoning of public biopolitics. As Steven Wilf quips, "perhaps nothing suggested how the specter of monopoly haunted early twentieth-century trademark law more than the repeated denial of this fact" (2008, p. 154). Public biopolitics embedded a concern with markets as producers of social welfare,

---

[13] As Beebe (2014) recently noted, Schechter's appropriation of the *Odol* case is an odd one, because it strategically downplays the extent to which *Odol* was not, in fact, a trademark case: it was a misappropriation case. The statutes in question sanctioned conduct "against good morals," and were designed to preserve fair market competition. How the misappropriation in question was immoral is never explained, and much of market competition involves, for example, companies copying marketing strategies from one another. Beebe suggests that Schechter's dissimulation was designed to insulate himself from critique by legal realists, an endeavor that failed, since "Rational Basis" is singled out for negative treatment in Felix Cohen's "Transcendental Nonsense" (1935). It seems to me that the larger point – that Schechter wanted to be identified with realism – is underscored by his quip about "subtleties and metaphysics" in *Historical Treatise* noted later.

a view that extended even into Hayek. However, the neoliberal extension of market logic into all social relations, as well as its reformulation of antitrust doctrine, dictated a different result. The idea that there can be no monopoly around a mark, and that robust protection of a mark allows firms to efficiently maximize their wealth, is closely aligned with Chicago school neoliberalism. If consumers pay higher prices, that is because they value the branded products more, even if the process of branding creates the enhanced valuation. As Bork put the argument:

> Efficiency does not arise solely from cutting costs. It also arises from offering products that people want more, even if those products cost more to produce. It is wrong to say that the Mustang is produced more efficiently than the Lincoln Continental because it costs less. Raising average costs through promotional and informational expenditures is no different from raising average costs through expenditures on larger engines. Both are efficient and procompetitive if consumers like them.
>
> (1993, p. 319)[14]

In other words, once all social welfare is measured in consumer, market-based terms, then the increase of consumer attachment to particular brands can only enhance that welfare.

At the point dilution doctrine emerges alongside the tendency to assign value to brands themselves, trademark takes a distinctly neoliberal turn. This happens in at least two ways, one about internalization and the other about monopoly and subjectification. First, the logic of brands is less about benefits to the consuming public and more about allowing brand owners to internalize the value of people's attachment to and feelings about brands. The logic is thus fundamentally Demsetzian. One of the externalities associated with a highly successful brand that is easy to lose in the translation of social welfare into market terms is what Rochelle Cooper Dreyfuss (1990) calls its "expressive genericity," its availability as a difficult-to-substitute tool for expressing social meaning. Successful brands – consider the term "Olympics," which the USOC infamously succeeded in preventing a group from using as part of its "Gay Olympics" – become essential means for expressing the affect associated with them. "Gay Track and Field Events" simply does not mean the same thing as "Gay Olympics." The opposing assumption of substitutability, central as early as Schechter's claim that competing brands could simply make use of other symbols, underscores the dependence of the process on a market logic where the value of symbols is only measurable in commodity terms.

Dreyfuss's argument is that in such cases, the trademark question is misplaced because the value in question accrues to the public at large, and not (only) a market competitor. For example, when Mattel sues another company for using Barbie, "the choice for assigning surplus value is not between a trademark owner and a trademark

---

[14] For some discussion, see Desai (2015, pp. 607–611).

user ... but between trademark owners and the public" (1990, p. 407). This is because absent the trademark, the price of the competing products would tend to decline to marginal cost – directly dissipating the surplus value into consumer surplus. Moreover, some of this value is virtually impossible to monetize. For example, when Nadia Plesner wanted to use the image of a Luis Vuitton bag in work designed to promote awareness of the famine in Darfur, that awareness does not translate into market terms (Katyal, 2015). The sense that trademark asks the wrong question is similar to the problem with parody in copyright discussed in Chapter 3: In focusing narrowly on the commodity being parodied, it loses sight of the extent to which the work being parodied might serve as a shortcut or metaphor for cultural values. In both cases, the question is one about positive externalities – spillovers – and the extent to which they can first be made legible in market terms, and then made available for internalization by property owners.[15]

Another, more directly market-oriented, of the externalities of a successful brand is the goodwill of consumers. To some extent, this value accrues to the brand owner in the form of product sales. Brand owners also capture this value by tying and sponsorship arrangements. Trademark law historically protects these efforts at internalization in various ways, for example, by protection against sponsorship confusion. For instance, in an early 1948 case, the owners of *Seventeen* magazine were able to enjoin the production of "Seventeen" girdles on the grounds that "purchasers would have the erroneous belief that the girdles had been editorially approved by or advertised in the magazine and that this belief would aid" the sales of the girdle manufacturer (*Rohrlich*, p. 971). As I will note later, dilution theory emerged out of unfair competition, and that genealogy is evident here as well, in that the court actually decided the case on the basis of unfair competition, and so declined to reach the trademark issues. The court also declined to allow for accounting of the defendant's profits in damage assessment.

[15] In highlighting two steps, I want to underscore the difficulty in the initial translation process. The only obvious way to translate affect into market terms is as willingness to pay the higher price for a branded good. It is not clear that the value of linguistic expression can be commodified in this way, since the social value of any expression is partly in its uptake by whoever hears or sees it. Unless the only effect of the use of the mark is narrowly commercial, the value of this uptake will be impossible to measure in market terms. Not only that, if the expressive use of the mark is one that the auditor does not enjoy, it might be socially important but have a negative market value insofar as the auditor would in principle pay to *avoid* hearing it. In addition, the usual objections to willingness-to-pay apply. For example, the mark's owner might charge more than the user (especially a marginal one, who is trying to convey something with a high public or social value but a low commercial one: see Benkler (2000)) is able to pay, and the transactions costs of negotiating a use might be prohibitive (especially when owners could unilaterally refuse uses they do not endorse; fair use is only a partial solution to that objection in this context, because the costs of defending one's fair use can be high, and side constraints like the need for insurance could make fair use irrelevant. On this, see Gibson (2007)).

Twenty years later, the same court, citing the intervening Lanham Act, explicitly overruled that part of the decision, in *Monsanto* v. *Perfect Fit* (1965). Monsanto, the maker of "Acrilan," an acrylic fiber, objected to Perfect Fit's use of the label in low-quality mattress pads that actually contained very little Acrilan (and a lot of filler, including sawdust and other allergens). In allowing Monsanto to pursue Perfect Fit's profits, the Court considered two views of trademark. According to one, "it is merely a means of protecting a businessman from injury resulting from another's use of his mark." According to the other, "the trademark right is that it is a form of property, similar in this respect to a copyright or patent right." The second view would allow accounting for profits; it is grounded "in the principles of unjust enrichment traditionally applicable where property is used for profit without the owner's permission" (*Perfect Fit*, p. 392). The court then further expresses "doubt whether ... protection of the trademark owner, is adequately served by a rule which would allow accountings only where the parties directly compete" (*Perfect Fit*, p. 395). That the two parties in the case at hand did not directly compete, then, was not an obstacle to accounting for the defendant's profits, since "it seems obvious that there must have been some economic injury to Monsanto, such as loss of sales to legitimate producers and the loss of the goodwill of some of the retail purchasers of Perfect Fit's inferior 'Acrilan' mattress pads" (*Perfect Fit*, p. 396).[16]

At the same time, the court is careful to argue that Monsanto's interests align with that of the consuming public. It reasons that individual consumers will never individually lose enough to warrant litigation, so their interests can only be furthered by allowing plaintiffs to deter such deceptive practices by making them unprofitable. The beneficiary of litigation will not be individual consumers, who cannot be plausibly compensated; rather, it will be the public as whole. The court cites evidence that Perfect Fit is essentially a "commercial racketeer" that has "taken up trademark infringement as its principal line of business" (*Perfect Fit*, p. 396). Such entities will stop their behavior only if it is unprofitable.

Cases such as these indicate how the law allows brand owners to capture the goodwill their brands have accumulated. Although they move in the direction of dilution – and, as noted earlier, Schechter cites goodwill as a preferable theory of trademark – the stated underlying rationale still notably relies on consumer confusion and protecting the consuming public. What matters for these cases is that consumers might be misled into thinking a brand owner associated with a product that they did not wish to. At the same time, the logic, initially based in

---

[16] *Cf.* Bone: Historically, "the goodwill-as-property theory had an advantage over Schechter's dilution theory. The goodwill-as-property theory was capable of reconciling seller protection with the dominant and persistent consumer protection strand of trademark law. The way a defendant injured or appropriated a plaintiff's firm goodwill was by confusing consumers about sponsorship. Therefore, protecting a mark against sponsorship confusion prevented harm to the seller at the same time as preventing harm to the consumer" (2008, p. 493).

unfair competition, explicitly moves toward one of proprietization and internalization. Because it is still tethered to unfair competition, the law can still be said to be supporting the fair operation of markets and correct pricing of goods. With dilution, by contrast, the market logic substantially recedes from view in favor of a logic of ensuring that the goodwill externalities surrounding a brand remain available for internalization by the brand owner, even when there is no market-fairness rationale. Although dilution is on the same trajectory as protection against sponsorship confusion, it also presents something different, something more aligned with both Demsetzian theory and an era when increasing amounts of value accrue to brands, and relatively less to products.

A second way that dilution evidences a neoliberal turn in trademark is that it reflects the shifting weight of market and monopolies in economic theory, a shift that has significant implications for subjectification. Traditional trademark doctrine was explicitly designed to promote markets and fairness in markets. Dilution subordinates markets to the ability of brands to generate consumer welfare. After all, disallowing noncompetitive uses of a trademark could easily be seen as antimarket. It instead treats the consumer welfare model as detachable from markets. On this logic, monopoly providers of certain signifiers are better for consumer welfare than markets. Indeed, even competition is in this instance subordinated to the logic of consumer welfare. A clear moment of transition occurs in Bork. After defending an informational view of advertising (in which he concedes that advertising does not in fact provide much information), as one might associate with a search-costs rationale for trademark, Bork notes that "advertising has other functions," that "advertisers often attempt to wrap their product in an aura, a daydream" and that "only a modern Puritan can object to these evanescent satisfactions which advertisers provide us" (1993, p. 318).

Advertising has not been primarily informational since the nineteenth century. As Bone notes, psychological advertising, which relies on manipulating basic needs and emotions, was celebrated in the early twentieth century for "its ability to align consumer preferences with the needs of a vigorously expanding economy" (2008, p. 479). Part of this effort was involved in constructing markets and types of consumers. Early magazine advertising, for example, segmented readers into largely imaginary types of households; this later gave way to empirical analysis through mechanisms such as focus groups (Arvidsson, 2004). Brands can also serve to create market segmentation. For example, Barton Beebe suggests that intellectual property (IP) law can increasingly be seen to function as a reinforcement of a sumptuary code, i.e., a "system of consumption practices ... by which individuals in the society signal through their consumption their differences from and similarities to others" (2010, p. 812). By offering legal protection to luxury goods in particular, trademark allows for consumers to sort (or be sorted) into different social groups based on their available human capital; signaling group affiliation can in turn be a mechanism for attaining further human capital. Examples such as these underscore that the value assigned to such immaterial markers is an effect of an IP regime, not its cause. If there were no trademark, there would be no scarcity in logos, they would lose economic value, and the creation and sorting of consumers would have to be enacted differently. My desires as an agent, in other words, cannot be separated from the social environment in which I find myself; this environment quite literally structures my sense of who I am and what my possibilities are.

This commodification of affect then becomes an important aspect of subjectification, as individuals are encouraged to become entrepreneurs of themselves by consuming a portfolio of such affects, "seeking to maximize their 'quality of life' through the artful assembly of a 'life style' put together through the world of goods" (Miller and Rose, 1990, p. 25). In this sense, trademark becomes a technology of subjectification, in the sense of a "matrix of practical reason" that:

> Permit[s] individuals to effect by their own means or with the help of others a certain number of operations on their own bodies and souls, thoughts, conduct, and way of being, so as to transform themselves in order to attain a certain state of happiness, purity, wisdom, perfection, or immortality.
>
> (Foucault, 1988b, p. 18)

Specifically, as with the Greek technologies of the self studied by Foucault, encouraging individuals to develop affective attachments to brands serves to prepare them as citizens of the *polis*, with the caveat that the neoliberal blurring of the economic and the political means that social welfare is measured as consumer welfare. Sonia Katyal underscores the confluence of individual subjectivity and corporate interest: "brands permeate the fabric of our lives – they help construct our identities, our expressions, our desires, and our language. Yet inasmuch as they serve as powerful expressions of consumer identity and desire, they are also an important vessel of corporate identity and property" (2010a, pp. 796–797).

If copyright law constructs authors and audiences, trademark constructs consumers. The stylization demanded by capital and abetted by neoliberal trademark is in terms of proprietization. We are to produce ourselves as an assemblage of various brand identities. This particular assemblage identifies us; that the components of the assemblage are not owned by us serves to govern in advance the various processes through which individuation could take place. The tensions in these subjectification strategies are evident precisely in the difficulty of explaining dilution doctrine on economic grounds noted earlier. Desai points to the incoherence of trademark's construction of consumers. On the one hand, the efficient-search version of the law presupposes that individuals are deliberative, calculating rational choice actors. On the other hand, "when it comes to issues of infringement and protecting the consumer, this highly rational consumer morphs into a dullard who must not be asked to use any extra thought to discern what a mark may signify" (2012, p. 1029). Desai continues:

When the law abandons the rational consumer model, it inserts a view that is not only suspect, but rejects what brand literature acknowledges: consumers are rather savvy about brands, to the point where they take brands and imbue them with personal meanings. Insofar as the law adheres to a behavioral model, in which the company pushes the psychological buttons of the consumer who is shaped by the message and helpless to resist that message, the law adheres to a view that business practice has questioned and in some cases rejected ... as the full ownership of the consumer is discredited in consumer brand theory ... Ironically, trademark law's role has been to use consumers as a lever in prying trademark law away from consumer protection towards brand protection.

(2012, pp. 1029–1030)

It is in this precise sense that trademark is engaged in a process of subjectification, one that renders consumers as the passive recipients of corporate meanings. As Desai puts it in a slightly different context, "insofar as companies use brands to build relationships with customers and offer them ways to embrace the brand as a way of life in many if not all parts of their lives, merchandising rights protect a company's interest in generating and controlling consumer identity" (2012, p. 1018). In this regard, it does not seem accidental that trademark law's move to neoliberal biopower favors corporate over noncorporate uses of a mark. For the neoliberal, all usage is market based, just as in neoliberal patent law, where even university research is commercial, or in copyright where all legitimate use is passive consumption.

4.1.2 *Victor's Little Secret*

In early 1998, Victor and Kathy Moseley opened a small adult products and novelty store in Elizabethtown, Kentucky (near Louisville), called "Victor's Secret."[17] The couple advertised in a weekly publication distributed at nearby Fort Knox: "GRAND OPENING Just in time for Valentine's Day!" The ad offered "Intimate Lingerie *for every woman*," "Romantic Lighting," "Lycra Dresses," "Pagers" and "Adult Novelties/Gifts." An army colonel who saw the ad was offended on Victoria's Secret's behalf, and forwarded the company a copy. A cease and desist letter followed; Victor's Secret (improbably claiming not to have heard of Victoria's Secret) renamed itself "Victor's Little Secret."[18] Victoria's Secret was unsatisfied with the change and filed suit. Although the initial suit made several confusion-based trademark claims, Victoria's Secret lost these in district court and did not appeal them; the appellate decisions dealt only with the question of whether Victor's Little Secret's "unwholesome, tawdry merchandise" (in the words of the army colonel) tarnished the Victoria's Secret brand.

[17] The facts here are as recounted in the Supreme Court decision. See *Moseley* (p. 423). References are to this decision, unless noted. I will mark the appellate decisions as such, and distinguish them by date.
[18] The Sixth Circuit reports this narrative as uncontested. See *Moseley (6th Cir.)* (pp. 466–467).

In 2003, the Supreme Court ruled that the Federal Trademark Dilution Act (FTDA) required a showing of actual dilution of brand value. That is, for a dilution (and thus tarnishment) claim to succeed, the claimant would have to show actual harm to its brand. The court reasoned that this bar had not been met:

> The record in this case establishes that an army officer who saw the advertisement of the opening of a store named "Victor's Secret" did make the mental association with "Victoria's Secret," but it also shows that he did not therefore form any different impression of the store that his wife and daughter had patronized. There is a complete absence of evidence of any lessening of the capacity of the Victoria's Secret mark to identify and distinguish goods or services sold in Victoria's Secret stores or advertised in its catalogs. The officer was offended by the ad, but it did not change his conception of Victoria's Secret. His offense was directed entirely at petitioners, not at respondents. Moreover, the expert retained by respondents had nothing to say about the impact of petitioners' name on the strength of respondents' mark.
>
> (*Moseley*, p. 434)

In the absence of conflicting evidence to the contrary, the Court concluded that Victoria's Secret had failed to show that its mark had actually been damaged.

The Court's reasoning should be contrasted with the argument Victoria's Secret made in its brief. The bulk of this document was designed to refute the contention that an actual showing of economic harm was needed, an effort at which the brief was unpersuasive to the Court. The company also argued two additional points. First, its mark was both well known and highly distinctive, and subject to dilution by the exposure of consumers – who almost certainly had "already formed strong associations with the mark" – to Victor's Little Secret (*Moseley (Brief for Resp.)*, p. 42). Second, it repeated the assertion that not only did Victor's Little Secret sell competing lingerie (p. 42), but that Victor's Little Secret's "sex toys and lewd coffee mugs" were, as Moseley himself once said, "extremely offensive to the general public" and sufficient to tarnish Victoria's Secret's trademark by the "tawdry association" (p. 40). Even the district court concluded that "while the Defendants' inventory may not be unsavory to all, its more risqué quality widely differentiates it from that of the Plaintiffs."[19]

All three of these claims ask the Court to construe the issues as one of subjectification by way of branding: the dismissal of economic harm as a competing standard, the appeal to consumers having "strong associations" with the Victoria's Secret mark, and the insistence that – despite selling at least some "similar" products – the Victor's Little Secret line was unwholesome or "risqué." Victoria's Secret, in other words (we will return to this later), staked the case on a carefully curated image of safe sexiness. The construction is also significant in that it asks for

[19] See *V Secret Catalogue v. Moseley*, 2000 U.S. Dist. LEXIS 5215 (2000), 15–16.

the Court to condone Victoria Secret's monopoly, but without engaging in the sort of market analysis that traditionally undergirds even Chicago antitrust theory.

The contrast between the companies is evident in the Court opinion. Victor's Little Secret was perhaps best described as an adult novelty store, carrying a wide range of products designed either to be used in sex, in association with sex, or to invoke ideas of sex. It certainly lacked the brand identity of Victoria's Secret. At one point, the store described its merchandise as follows:

> [it] sell[s] novelty action clocks, patches, temporary tattoos, stuffed animals, coffee mugs, leather biker wallets, zippo lighters, diet formula, diet supplements, jigsaw puzzles, whyss, handcufs *[sic]*, hosiery bubble machines, greeting cards, calendars, incense burners, car air fresheners, sunglasses, ball caps, jewelry, candles, lava lamps, blacklights, fiber optic lights, rock and roll prints, lingerie, pagers, candy, adult video tapes, adult novelties, t-shirts, etc.

(Moseley, p. 424 n4)

Both parties conceded that relatively little of the store's overall sales came from lingerie, and so the case was about the additional presence of these various novelty items.

Victoria's Secret, by contrast, and as it argued in its brief, presented a case of enormous investment in brand image and cataloguing. The lingerie industry is not small; a recent industry report suggested a global market of approximately $30 billion, and a 9 percent growth rate for the next several years ("Lingerie Industry," 2014). The Victoria's Secret brand presents itself as "one of moderately priced, high quality, attractively designed lingerie sold in a store setting designed to look like a wom[a]n's bedroom" (qt. in *Moseley,* p. 422). The brand image is then heavily marketed through the company's catalog and fashion show. This combination of product and stores constituted the brand's "personality," and the strategy is consonant with research indicating that "in terms of symbolic capabilities, the trading format [e.g., store format and layout] can be used by a retailer to tangibly reflect the brand's personality thereby creating an advantage over competitors when combined with the other dimensions of brand orientation" (Bridson and Evans, 2004, p. 509).[20]

The Victoria's Secret brand is sufficiently established that it has itself been the subject of marketing research, and this marketing research largely supports both the company's self-presentation and its effort to market itself as a brand with a strong, specific personality, one that differentiates it from other lingerie brands. Consumer research suggests that women largely perceive the purchase of lingerie on utilitarian

[20] There is also literature (looking at a successful campaign against the amount of paper used printing Victoria's Secrets catalogues; as a result, the company agreed to at least use recycled paper) suggesting that consumers with a high engagement in a product category will be more resistant to antibranding or negative campaigns aimed at a company's product. See Cervellon (2012).

lines, with a concern for features like comfort, fabric quality and durability. Women will be drawn to products that, in their experience, display these characteristics, and tend to be repeat purchasers (Hume and Mills, 2013). This view of consumer behavior "assumes customers rationally evaluate the purchase by evaluating performance expectations and actual performance." In other words, the view assumes that "the consumer adopts the rational man [sic!] theory" (Hume and Mills, 2013, p. 465). This view is broadly convergent with the behavior encouraged and protected by traditional trademark doctrine's economic justification. On the one hand, consumers are likely to be looking for a specific brand, to which they should be efficiently directed; on the other hand, that consumers value that brand for utilitarian reasons incentivizes brand owners to maintain and improve their product quality.

An alternative pattern of consumption applies to "hedonic" products, one that "challeng[es] traditional product marketing perspectives such as the utilitarian view" (Hume and Mills, 2013, p. 466). The purveyors of hedonic products, in other words, are going to be less concerned about traditional trademark protections. Hume and Mills cite earlier research to propose that "lingerie and inconspicuous fashion used for erotica and sexuality . . . fall into this category" and that "the greater the emphasis or importance of the symbolic and hedonic aspects of the product/service the less relevant the major functionality of the good or service is to the consumer" (2013, p. 465). In other words, for undergarments marketed as erotic goods, or for the higher end of the market, traditional trademark protection is less important than brand differentiation and the ability of that brand to consistently evoke the correct affect.

Hedonic brands are a version of luxury goods, a market that is, as Ann Bartow has noted, often suffused with complex patriarchal norms. The following section on geographical indicators will point out some of the orientalist and colonialist constructions on which that market trades. Here, consider the color pink (or, in the case of Victoria's Secret, the word "pink"), which is often used to denote a certain safe femininity and to signal corporate endorsement of that safe femininity. This subjectification process is independent of any particular utility or traditional economic function of trademarking. As Bartow sardonically notes, when a company markets "Breast Cancer Awareness Can Insulators" adorned with a pink ribbon, the goal cannot plausibly have anything to do with product differentiation on utilitarian grounds: Someone who made such a utilitarian calculus must think "wow, thanks to breast cancer, my beer has remained deliciously chilled" (2015, p. 165). This association of pink and women serves to frame the ways that women can express themselves socially; the more the market produces pink as a marker of femininity, the more people come to desire pink goods as a form of expression, and so "pink or the absence of pink will unavoidably be a visible component of every woman's brand" (2015, p. 167). This is an issue that confronts women their entire lives, well before they make conscious brand decisions, as anyone who has tried to dress a baby knows. In other words, the possibilities for both the expression of norms and resistance to them are substantially framed by corporate brands.[21]

Here, Hume and Mills found that "brands like Victoria's Secret were seen as higher end and were discussed [by study participants] related to the Victoria's angels and some of the supermodels" (2013, p. 475). The study subjects also made the distinction that Victoria's Secret relied on in its case against Victor: "in most subjects there was a clear distinction between lingerie and lewd attire" (2013, p. 476). Perhaps one reason for this distinction is noted in an industry report that cited earlier research suggesting that consumption of luxury lingerie was "more about luxury for oneself than the display of luxury for others" ("Lingerie Industry," 2014, p. 20).

That is, Victoria's Secret's customers are encouraged to view themselves as sexy and indulgent but not lewd; and, as Hume and Mills note, "women with a strong sexy self-image preferred brands that reflected this whereas subjects with a more functional perception of self aligned their consumption to more functional brands" (2013, p. 477). This distinction between sexy and lewd constitutes the economic geography (Pike, 2013) of Victoria's Secret. Although the company is headquartered in Ohio, the brand projects the space of a luxurious Victorian boudoir, where Victorian mores prevent lewdness but contemporary suspicion of those mores suggests that the space is also erotically charged.

A parallel line of research suggests that the amenability of consumers to such brand signaling is related to their views of selfhood. Dividing people into "entity theorists" (who view basic personality as largely static) and "incremental theorists" (who view personality as malleable, even at a deep level), this literature suggests that "consumers are attracted to brands with distinctive personalities when they wish to express, affirm, or enhance their sense of self," and that "although these effects may not be permanent in nature, we find that self-perceptions are altered regardless of whether the brand experience is short-lived or repeated over time, in a public or private consumption context" (Park and John, 2010, p. 656). This is particularly true for so-called entity theorists, who view brand association as an opportunity for signaling their perceived personality traits. Indeed, one experiment, which involved recruiting subjects to walk around a mall carrying either a Victoria's Secret shopping bag or a plain pink shopping bag concluded that:

> Entity theorists perceived themselves as better looking, more feminine, and more glamorous after using a Victoria's Secret bag than after using the plain pink shopping bag. Incremental theorists were not affected by the shopping bag they carried.
>
> (2010, p. 659)

---

[21] For an extended discussion of this in the context of global branding and antibranding campaigns, see Katyal (2015), noting that the dynamics of branding vs. antibranding by activist groups "have reframed the relationship between advertising and consumers into a much more dialogic relationship, as opposed to a one-way relationship of corporate inculcation" (p. 328).

Not only that, but implicit-self theory is malleable. Advertising or information promoting either entity or incremental versions of selfhood is capable of modifying subjects' views of personality. Park and John were able to manipulate consumer attitudes such that those who read an article promoting entity theory also perceived themselves as better looking, etc. (2010, p. 664). In later work, Park and John (2012) – again using Victoria's Secret – were able to show that consumers with entity theories of self responded well to advertising, suggesting that products signaled personality traits, but that those with incremental theories responded well to advertising that emphasized that use of the product could promote those traits in themselves.

What all of this suggests is that investment by corporations in brands is closely tied to Foucauldian questions of subjectification. By presenting a brand with a distinct-ive, strong and "sexy" persona, Victoria's Secret is both encouraging consumers to express these aspects of themselves, and encouraging them to view consumption of Victoria's Secret products as signaling or enhancing their sexiness. This sexiness does not appear in consumers' minds to be associated with "lewd" or overtly sexual behavior, but with an erotics centered partly around being on display and partly on a romanticized English Victorian boudoir. Traditional trademark does little to protect such strong brand personalities, but dilution doctrine is designed to do exactly that.[22]

The Supreme Court's insistence on actual harm evidences traces of concern with public, social welfare grounded in unfair competition of the sort that caused the Second Circuit to decline to award profits to *Seventeen* magazine. It also evidences an unwillingness to treat claims of harm to a monopoly property owner without market-based evidence. Following the decision, Congress promptly passed the "Trademark Dilution Revision Act" (2006), revising the statute to require only an "association" to ground a tarnishment claim. In relitigation, the Sixth Circuit ruled that the new statute establishes "a kind of rebuttable presumption, or at least a very strong inference, that a new mark used to sell sex-related products is likely to tarnish a famous mark if there is a clear semantic association between the two" (*Moseley*, 2010, p. 382).

The economic logic of the revised dilution statute moves dilution further in a neoliberal direction in a manner analogous to the way that the Second Circuit's award of profits to Monsanto moved consumer-confusion-based trademark: *Some loss is to be expected.* Dilution of course moves the needle further, as the need for an unfair competition rationale has completely disappeared. The case thus demon-strates the congruence of neoliberal biopower and subjectification. In addition to

[22] Questions of dilution are likely to turn out to be much more complicated than appears. For example, one recent study suggested that when companies attempt to extend their product lines, incremental theorists reward extensions into areas where the extension is a "poor fit" for the brand personality, and requires considerable effort to achieve. However, extension into areas where the new products are seen as a good fit with the brand are likely to lead to a dilution of the brand personality in the minds of incremental theorists. See Mathur, Jain, and Mahes-waran (2012).

illustrating the disciplining of consumers and producers into approved paths of subjectification, the fate of Victor's Little Secret offers a very precise example of the functioning of "sexuality" under affective, brand capitalism.

To return to the layout of the stores, Victoria's Secret presents a very particular-ized projection of what a woman's bedroom might look like. To begin with, the décor trades in what is clearly meant to be a "romantic" color scheme of pinks and reds, vaguely recalling consumer stereotypes about the Victorian era. It also features pictures and mannequins of sexualized women wearing the company's products. The stores also lack any representation of the normal accoutrements of a bedroom, most notably a bed. What is featured instead are drawers and other space for storing products. That is, there is a lot of "sexiness" in a Victoria's Secret, but evidence of the sex that all of this lingerie is presumably designed to lead to is conspicuously hidden, apparently on account of being "tawdry." The brand identity revolves around inducing the affect of "feeling sexy." As Jane Juffer noted twenty years ago, this emphasis on both the boudoir and the sexualized body is essential to the company's efforts at self-presentation, and how it differentiates itself both from other lingerie lines and – perhaps more importantly – from an overt sexualization that might be perceived as threatening:

> The company's insistence on the private and intimate maintains a proper image of femininity which distances itself from pornography even as the catalog builds its profits on its pornographic overtones. On the one hand, the catalog represents the lingerie as Victorian, playing on popular stereotypes about a kind of sexual prudery in Victorian England and in so doing appealing to a kind of Murray-esque vision of proper female sexuality. On the other hand, it seems to revel in constantly telling its secrets, displaying the female body in a manner that is not at all shy or repressed but close to soft-core pornography, with models who also pose for Playboy wearing black lace garter belts.
>
> (1996, p. 31)

Juffer's language immediately recalls Foucault.

On the one hand, sexualization, *à la* Victoria's Secret, exemplifies the demand to talk about sex, and to do so using narratives that are acceptable to the logic of commodification protected by trademark. Sex is a secret, but a safe secret, bounded by Victorian reticence and the private walls of the bedroom; access to this secret is mediated by the company's lingerie. At the same time, the lingerie is presented as a way to move past the repression implicit in representations of the Victorian era. Indeed, to the extent that the secret is associated with actual sex, the act of sex becomes overdetermined by the approved commodity relations instantiated in Victoria's Secret products and their role in overcoming repressive Victorian social norms against sexiness. As Foucault puts the point, one sees "a policing of sex: that is, not the rigor of a taboo, but the necessity of regulating sex through useful and public discourses."

On the other hand, the act of sex itself (or, perhaps any representation of the act of sex itself), insofar as it is not part of the approved narrative of sexuality as commodified and protected by trademark, is subject to a sovereign ban as "lewd."[23] Whatever happens in the boudoir stays in the boudoir, and so the suggested privacy of the boudoir store serves to domesticate female sexuality and allay any fears that it might find a place outside the private space of the boudoir. At the same time, the commodified bedroom is presented as a place that escapes the abstractions of commodification, as the imagery "plays on a nostalgia for clearly defined and bounded locations in these post-Fordist times of globalization, high-technology communications, and decentralized production" (Juffer, 1996, p. 36). Female sexuality is presented as a possibility, but that presentation is subject to the framing of the merchandise. As Juffer puts it:

> Victoria's Secret ... presents, within the cohesiveness of the white, classical body ... a series of contradictory images and textual messages as to what constitutes femininity. One such gap occurs in the concentration on female pleasure, which could be subsumed to a male gaze – looking beautiful for him – but is sufficiently distanced from it so as to leave open the possibility that female pleasure, of various kinds, will be pursued.

(1996, p. 41)

In sum, the affects associated with sex are to be experienced by way of attachments to the Victoria's Secret brand. Again, Foucault: Modern societies have "dedicated themselves to speaking of [sex] *ad infinitum*, while exploiting it as *the* secret." (1988a, p. 35, emphasis original).

4.2 DISPARAGEMENT

Assuming that they are the first to use it in commerce, trademark owners are entitled under common law to certain protections for their mark, including exclusive use of it in specific markets. There are, however, numerous benefits to federal registration of the mark, such as exclusive rights to the mark across the United States (as opposed to one region), as well as several advantages in litigation surrounding it (Anten, 2006, pp. 396–398). Registration is meant to be a fairly automatic process; most of the hurdles are procedural. The substantive hurdles are found in Section 2 of the Lanham Act, and include, for example, bans on trademarking official insignia of

---

[23] As Juffer notes, speaking of the company's formerly ubiquitous catalogues, this is evident in a comparison between Victoria's Secret and the more overtly sexual Frederick's of Hollywood (which has since declared bankruptcy and moved online only): "Victoria's Secret, with its provocative lace teddies and garter belts, its cleavage-producing Miracle Bras and thong bikinis, enjoys a kind of privileged status that Frederick's doesn't precisely because, throughout its eighteen-year history, it has been careful to sell its sexuality under the guise of privacy. It's a 'secret,' distributed within the privacy of one's home, whose products are delivered to one's doorsteps in the name of a model, Victoria, whose whereabouts are hush-hush" (1996, p. 33).

governmental entities or the identifying name, signature, or portrait of a living person without their consent. The statute also prohibits registration of a mark that:

> Consists of or comprises immoral, deceptive, or scandalous matter; or matter which may disparage or falsely suggest a connection with persons, living or dead, institutions, beliefs, or national symbols, or bring them into contempt, or disrepute.
>
> (15 USC 1052(a))

In denying registration to scandalous or disparaging material, the Lanham Act evidences a sense of public biopolitics. Independently of its viability in commerce, putting governmental imprimatur on a scandalous or disparaging mark is viewed as bad for the polity. In the case of disparaging marks, the idea is that the use of the mark would be damaging to those targeted by the mark in question. The First Amendment means that the government cannot stop such use, but it is also not required to reward it in commerce with the benefits of trademark registration, and so the policy explicitly values a vision of civil discourse over commercial benefit.

Various marks have been denied registration under the disparagement clause, including both those that repeat slurs assumed to disparage others (the NFL's Washington "Redskins") and those where members of targeted groups intend to reappropriate the terms, as in "Dykes on Bikes." In *Matal* v. *Tam* (2017), the Supreme Court ruled on First Amendment grounds that the government did not have the right to refuse registration to disparaging marks. The case pitted Simon Tam, an Asian-American who wanted to register the name of his band – the "Slants" – in order to reclaim a racial slur, against the PTO, which argued that the term disparaged Asian-Americans, many of whom would find it offensive.

In what follows, I will trace the logic of the *Tam* decision as an attempted exercise in juridical power. As I will argue in Chapter 5, the Supreme Court has attempted to curtail patent rights, often with an implicitly juridical understanding of power. The *Tam* decision evidences a similar logic, this time in its application of the First Amendment. In the present context, *Tam* is of interest for two reasons. First, it carefully avoids biopolitical reasoning: There was a readily available biopolitical precedent by means of which the Court could have either upheld the disparagement clause (disallowing both the Redskins and the Slants), or upheld it as facially valid but invalid as applied to Tam (disallowing the Redskins but registering the Slants). As the decision's refusal of the public biopolitical rationale behind the disparagements clause would suggest, the decision also does not endorse the neoliberal reasoning behind trademark dilution. *Tam* thus evidences the tensions within current trademark doctrine.

Second, the outcome poses difficult questions for understanding how trademark regulates cultural expression and how the assertion of free speech and trademark rights affects larger processes of economic neoliberalism. The *Tam* decision's assertion of Free Speech rights may paradoxically weaken the substantive power of minority speakers and further entrench the privatization of expression. A look at ongoing litigation about "scandalous" marks serves to underscore the point. As the following section on geographic indicators will explore at greater length, the question of how trademark regulates cultural expression can be contextualized as a larger question of the relation between property rights and culture more generally; in that larger sense, the role of property rights in protecting cultural minorities is deeply ambiguous.

Tam can be contrasted with a more straightforward example, the NFL's Washington Redskins, whose registration the PTO canceled three years before the *Tam* decision, almost to the day. (The registration has since been restored.)[24] That case presaged many of the issues decided in *Tam*, but can be clearly distinguished in at least two ways. First, it concerned a direct cultural appropriation by a large corporate entity of a name that almost no one in the community it designates finds inoffensive. In other words, "Redskins" is straightforwardly derogatory, and there is no evidence that the NFL franchise or its owner has any interest in the cultural history of the term or is engaged in some effort to reappropriate it. Second, because it concerns a sports team, the term also involves a large number of enthusiastic fans for whom the name is important. At one level, of course, the interests of fans ought to be subordinate, and it is not difficult to think of hypothetical names ("The Nazis") that a sports team should not have, no matter how enthusiastic its fan base. Rosemary Coombe compares the name to blackface, and makes the case for the implicit colonialism behind the Redskins: "[T]he violence instrumental to the creation of America is forgotten, as is the actual life of indigenous peoples, whose return is nonetheless staged by the occupation of their bodies in forms of caricature" (1998, p. 196).

That said, the broader issue of the appropriation of Native American tribal names, as opposed to obvious racial slurs, by sports franchises has been a difficult and longstanding one, as the NCAA's prohibition on nonconsensual uses of Indian names brought to light. On the one hand, because fans often form their own community around the mascot as a symbol, it is often unclear the extent to which that mascot in any meaningful sense refers to any actually existing people or culture, even if the term functions as a racial slur. (Of course, as the passage by Coombe indicates, the very lack of referentiality in sports names can itself be problematic.) On the other hand, because of the legacy of colonial violence against Native Americans, it is also not clear who should represent a tribe. For example, in the case of NCAA team mascots, the Florida Seminoles endorsed the use in the Florida State team name, but the Oklahoma Seminoles objected.[25] Cases like the Redskins cut directly to the center of deeply contested and difficult social issues around group

---

[24] USPTO Trademark Trial and Appeal Board: *Amanda Blackhorse, Marcus Briggs-Cloud, Philip Gover, Jillian Pappan, and Courtney Tsotigh* v. *Pro-Football, Inc.*, Cancellation No. 92046185, at: http://ttabvue.uspto.gov/ttabvue/v?pno=92046185&pty=CAN&eno=199.

[25] The Attorney General for the Oklahoma Seminoles did not mince words: "I am deeply appalled, incredulously disappointed ... I am nauseated that the NCAA is allowing this 'minstrel show' to carry on this form of racism in the 21st century" (Wieberg, 2005). For all

identity and membership. Particularly insofar as decisions whether to award trademark registration are made by a government administrative agency, it would appear to be almost a paradigmatic case of public biopolitics.

Existing precedent enabled the Court to reach a decision on more or less biopolitical grounds. Such a decision would interpret trademark registration as a government subsidy, and ask whether individuals have a right to government subsidy of their speech, and whether government could exercise some sort of editorial discretion about what speech it wanted to subsidize. The government subsidy argument is grounded in abortion funding cases, *Rust* v. *Sullivan* (1991) in particular, and the conclusion there was that the individuals did not have a right to government subsidy of their speech. On the subsidy view, trademark registration essentially gives the government's imprimatur to a monopoly right, as well as conferring substantial benefits to those who receive it. Accordingly, by spending money on the registration process, the government is subsidizing the speech of some trademark owners.

Rust v. *Sullivan* was one of the so-called gag-rule cases, where the government prohibited agencies receiving public money from discussing abortion with their patients. The Court there addresses the subsidy issue directly by unequivocally refusing to frame the question as one of viewpoint discrimination under the First Amendment:

> The Government can, without violating the Constitution, selectively fund a program to encourage certain activities it believes to be in the public interest, without at the same time funding an alternate program which seeks to deal with the problem in another way. In so doing, the Government has not discriminated on the basis of viewpoint; it has merely chosen to fund one activity to the exclusion of the other ... "There is a basic difference between direct state interference with a protected activity and state encouragement of an alternative activity consonant with legislative policy."
>
> (Rust, pp. 192–193, internal citation omitted).

There are many ways that the regulation *Rust* upholds is deeply problematic, and perhaps the fact that the Court decided the *Tam* decision in one way and the *Rust* decision in another says more about the Court's susceptibility to political ideology

---

of this, see Mezey (2007). Sports team mascots may in this sense represent brand communities: "A given brand community collectively negotiates with companies regarding the brand. The members of a brand community experience a connection to the brand, but they experience an even stronger bond with the other members of the brand community" (Desai, 2012, p. 1002). In other words, the nature of the mascot is incidental to the community. Of course, if the particular mascot is incidental, then that becomes an argument for the replacement of offensive mascots with inoffensive ones; the problem is the accreted history of the brand community around the offensive mascot.

than anything else.[26] Following this logic, the government argued in *Tam* that registration was a subsidy, and Judge Dyk's dissent in the appellate decision argues "that registration is a subsidy is not open to doubt," that the registration program is not a regulatory regime and that it does not ban any speech. Refusal thus "merely deprives a benefit" (*In re Tam*, 2015, p. 1368).[27]

A theory of the case congruent with *Rust* would argue that because trademark registration confers public benefits, the PTO has chosen to value nonracist speech over racist speech, and to implement that judgment by the allocation of public funds. The PTO is not interfering with speech, but encouraging a different kind of speech consonant with legislative policy. The *Rust* Court continues that "a doctor who wished to offer prenatal care to a project patient who became pregnant could properly be prohibited from doing so because such service is outside the scope of the federally funded program" (*Rust*, p. 193). By analogy, a team owner who wished to use racist speech could be denied trademark registration because such service is outside the scope of the federally funded trademark doctrine. He could still use racist speech, but would have to do so without government assistance. The analogous doctor could still provide abortion care as long as it was provided to people outside the subsidy program. The *Rust* Court further argues that "our 'unconstitutional conditions' cases involve situations in which the government has placed a condition on the *recipient* of the subsidy rather than on a particular program or service, thus effectively prohibiting the recipient from engaging in the protected

[26] Perhaps it also signals that the abortion funding cases were poorly decided. *Rust* essentially imposed governmental restrictions on medical speech, and medical speech has a strong tradition of being governed by independent norms. In arguing that *Tam* is not a subsidy case, Justice Alito relies on the idea that trademark registration is a service that enables speech, not a direct funding of speech. One could easily argue that the family planning programs created a framework in which speech about abortion or other family planning services was made available. If that analogy is correct, then the logic of the decision to strike down the commercial speech regulation in *Tam*, which Alito says does not even survive intermediate scrutiny, should indicate that *Rust* was poorly decided, since the speech in question was not commercial.

[27] Alito also rejects a comparison to *Walker* v. *Texas Sons of Confederate Veterans* (2015), in which the Court ruled that Texas' refusal to allow Confederate flag license plates was legitimate because the license plates were government speech, and the government could not be forced to say something with which it fundamentally disagreed. *Walker* itself made favorable reference to the abortion cases. In *Tam*, Justice Alito dismissed this comparison on the grounds that trademark registration is, with the exception of the disparagement question, essentially automatic. Thus license plates are government speech because the government controls the entire process, whereas trademark registration is private speech that the government registers. Alito emphasizes the diversity of trademarks; treating them all as speech would make the government an incoherent subject: "[I]f the federal registration of a trademark makes the mark government speech, the Federal Government is babbling prodigiously and incoherently. It is saying many unseemly things . . . It is expressing contradictory views. It is unashamedly endorsing a vast array of commercial products and services. And it is providing Delphic advice to the consuming public" (*Tam*, p. 1758). This by itself does not distinguish the cases. Although there are fewer license plates to choose from, they do not necessarily express a coherent worldview. North Carolina, for example, allows both Duke University and UNC license plates, a position that most basketball fans would consider incoherent babbling.

conduct outside the scope of the federally funded program" (*Rust*, p. 197). In other words, if the PTO had tried to ban the use of the Redskins brand altogether, or to prohibit Tam from naming his band the Slants in the first case, *that* would have been clearly unconstitutional.

Judge Dyk grounded his subsidy interpretation in a different pair of cases (neither of which cites *Rust* directly), pointing to two instances in which the Court had upheld government involvement in facilitating the collection of union fees. Underscoring that these are not cases of direct subsidy, he argued that:

> Federal trademark registration, like the state-bestowed collection mechanisms for unions in *Davenport* and *Ysursa*, is a government-bestowed collection mechanism for enforcing trademarks. It opens the federal courts to enforce trademark rights by providing, *inter alia*, original jurisdiction in federal courts for infringement claims, eligibility for treble damages for willful infringement, the ability to petition Customs to prevent the importation of infringing articles, and various enhanced protections for marks. These benefits all "enlist" the government in support of the mark holder's commercial identification, much like the collection of nonmember fees in *Davenport* and the payroll deductions in *Ysursa* enlisted the states in support of the unions' political speech. Just as the states were not obligated to enable labor unions to collect nonmember fees or take payroll deductions in the first place, the federal government is not obligated to provide these benefits of a trademark enforcement mechanism. And just as the unions remained free to speak for election-related purposes using all other funds, trademark holders remain free to use their marks – however disparaging – as far as the federal government is concerned. That states may deny state-law protection to these marks cannot make the denial of the federal subsidy any less constitutional.
>
> (In re Tam, pp. 1369–1370, internal citations omitted)[28]

In sum, there was considerable precedent for viewing the case as one of a subsidy.

Given a general framing of trademark registration as a government subsidy, and a principle that no one was entitled to a subsidy of their speech – that the government could choose to advance certain policy objectives by way of subsidies or their refusal – self-disparagement becomes easy to distinguish from a case like the Redskins. Rather than banning all disparaging marks, the provision should look at how those marks are used. As Todd Anten (2006) argues, there is a good case to be made that self-disparaging marks serve an important social function.

---

[28] Alito rejects the comparison to *Davenport* and *Ysura* as follows: "[T]he challenged laws [upheld in those cases] did not go further and provide convenient collection mechanisms for money to be used in political activities. In essence, the Washington and Idaho lawmakers chose to confer a substantial non-cash benefit for the purpose of furthering activities that they particularly desired to promote but not to provide a similar benefit for the purpose of furthering other activities. Thus, *Davenport* and *Ysursa* are no more relevant for present purposes than the subsidy cases previously discussed" (*Tam*, p. 1762). He does not address the claim that *Davenport* and *Ysura* were subsidy cases.

The reappropriation of racial and other slurs by minority groups can be an important part of both empowering members of those groups, and in defusing racist terms of their power to injure. Anten accordingly argues that the PTO should treat cases of self-disparagement as presumptively valid, conferring registration benefits unless someone later raises specific objection. On this logic, the same policy that disfavors racism by refusing to subsidize racist speech could in turn presumptively subsidize reappropriation of that speech.[29] The logic here – using property rights as a way to advance social value – might be seen as imperfectly analogous to that applied to certain aspects of fair use in copyright. Parody, for example, is a paradigmatic example of fair use, on the grounds that restricting property rights on those grounds advances a social good.

Justice Alito rejects the subsidy interpretation on the grounds that trademark registration does not constitute an actual transfer of money beyond that needed to process the registration. Trademark registration is a "service" but not a "subsidy." His argument here is very brief: trademark registration costs money, rather than conferring it, and as for the idea that benefit flows from registration, "just about every government service requires the expenditure of government funds" (*Tam*, p. 1761). Conferral of benefits is not analogous to a direct grant of funds, and funding for the transaction costs of operating a service is not the same as funding the activity the service promotes.

As a First Amendment matter, *Tam* presented an easy example of viewpoint discrimination; a separate concurrence by Justice Kennedy (joined three others) thought the viewpoint discrimination argument was sufficient to resolve the case on its own. The core difference between this view of the case and a biopolitical one is that the viewpoint discrimination interpretation takes the issue as being between a sovereign and a citizen whose views it deems offensive. As I argued in Chapter 2, this focus on sovereign–subject relations is central to juridical power. Judge Dyk offers the alternative reading: "[T]he statute is designed to preclude the use of government resources not when the government disagrees with a trademark's message, but rather when its meaning 'may be disparaging to *a substantial composite of the referenced group*'". On that view, the government's role is to try to mediate between opposing social groups, and "the purpose of the statute is to protect underrepresented groups in our society from being bombarded with demeaning messages in commercial advertising" (*In re Tam*, p. 1364, internal citation omitted and emphasis Dyk's). This sense of protecting citizens from each other (and the market) is completely lost when the question is one of protecting citizens from the state.

---

[29] Judge Dyk's dissent in the appellate decision distinguishes between commercial speech and core First Amendment speech. It finds the statute facially valid (since commercial speech is less protected) but not as applied (interpreting Tam's speech as political). See *In re Tam* (pp. 1365–1368). Another way would be to revise the statute.

Justice Alito found two other asserted government interests. One was protecting against speech that offends, and he dismissed that argument on the grounds that the "the proudest boast of our free speech jurisprudence is that we protect the freedom to express 'the thought that we hate.'" The second interest was in the protection of the orderly flow of commerce. Here, he argues that the statute was in no way narrowly drawn, as even intermediate scrutiny would require. Only the last of these reasons recognizes the relations of private parties between one another, and the last one does not require invalidating the entire clause, only its application to cases of self-disparagement.

I emphasize the *Tam* Court's reluctance to frame disparagement as a biopolitical question in order to note the very different conceptual structure of its juridical frame. As a formal question, both *Rust* and *Tam* concerned whether or not the government was required to put its imprimatur on speech with which it disagreed. Distinguishing the cases on the basis of whether the government was "directly" spending funds on the program in question makes it easy to protect Tam's First Amendment rights (and more difficult to reach the same result in *Rust*). On the other hand, since trademark registration provides unquestioned benefits, treating these benefits as not part of a government program has the effect of occluding the extent to which trademark registration (like copyright) is an intervention that strengthens the private property rights of some individuals. That is, and for better or worse, the logic manages to strengthen the extent to which expressive speech is subject to proprietization.

Justice Alito suggests that if registration and subsidies were treated analogously, other government registration programs, like copyright, would be potentially subject to the same sort of regulation. He then notes that trademarks are often expressive. While it is true that copyright protects expressive speech, copyright *registration* protects the class of expressive speech whose creator presumes it to have commercial value, wants to leave their litigation options open, and who has the resources and savvy to register the speech (Tehranian, 2012). Copyrighted speech can be for many purposes; commercial gain is only one, even if, as I argued in Chapter 3, the dominant narrative around incentives obscures the point. Trademarked speech is much more closely tied to the market. From the point of view of a trademark owner (registered or otherwise), a mark primarily has value either as a referent to a commodity, or as a commodity in itself. As Rochelle Cooper Dreyfuss (1990) pointed out, genuinely expressive uses of trademarks – uses with value that can primarily be measured in non-market terms – tend either to separate from the market or even operate in opposition to it. As Judge Dyk notes, "it is difficult to imagine" that attaching racial slurs to product marks "further[s] any legitimate 'informational function' associated with the relevant product" (*In re Tam*, p. 1373).

Like copyright registration, trademark registration significantly strengthens a property entitlement insofar as it both provides evidence of the mark's validity and substantially increases the ability of owners to enforce their rights. It also imposes procedural requirements and expense. Registration favors the same set of owners that copyright registration does – savvy, well resourced, and commercially minded – and rewards them with stronger rights. It offers heightened protection to marks insofar as they function in the market, at the possible expense of expressive uses. The formal logic of protecting speech, divorced from the fact that the speech is commercial, tends to facilitate the expansion of the market further into the symbolic sphere by removing a barrier to fully marketizing certain kinds of marks. In that sense, it facilitates the neoliberal extension of market values into all social relations.

Treating the question as one of formal rights, rather than as government endorsement, also occludes social relations of power. It is true that Simon Tam's effort to reclaim the term "slants" is a beneficiary of the decision. The Washington Redskins' continued use of a racial slur is also a beneficiary. That one of them is trying to reclaim the slur and the other appears to simply be using it becomes legally invisible. What is certain is that the Washington Redskins have more resources invested in developing and protecting their mark; it seems predictable that this situation will generalize for other mark owners representing hegemonic uses. In other words, there is little substantive equality between Tam and the Redskins. Alito complains about the flattening of differences when he observes that the disparagement clause is overbroad; by banning "any" disparagement, it applies equivalently to both racist speech and "down with racists." As such, "it is a happy-talk clause" (*Tam*, p. 1765).[30] In this regard, both the disparagement clause (without an exemption for self-disparagement or core political speech) and Alito's deference to the market make the same mistake of failing to see the role that the government plays in mediating competing interests between different social groups. Rosemary Coombe argues:

> A radical democratic politics ... will involve more than simply a libertarian celebration of regimes of freedom for appropriation. Post-colonial circumstances cut across the grain of postmodern practices and urge upon us a heightened sensitivity to the differential relations of others and their relationship to dominant practices of othering".

(1998, p. 274)

The following section considers in detail one example of an attempt at such a radical democratic politics, one that attempts to use the resources of trademark to its own advantage.

In the case of registration requirements, the blind spot about corporate interests – and the way that recognition of formal, juridical rights can advance those interests – is readily apparent in litigation around the ban on scandalous marks. Following *Tam*, the Federal Circuit ruled in late 2017 that provision also violated the First Amendment. *In re Brunetti*, the PTO had denied registration to the apparel line

---

[30] The comparison seems stretched; disparaging statements rely upon associating attributes with a person or group. "Down with racists" does not.

"FUCT" on the grounds that the mark was scandalous. The court canvassed the expected First Amendment grounds, and concluded that "the provision impermissibly discriminates based on content in violation of the First Amendment." In early 2019 (thus, as of this writing), the Supreme Court agreed to hear the case. One argument in the Brunetti litigation that is not particularly relevant in *Tam* is the claim that the regulation is impermissibly vague. The court produces substantial evidence that the PTO's determination of what constitutes vulgar or scandalous speech (and thus whether marks can receive registration) appears arbitrary. For example, seemingly equivalent references to "MILF" or "F'N" were alternately granted or denied registration. Similarly, FUCT was denied but FCUK was granted (*Brunetti*, p. 1354). As the opinion summarized, "subjectivity in the determination of what is immoral or scandalous and the disparate and unpredictable application of these principles" is a problem (*Brunetti*, p. 1355).

Once framed as a question of the First Amendment, these cases are straightforward. What I would underscore here is that cases like *Tam* and *Brunetti* (assuming the Court also strikes down the ban on scandalous marks on First Amendment grounds) do not create a space where speech is less regulated or where regulation is more predictable. Rather, they transfer the power to regulate uses of these terms to the owners of the marks themselves. In this regard, the cases end up endorsing the same neoliberal logic of power that they superficially deny in their invocation of the First Amendment. In this regard, they are much more like dilution than they at first appear. Dilution allows a private party to use the government to stop speech by another private party on the grounds that some people will find that speech offensive, even though no evidence of actual harm is required. The only difference between this and *Tam* is the agent doing the determination that some hypothetical audience will be offended. Even the more neutral dilution theory – that the mark being enjoined will somehow diminish the specificity of affect that consumers feel for a given brand – requires an assumption about consumers' uptake of a given expression in the same way that the ban on scandalous marks does. In both cases, the harms are speculative. In both cases, the determination of those harms is left to private actors.

4.3 GEOGRAPHIC INDICATORS: RESISTANCE AND THE LIMITS OF PUBLIC BIOPOWER

4.3.1 *Introduction*

Although law and the judicial system can impose limits on the extent and power of branding culture, I will argue here that those limits are not without cost to those who might seek to impose them, or who might be seen as most obviously to benefit from them. Brands directly affect the *bios* of different communities insofar as they necessarily interact with local geographies, with effects on producers, consumers, and regulatory processes; in essence, as Andrew Pike notes, "branding seeks to destabilize existing markets and reinstitutionalize them around new, strategically calculated produce and service brand definitions" (Pike, 2009, p. 633). Geographical associations are an integral part of branding strategies. As Pike argues, brand owners engage in a strategy of selectively "playing up certain desirable and valued meanings – such as the heritage, quality and reputation connoted by particular places (*e.g.*, Milanese design or Thai silks)" while downplaying negative associations (2013, p. 323). As Pike emphasizes, this process necessarily has distributive effects, as for example, geographies that are perceived as high value are able to monetize that consumer perception.

Consumers assign value to products based on their place of origin, and Western companies frequently attempt to profit by association with the "traditional" products and methods of non-Western cultures and places. In Western countries, IP law – particularly trademark, since it is concerned with the naming and branding of goods – has traditionally been invoked to keep freeloaders away from the goodwill accreted to a brand. Could a similar strategy help the producers of traditional products? The logic is clear enough. Global consumers demand "Coke," and they are rewarded with the product of one, specific corporation. If global consumers are going to demand "Darjeeling" tea, then it only seems just that they should get something from India, and not from Benetton. Indeed, such global standards seem to be needed to stop Western companies exploiting indigenous products for their own profit. In one famous example of such "biopiracy," the Texas company RiceTec imported basmati rice from India and sought patent protection for it; it took a lengthy battle and global pushback to prevent RiceTec from calling its products "basmati" (Boyle, 1997; Shiva, 1999).

IP, on the theory behind GIs, can do more than protect Western products like pharmaceuticals. It can protect indigenous ones.[31] Europeans see in source protection a way to preserve and develop rural areas, while at the same time preserving a

---

[31] As will become apparent, I think the best advocate of this view – in substantial part because of the nuance she provides it – is Madhavi Sunder. I draw from her original "Invention of Traditional Knowledge" (2007), an anthology paper, "Intellectual Property and Development as Freedom" (2008), and the revisions of these in her *From Goods to a Good Life* (2012). Sunder's main target is the dichotomy between property and the unowned "public domain;" at the risk of oversimplification, her central claim is that this dichotomy leaves indigenous cultural production open to exploitation by the very actors against whom it was supposed to protect (an argument she also pursues forcefully in Chander and Sunder (2004)), while reinscribing Western notions of indigenous peoples as the objects or curators of knowledge, but Westerners as producers of knowledge. This reification involves a reification and flattening of cultural forms into essences. As she underscores, "the concept of traditional knowledge, too, is a modern invention" (2012, p. 139). My concern in what follows is to underscore limitations of the "poor people's knowledge" strategy imposed by the logic of commodification. As will become apparent, and as I will explicitly argue in the conclusion of the book, I also do not think that the "opposite of property" strategy that Sunder critiques – the one that works with a dichotomy of property/public domain – is viable.

sense of *terroir*, the traditional association between land and culinary traditions. A global regime of source protection would ensure that anything labeled "Champagne" is produced in that region of France, for example. Indigenous groups see that trademark law could go well beyond food to ensure, for example, that "Mysore" silk *sarees* were produced in India and "Persian" rugs in Iran. The traditional producers of these goods would thereby be the beneficiaries of people's positive associations with them. Such a strategy would return both economic value and cultural recognition to their producers. In this regard, the GI would function as what Sunder calls "poor people's property." As she notes, "creating a protected *brand* ... rewards the local community for having created a valued reputation and protects that reputation from the forces of global commerce." On balance, she argues that these benefits are worth pursuing despite the risks, and "it may be more important to think of GIs as part of a larger framework in which the poor learn the secrets of Madison Avenue" (2012, p. 143).

In the terms developed in this study, the strategy is also an effort to tweak trademark-as-branding – which, as the previous sections have shown, is most easily tied to a neoliberal biopolitics – into a more public version. That is, claims of "poor people's knowledge" are explicitly designed to insert a sense of "public" good into what otherwise appears as a regime of privatized gain. This is apparent in at least two ways. First, the focus is on maintaining externalities. For example, the economic viability of rural areas and the attendant aspects of human capabilities and quality of life that follow from it are considered to be valuable in themselves, and are not subject to either economic accounting or specific capture.[32] The strategy thus attempts to articulate the public value of property claims. Second, the focus is explicitly on noneconomic benefits. As Sunder draws the contrast, "for the United States, establishing intellectual property law is itself development – such law will attract foreign direct investment and spur indigenous creation." However, IP also can help "expand capability for central freedoms." Accordingly one should not just incentivize production, but recognize the importance of "participating in the process of knowledge creation" because "recognizing people's humanity requires acknowledging their production of knowledge" (2008, p. 470). In other words, "failing to promote poor people's capacity for creative work and their participation in global culture and commercial markets hinders development as freedom" (2012, p. 144). This attempt at reconfiguration of trademark rejects the neoliberal version of property both by rejecting the incentives and internalization narrative in favor of a richer notion of public goods, and by rejecting the view of individuals as primarily economic actors.

---

[32] Although the discussion here follows Sunder and is thus specific to developing countries, it should be noted that European nations have long pursued geographic source protections (and the specificity of rural food especially) as part of a strategy of rural preservation and development. See, e.g., Bessière (2002), Hughes (2006), Ilbery and Kneafsey (2000).

Nonetheless, this is a high-risk strategy because traditional products are also typically associated, not with a corporate identity, but with specific places and the cultural groupings presumed to inhabit those spaces. That is, not only does the strategy attempt to use the tools of neoliberal capitalism against neoliberal capitalist accumulation, but it involves an obvious fetishization of the land and people who live there. There is an analogy to be drawn with hip hop's ambivalent relation to copyright, on the one hand relying on sampling and on the other hand using copyright. As Richard Schur puts it, this ambivalence "exists because property law seems either too individualistic or too interwoven with white supremacy. Any attempt to reconstruct IP law would likely rely on an essential, authentic, or romantic subject, which hip hop aesthetics constantly distrusts and defers" (2011, p. 167). Simply put, it is unclear the extent to which resistant forms of proprietization can be used as a strategy against other kinds of proprietization.

The GI strategy also tends to entrench traditional hierarchies embedded in the production process by giving legal imprimatur to that process as it exists in the status quo.[33] The argument here is that there is a particular risk that this effort at making branding public poses: the reinscription of the neoliberal version of branding at a cultural level. The move to GIs generates numerous avenues and incentives for cultural fetishization by both producers and consumers, and although this fetishization does generate value, it is a value that is easily internalized by existing cultural elites. The move to branding will therefore potentially exacerbate the risks of fetishizing land and communities, while undermining its public benefits. As a result, the logic of trademarks in late capitalism risks pushing geographic source protections toward becoming *de facto* IP rights in culture. In short, there is considerable risk that the poor remain poor. This risk is most acute when fetishized notions of cultural authenticity can be used to disrupt innovative activities on their part.

The next section uses the theoretical frame developed earlier, tracking the emergence of branding as part of the process of commodification, to discuss the risk that geographic source protections will tend to reduce cultural diversity, both by tending to promote exoticized images of cultures and by increasing the importance of standardization. The following section explores how the reification of culture can be used as a tool by cultural elites to suppress dissent and treat the source protection as IP rights in culture.

4.3.2 *Eating Culture?*

Empirically, consumers care about geographic origin and the "authenticity" it confers to the point that they will pay more for products manufactured at a corporation's "original" factory over other production facilities owned by the same corporation (Newman and Dhar, 2014). Consumers will also pay more for products with

---

[33] On these, see especially Hughes (2006), Parry (2008), Sunder (2007).

country-of-origin labeling that points to favored countries, and this effect is more pronounced if the origin is a GI (Menapace et al., 2011). Meta-analysis of mostly European research also finds that consumers are willing to pay more for food products containing GIs, especially in markets where there are not already strong brands (Deselnicu et al., 2013). This result comports with work by, for example, David Aaker, who argues that establishing the authenticity of one's own brand is a way to create barriers to the entry of competing products, and that where there are competing brands, association with a specific region bolsters the authenticity of any product that can credibly claim that association (Aaker, 2011, pp. 283–286). In short, credible claims of geographic origin appear to increase the willingness of consumers to pay for goods bearing those claims. What, then, is the cost for the high(er) price of authenticity?

As noted earlier, brands and trademarks inherently fetishize the origin of products, by presenting them as originating in a corporate entity. Geographic source trademarks inherit this feature, most obviously in that they seem to strangely fetishize a geographic space and the culture presumed to inhabit it (Hughes, 2006, p. 360; Parry, 2008). However, it is not just the land that is fetishized: The term also subsumes consideration of the production process into the geographic designator, since it is products that involve both land and a "traditional" production process that can receive source protection. It is in the subsumption of the production process that the concern lies.

The problem (as advocates like Sunder acknowledge) is that GIs smuggle in a dated and arguably dangerous conception of culture under the banner of the mystified land on which that culture traditionally resides. For a given parcel of land, the regime seems to propose, there is a univocal, well-defined cultural grouping that can, because it inhabits that land, be designated as the "source" of the products in question. The difficulties with this view of culture are well-documented, and need not be of direct concern here. Instead, I wish to emphasize how the economic logics of standardization and differentiation encourage the problem. Consider the case of Indian handlooms (the following derives from Vinaya, 2012). Highly distinctive, local, and economically significant to those who weave them, this sector is the second largest employer in India outside agriculture, and is under constant threat from machine looms. Most handlooms are produced in individual households in rural areas. The challenges in standardizing production enough to guarantee "quality" in such a case are significant, not least because the model of production makes economies of scale difficult to achieve. Not only that, there are problems with supply chain integration, legal paperwork, and marketing, all of which require resources beyond what local households can supply. On top of this, there are further problems with the tendency of the caste system to undermine the trust necessary among individual weavers. Finally, as Soumya Vinaya emphasizes, "[T]here exists a near absolute disconnect between the individual weaver and the market. The weaver who often works for the master weaver or cooperative has no information for whom the product is produced or how it is marketed" (2012, pp. 62–63). Overcoming these problems pushes such distributed production systems in the direction of Western firms, with their centralized and hierarchical structures. Beyond the increased resources centralization brings, there are economic incentives as well: Empirical research also suggests that for products with a complex production process (say, olive oil, as compared to fruit), the more tightly the designation of source controls that production process, the greater the price premium it commands (Deselnicu et al., 2013).

The risk is that trademark protection, in this way, serves to create the cultural homogeneity that supposedly legitimates it. If traditional producers of *sarees* from Mysore do not produce scarves that meet the designation, they have little choice but to adapt their production process to the standard. This process is endemic in that if source indicators are to perform their differentiating function, they have to standardize as well. All products that claim to be "Mysore" *sarees* will have to comply with the strict requirements encoded in the source designation. The more such goods and services become homogenized under the source appellation, the more diversity in their production process is lost to the logic of commodification.

The focus on branding can be expected to make this occultation of the production process worse. Recall that, in a globalized economy, consumers will often know very little about the places where their goods are produced, even when (as in the case of GIs) those places are used for product differentiation. From the point of view of the consumer, GIs serve as a cognitive shortcut in that they enable consumers to feel that a product's invocation of attributes associated with its stipulated origin are authentic. What is valuable in this process, however, is not obviously the product or its connection to the place itself; it is the feeling of *terroir* or the sense of authenticity consumers experience. It is true that with source protection designation, the products allowed to evoke the relevant source associations will in fact have to come from the designated areas, but nothing about this process implies that the consumer will be in a position to care about the actual production of the commodities. There is empirical support for this proposition. Here are two examples. First, if the process of making Parmigiano-Reggiano cheese has technically remained constant for several hundred years, the cattle have not: The local stock has been replaced with descendants of American and Dutch varietals that no longer graze freely outside (Hughes, 2006, pp. 360–361). It requires a careful construction to claim that nothing relevant has changed here. Second, as Hébert (2010) demonstrates, the production of "quality" salmon involves producing wild salmon that have some of the aesthetic attributes of aquaculture salmon. These features become more important than any actual connection to the Copper River where the salmon are fished.

Indeed, very few consumers will have been to the relevant place and experienced the products directly, and so the majority will have to rely on intermediary sources for their perceptions. In other words, it is their perception of cultural authenticity that matters, and there is no necessary relation between that perception and the people it represents. Some of these intermediaries that shape consumer perceptions can be family and friends, but media and other images are also a significant source of consumer information, particularly for goods where family and friends may also lack direct cultural experience. To this extent, consumers have to rely on a brand and its interaction with their cultural stereotypes. Consumers do not want their stereotypes undermined, and one recent study suggests both that country-of-origin labeling affects consumers' subconscious, emotional responses to products (even when they deny it consciously), and that advertising needs to match these stereotypes in order to improve brand evaluations. Mismatches make consumers *less* likely to intend a purchase to the point that "as far as purchase intentions and positive word-of-mouth are concerned, it is better *not* to evoke the COO [country of origin] at all rather than to communicate it in a way that is dissonant to the underlying country stereotype" (Herz and Diamantopoulos, 2013, p. 412). Not only that, the more exotic the image is, the more distinctive it will be in the competing market-place of brands, and the better a trademark it will be. Consumers will likely require increasing levels of cultural fantasy to be persuaded to purchase the source-differentiated product. Why should one choose "Persian" rugs over "Arabian" ones?

In short, consumers are necessarily part of the process of product qualification (Callon et al., 2002, p. 201), and there is no reason to suppose that disconnected indigenous producers will be able to impose their specification of protected products on Western consumers. For one, consumer ignorance of granular details in a different place's geography risks the need to dilute that in global marketing. For example, Newcastle Brown Ale developed a very specific, geographically mediated meaning in Northern England and the city of Newcastle, a meaning tied to local economic and cultural traditions, as well as local water and hops. When the beer was later marketed successfully in the United States, "Imported from England" became its marker of geographical specificity, reflecting the belief that Americans did not generally know or care about regional differences within England (Pike, 2011). More generally, and particularly with regard to more "exotic" locales, not only will consumers likely be ignorant of subnational or subregional geographic differentia, but they will also likely arrive with any number of highly mediated assumptions about the place that produces protected products. Trademark protection serves to protect an imagined pure culture and its products, even if the products protected are substantially the result of exoticized images in consumers' heads.

A combination of the coproduction of the producer–consumer relation and the location of economic power in Western consumers drives both of these processes, which together risk generating the sorts of problems bell hooks outlines in "Eating the Other" (1999). As hooks proposes, trade in the bodies and products of "authentic" indigenous peoples tends to uncritically absorb nostalgia for a (manufactured, imaginary) "primitive" cultural otherness. At the same time, and equally problematically, it can embody a sense of the Westerner as a cultural tourist, able to move freely between and among cultural associations, with an identity created at the intersection of an eclectic mosaic of components. While this understanding of selfhood perhaps has much to recommend it on its own, when it is paired with branding strategies that emphasize cultural authenticity in products, cultural eclecticism becomes a privilege accorded only to Western consumers. These consumers, as it were, produce themselves, whereas indigenous producers express their culture. GIs attempt to remedy some of the asymmetrical distribution of power implied in all of this by relocating the production of indigenous cultural products from multinationals like Benetton to actual indigenous producers. As the following section analyzes in detail, however, this relocation generates a new kind of problem: the feedback loop between Western consumer stereotypes and indigenous product specification enhances the ability of indigenous elites to deploy that loop to their own advantage.

4.3.3 *Uneven Development*

As I noted in Chapter 2, the public biopolitics arose more-or-less contemporaneously with modern capitalism, which arose in tandem with colonialism. GIs emerge partly to shield against a repetition of this problem by purely economic means. It seems unquestionably to be the case that multinational corporations will use IP to attempt to shut indigenous communities out of profits derived from goods associated with them, as the early experiences with basmati rice, rooibos tea, and other goods indicate.[34] The reification of culture and space presupposed by geographic source protection risks repetition of these dispossessions at a local level. That is, if it is the case that Western producers can appropriate the value associated with culturally identified products, shutting out local producers, it is also the case that local elites can appropriate that value for themselves. The way for doing so is prepared by the standardization process itself, which, as the case of Indian handlooms illustrates, can push decentralized and distributed production processes toward the model of firms, establishing numerous points of hierarchy in marketers, master weavers, and so

---

[34] For rooibos, see D. Smith (2013). For basmati rice, see Rai (2001). Of course not all of these are trademark cases; RiceTec had attempted to patent basmati rice. Citing a "list of crops or plant genetic resources implicated in the practice of biopiracy [that] includes the following: Rosy Periwinkle (Ethiopia), Neem and Turmeric (India), Basmati (Indo-Pakistan), Enola Bean (Mexico), Hoodia Cactus (South Africa), Cow Pea (Nigeria), and Karela juice (India)," Chidi Oguamanam writes: "[S]hortly after it came into effect, the devastating consequences of a hegemonic intellectual property order imposed by TRIPS have been felt at diverse intersections, including health and access to essential drugs; human rights, biodiversity conservation, bioprospecting and biopiracy; market access and balance of trade; and technology transfer and questions about indigenous knowledge. Each of these implicates a complex intellectual property instigated socio-economic and moral crisis, resulting in the marginalization of the developing countries and the rest of the world's indigenous peoples. This state of affairs facilitates a trend in which second comers easily fritter away indigenous knowledge and resources in ways that aggravate the development divide between them and the rest of the world" (2009, p. 140).

forth. In so doing, by excluding other meanings and forms of those products, these processes risk dispossessing individuals both of their own cultural self-understandings (as experienced in the goods they produce) and whatever economic opportunities those different meanings might have afforded.

Beyond handlooms, one can cite numerous examples of this process in areas that are closely analogous to trademark; I will briefly discuss three. First, Sunder (2001) notes how a US Supreme Court decision allowed the Boy Scouts to dismiss gay leaders on the strength of assertions by the national leadership that the organization condemned homosexuality.[35] However, not only did the decision ignore considerable evidence that the leadership's assertions masked a great deal of dissent and discussion among rank and file members of the organization, the decision also empowered the organization to then punish and expel members that disagreed with its chosen brand identity. In other words, assigning legal imprimatur to the cultural definition of a group by elites allowed those elites to impose traditional power structures on the group in a way that they had been unable to before; as Sunder puts it, law in this sense "regressively treats cultural meanings like the private intellectual property of a culture's leadership" (Sunder, 2001, p. 552).

For a second example, consider the release of the diaspora Indian film *Fire*, which depicts a same-sex relation between two middle-class Hindu women. The film caused a cultural firestorm among Hindu cultural nationalists, who tried to have it suppressed, largely because it violated their view of the "good Indian woman." Ironically, this image was itself the product of the struggle against Western imperialism, and an effort to differentiate an essentially good "Indian woman" from a sexually promiscuous "Western woman." As Sunder notes, nationalists had "conceived Indian culture as having an essential meaning that needed to be legally preserved and protected against dilution by foreign influence, and sought an absolute right to define Indian culture and to exclude meanings that contradicted their definition" (2000, p. 75). In such a context, adding IP protection to cultural identities only makes the situation worse by giving legal imprimatur to the efforts at suppression. Hence, "where law has traditionally allocated rights to exclusive control and exclusion over intellectual products in order to provide *economic incentives* for production, it now contemplates awarding intellectual property rights in order to protect the identity of the property owner, regardless of the economic consequences of nonprotection" (2000, pp. 71–72).[36]

A third set of examples derives from the appropriation of Native American artifacts and symbols. Here the issue is not, as with disparagement, the use of terms that are pejorative, but the use of terms and symbols that have value, whether commodifying

---

[35] *Boy Scouts of America v. Dale*, 530 U.S. 640 (2000).

[36] The situation is even more complicated than this, however, as the director, Deepa Mehta, actually lives in Toronto. The film and debates surrounding it also implicate the rights of those in the diaspora to "represent" their culture. (For the argument that the film lapses into colonial images and stereotypes, see Goswami (2008).)

that value is appropriate, and (if so) where the returns on that commodification should go.[37] For example, the Navajo Nation pursued confusion and dilution claims against the retail clothing chain Urban Outfitters, after Urban Outfitters marketed a line of products including "Navajo Hipster Panties." Following testimony by Urban Outfitters indicating that consumers did not believe that Navajo Nation was the source of the products, a federal court refused to order summary judgment in favor of Navajo Nation on the confusion claims. The same court denied summary judgment on the dilution claim, arguing that although the Navajo mark was distinctive, and that the tribe had spent considerable resources curating it and marketing products bearing it, it was not sufficiently famous to receive dilution protection as a matter of law. Facing the prospects of trial and fact-finding, the parties settled.[38] The Zia of New Mexico have demanded compensation from the state government for appropriation of its religiously significant sun symbol, while simultaneously licensing the symbol to Southwest Airlines. The Zia have also pushed back against Navajo appropriations of Kachina dolls (M. F. Brown, 2003). Examining cases such as these, Peter Yu underscores the general point that cultural boundaries are often fluid and contested, with different groups claiming similar symbols, practices and products, and with different subgroups wanting to do different things with those symbols and products (P. K. Yu, 2008, pp. 488–490).

As the intersection of cultural symbols and the logic of commodification suggests, the trademarking process creates a source of wealth not so much in a product, but in a product insofar as that product is credibly associated with a traditional image of a culture. Insofar as cultural elites will be in a position to capitalize on that wealth and those property rights, they will be in a position to dispossess both the initial creators of the cultural image and those who dissent from it, of the value (either economic or personal) of their cultural meanings. That is, what source protection gives a cultural grouping as a whole, it risks taking away from marginal members of that culture, precisely to the extent that it offers the group protection as a whole.

Insofar as global trademarks increasingly focus on brand images and less on goods, the risk will increase, since the percentage of the value associated with the traditional image, as opposed to the product itself, will also increase. This, in turn, increases the risk that a geographic indicator, serving as a proxy for culture, will become a de facto IP right in that culture. One can identify at least two pressures. On the one hand, the accretion of value to the cultural image will tend to reinforce the dominance of the reproduction of the image at the expense of the reproduction

[37] Some of the tensions about who has the right to speak for the group in question also persist. For example, an appeals court upheld the conviction of Richard Corrow for trading in sacred Navajo artifacts, despite the presence of conflicting narratives about the status of these objects from within the Navajo community. See *United States v. Corrow*, 119 F.3d 796 (1997).

[38] For confusion, see *Navajo Nation v. Urban Outfitters, Inc.*, 2016 U.S. Dist. LEXIS 136558 (2016). For dilution, see *Navajo Nation v. Urban Outfitters*, Inc., 2016 U.S. Dist. LEXIS 63599 (2016). For the settlement, see Woolf (2016).

of different commodities. Products of a culture – even those with robust brand identities – will be increasingly required to conform to the image that culture projects. On the other hand, as noted earlier, the cultural image itself – likely highly conservative already insofar as it is "traditional" – will need to be increasingly so in order to differentiate itself from the other cultural images on hand.[39]

Beyond concerns with disparagement, I want to focus here on one normative problem in particular, because it shows how IP allocations can function as coercive regimes of subjectification. Generally speaking, meaningful opportunities to dissent from the cultural environment in which one finds oneself (not to mention meaningful economic opportunities that require one to dissent) are necessary to any robust understanding of autonomy. As Sunder puts it, "dissent creates options within a culture and thereby offers individuals greater possibilities for autonomy and equality in their cultural lives" (Sunder, 2001, p. 561). Critics of allowing cultural dissent in this sense typically invoke an "exit right:" If you do not like the rules here, you are always free to leave. Dissenters can do so elsewhere. The relative difficulty in exit can accordingly serve as a measure of the extent to which the lack of meaningful opportunity to dissent functions as a form of coercive subjectification. Set aside for the moment concerns about very real difficulties in leaving, especially for those who are already disadvantaged.[40]

A globalized world of geographically based trademarks makes this constellation of problems more worrisome. At one level, the persistence of diaspora communities in different settings entails an inevitable heterogeneity among those who identify with a cultural grouping or set of cultural practices, and makes it much more difficult to say who "speaks for" the culture. The controversy surrounding *Fire* demonstrates this point clearly, as does Florida State's usage of the "Seminoles." At another level, however, globalization makes it increasingly difficult to exercise the exit right that enables dissent. The problem is precisely that the global nature of these rights extends them into diaspora communities, to whatever space into which affected individuals might try to exit. At that point, practicing at least some parts of a cultural identity requires doing so in conformity with trademark rules. The regime thus exists

---

[39] The argument here is in an important sense a simplification, because many of the "traditional" products and images of indigenous cultures are products of white culture, not of the indigenous cultures themselves. For a demonstration of this point with regard to symbols associated with Native Americans (such as sports mascots), see Mezey (2007). As Mezey notes, former University of Illinois mascot Chief Illiniwek's "real inspiration is the mythic Indians of the white imagination; he simply makes no sense outside white sports culture and even then, makes different sorts of sense when viewed in the light of the American tradition of playing Indian" (p. 2044).

[40] As Susan Moller Okin (2002) underlined, it is precisely the disenfranchised – Okin is thinking of women, but the argument clearly can be extended to other minorities – who will both be most in need of an exit option and least able to exercise it. Further, the perceived availability of an exit option can be used by elites to clamp down on dissent: if you do not like it, just leave!

as a form of subjectification, forcing a global compliance with the reified view of culture it expresses.

Imagine the case of a maker of "Persian" rugs who, for political reasons, now lives in Canada. Under a fully globalized regime of source protection, the owners of the trademark would be able to legally enjoin his production of identical rugs, simply because he was in a different location. Not only that, if he produced rugs in some way that was not incorporated into the official standard, he would be unable legally to produce "Persian" rugs anywhere in the world, no matter how many centuries his family had been in Persia making rugs. If a global source protection regime included dilution protections, then his problems might be even worse. One can easily imagine a tarnishment case in which a "Gay Persia" adult-goods store is sued by the owners of "Persian" rugs on the grounds that the adult goods damage the reputation of the rugs by associating the term with explicit sexual content. The Victor's Little Secret litigation shows that such a scenario is entirely plausible.

4.4 CONCLUSION: WHAT IS TO BE DONE?

The complexities surrounding GIs as a form of resistance occupy the same conceptual space as those around dilution and disparagement. In all three cases, trademark increasingly comes to directly regulate social and cultural practices by clearing the space for market actors to internalize, Demsetzian-style, the externalities of brand-centered, affective capitalism. Dilution doctrine provides legal backing to corporate strategies to manage and profit from consumer attachment to brands. Striking down disparagement doctrine on free speech grounds ensures that this process occurs without state interference based on how those brands are signified. Finally, GIs as source protection extend this process to "traditional" cultural identities. All three cases illustrate the ways that trademark can facilitate capital's expansion into the direct commodification of affective relations between consumers and brand identities, as well as internalize the wealth generated by this commodification. In so doing, they illustrate how trademark makes people.

In different ways, the judicial insistence on First Amendment rights against disparagement policy and indigenous efforts to reappropriate GIs to protect their own interests illustrate not only the Foucauldian dictum that power and resistance are always co-constituted, but also the point that resistance itself can express different models of power. The market-oriented strategy of indigenous GIs can be conceptualized along biopolitical lines. That is, as Sunder explains, the goal is to use property regimes to enable the emergence culturally and socially rich lives as indexed by notions of human capabilities. The juridical strategy rejecting disparagement is designed to protect the sphere of action of a classic, rights-bearing subject, and explicitly rejects any consideration of questions of the effects of this protection on larger, social and political issues. That said, these strategies are not without risk: free speech rejection of disparagement makes easy alliance with the neoliberal protection of corporate interests, and indigenous GIs risk interfering in dynamic cultural practices.

An issue underlying all of this can be seen as an example of what Sonia Katyal, following the work of critical race theorists such as Kimberle Crenshaw and of trademark theorists such as Rochelle Cooper Dreyfuss, has identified as the "intersectionality" of trademarks, which function as both commercial product identifiers and as expressive speech (Katyal, 2010b). The Victoria's Secret case shows the extent to which protecting commercial speech around sex risks subtly shaping culturally available modes of sexual expression. The resistant use of GIs raises question about whether the commodification process necessary to turn the expressive cultural symbol into a product-identifying form of speech has effects on the expressive use of the symbol. In other words, both raise the question of to what extent the commodification process might tend to ossify the expressive use of cultural symbols. For example, in the case of GIs, one has to balance thoroughly legitimate concerns about multinational expropriation against the worry that nearly every aspect of the process of registering and using them will tend to encourage the use of stereotypical and potentially disparaging signifiers as representative of a cultural practice. On top of that, the mark can then be used against dissident voices attempting to challenge their own representation.

One point that emerges in Sunder's work that might help to thread the needle between these alternatives is that not just any regime of source protection will serve resistant aims. That is, Sunder's optimism about GIs is in part because she views property as a narrative strategy that enables reimagining the cultural relations behind protected GIs. In other words, many of the risks outlined here are greatest when resistance strategies embrace a neoliberal logic of privatization, and they depend in part on the degrees to which GIs inherit the structures of the emerging, hegemonic global trademark regime. Sunder notes that the Indian source protection law allows ownership by collectives, and "multiple associations of artisans may be recognized as the authorized producers or users of a GI" (2008, p. 464). If ownership were in fact treated in this way, it would be considerably more resistant to some of the forms of relapse into neoliberal biopower outlined earlier. That is, and depending on the power relations between the associations, the Indian GI law also underlines that the revisioning of property attempted by GIs is, whatever risks it entails, an important contribution. Most fundamentally, it recognizes that IP need not follow a neoliberal model, a point to which I will return in Chapter 6.

At the same time, it underlines a lesson of the *Tam* decision: The move to return to a (Western) juridical conception of rights-bearing subjects can interact unpredictably with more market-oriented and biopolitical framings of trademark and the people it affects. Indeed, the entire debate I have attempted to develop here is about the way that IP interacts with, modifies, and creates cultural institutions and forms, and the individuals who inhabit them. As I will argue in the Chapter 6, one virtue of understanding IP as expressing different models of power is that it becomes possible to see that the model of power IP expresses is contingent. In other words, our current view of property is not a necessary one, even as it is tied to broader understandings of power.

5

Patents

The premise that economic growth is due to innovation leads naturally to an emphasis on promoting invention as central to overall economic policy. The development of the larger economy from Fordist factory production and into immaterial goods leads naturally to the expansion of patents into new areas like computer software and even into life processes themselves. The direct role of the pharmaceutical industry in pushing for patents, ostensibly as trade policy, has served to move patents to the forefront of innovation and economic policy over the last forty years or so.[1] As noted in Chapter 2, university research in particular has been increasingly driven by patentability, and less by basic research.[2] More generally, the high rewards associated with patented blockbuster drugs, combined with the ready availability of venture capital, encourage research into difficult but potentially very lucrative markets, such as gene therapies and other forms of molecular and personalized medicine.

---

[1] For the emergence of Schumpeterian theories of innovation, see the discussion in Chapter 2. For the expansion of the economy, especially into "life," see, e.g., Cooper (2008) (documenting a move from chemistry to biology and from assumptions about scarcity to an emphasis on life as generative). For patenting novel life forms, see the Supreme Court's unanimous ruling in *Diamond* v. *Chakrabarty*, 447 U.S. 303 (1980). Weaker, but patent-like protection has been available for plant varieties for significantly longer than that. See Bugos and Kevles (1992). For concerns about enclosure, which animate resistance to this expansion, see, e.g., Boyle (1997, 2008). For intellectual property (IP) as trade policy in the 1980s, see Sell (2003).

[2] One example is the 1980 Bayh–Dole Act, which encouraged universities to move away from bench research toward a focus on patentable inventions. As noted in Chapter 2, university scientists were to re-envision themselves as entrepreneurs (Strandburg, 2005). This push was further solidified in *Madey* v. *Duke* (2002), which substantially narrowed the research exemption for patents, essentially applying patent licensing and other aspects of the IP regime to nearly all university research. Facing funding cuts from state governments, cash-starved university administrators have heavily encouraged their scientists in this direction of producing patentable "innovations" rather than bench science (Mirowski, 2011).

That is, a focus on the internalization of the potential market value of research and a priority on innovation over distribution mark a move away from public biopolitics. There are at least two reasons. First, research is heavily oriented towards technologically intensive research, and away from more pedestrian aspects of health (Berlinguer, 2004). Public health programs produce positive externalities that are difficult to internalize, and so get less attention. Second, the system works in subtle ways to direct attention to the diseases of the rich. Margaret Chon compiles a number of well-known criticisms of the reliance on patents as health policy, which can perhaps best be summarized by noting where research dollars go:

> 99% of the global disease burden is concentrated in low and middle income countries. However, in 1992, less than 5% of the total global R&D was spent on their health problems. In 1996, only 0.5% of pharmaceutical patents related to tropical diseases such as malaria.
>
> (2006, p. 2884)[3]

The reason for this state of affairs is simple enough: A privatized, patent-based system will encourage research into medicines for which there are lucrative markets. Since the poor cannot pay for drugs, drug development bypasses their needs. What the poor often need is improvements in the various social determinants of health, and a system focused on internalization is not well equipped to address these.

That said, patent policy has not universally abetted this neoliberal trajectory. This chapter presents a selection of case studies that show that expansionary patent policy has met with only mixed success in the Courts. The Supreme Court in particular, adopting a more juridical view of power, coupled with concerns more typical of public biopolitics, has repeatedly attempted to limit the scope of patent protections. I begin with a detailed analysis of the ultimately unsuccessful effort by Myriad Genetics to secure patent protection for the isolated genetic sequence of the BRCA1/2 mutations that predispose patients to hereditary breast and ovarian cancer (HBOC). The Myriad story offers a window not only into how the development of biotechnology, as a significant component of the post-industrial economy, encourages new kinds of subjectivity, but also how strong patent protections help to nudge that subjectivity in neoliberal directions. I thus offer a detailed account of how biotechnology is changing our experience as medical subjects, and how policy surrounding the genetic test for HBOC in the United States does so specifically.

---

[3] Chon's larger point is to marshal a case against neoliberal, "Washington Consensus" doctrine as applied to patents and development, in favor of modeling development on the "human capabilities" approach pioneered by Amartya Sen and Martha Nussbaum. As Chon puts it, "the provision of basic food, health care, and education must be prioritized over the provision of intermediate public goods such as legal regimes that facilitate innovation through the grant of exclusionary rights. After all, basic education and adequate health status are prerequisites to any capacity-building for the technological progress that is one of the biggest rationales of TRIPS" (2006, pp. 2827–2828). On capabilities and patents, see also Sunder (2012, pp. 173–199).

The story is also important because the litigation surrounding it shows quite clearly how different implicit views of power can generate different views on the patentability of isolated genetic fragments. I trace the litigation in some detail. The district court rejected patentability on juridical grounds, the appellate court affirmed it on neoliberal grounds, and the Supreme Court rejected it with an inchoate mix of juridical and public biopolitical reasoning. Ironically, as I argue, the Court's rejection may not make much of a difference.

I then put the *Myriad* litigation into the larger context of Court efforts to define the scope of patentable subject matter under §101 of the Patent Act. Here the Court has been fairly consistent in pushing back against efforts to expand the doctrine. Its efforts rely on juridical mechanisms, but seem to evidence a concern about the ability of patent-holders to stifle downstream innovation with excessive enclosure of natural processes. The following section looks at the Court's recent decision emphasizing patent exhaustion and the limits of patent owners to profit from post-initial-sale uses of their invention. The decision is legible as a retrenchment from the full implications of Chicago antitrust policy, and can be read in the context of decisions in the 1940s limiting patent-tying arrangements as abuses of monopoly power. The final section looks at the Court's recent affirmation of administrative review processes, rather than Court proceedings, as an acceptable venue for challenging some aspects of patents. The decision clearly shows how the outcome depends on one's view of power, and it clearly rejects the juridical view proposed in the dissent in favor of a public biopolitics of administrative regulation.

5.1 GENETIC TESTING FOR HEREDITARY BREAST AND OVARIAN CANCER

5.1.1 *Actuarial Agency*

This section develops an account of subjectivity specific to the interaction of neoliberal biopolitics and patents, with an emphasis on the rise of genomics.[4] I call the model "actuarial agency." According to this model, individuals are to understand themselves as risk managers of their own health outcomes, rather than as citizens who benefit from public health measures. In particular, individuals are able to view their bodies as sources of information about their future health. However, like the anticipatory returns that drive the companies that market these sources of information, the information itself is ultimately probabilistic in that it defines risk categories and offers, at best, probable diagnoses, often far into the future. Actuarial thinking represents a radical departure from traditional, symptom-based clinical models of medical reasoning. At the same time, the US context tends to divorce

---

[4] Other emphases are possible, in particular the rise of pharmacology as a primary modality of contemporary medicine. See Camargo and Ried (2016).

agents from either a public policy or normative family context; in so doing, it makes individual patients responsible for managing their own health outcomes and for assuming much of the burden of obtaining, interpreting, and responding appropriately to the probabilities that present themselves to them. The actuarial agent in this sense is *homo economicus*: managing an uncertain health future as a stock portfolio, both empowered and burdened with an ever greater assumption of responsibility for that set of possible futures.

The emergence of actuarial agency is part of a profound change in the sociology of medicine. At its core, the change is from a view according to which a patient has a body that presents symptoms to one in which the patient's body is also viewed as a collection of information-rich parts that either enable the interpretation of symptoms or which present clinically relevant information.[5] Consider the change in the role of symptoms in some kinds of diagnosis. On the one hand, symptoms can be taken as evidence of a genetic risk. For example, being diagnosed with triple-negative breast cancer, particularly at a young age, is a potential indicator of the BRCA1 mutation.[6] On the other hand, genetic features of one's body are read as points of information, which then construct a risk profile predictive of future health outcomes. For example, BRCA mutation carriers have a substantially higher lifetime chance of developing breast and ovarian cancer. That happens before any traditional symptoms of disease appear; those at high risk for particular conditions are "presymptomatically ill" (N. S. Rose, 2007) or "previvors" (M. Dean and Davidson, 2018).[7] Those at high risk can then be tasked with managing their future health outcomes, a task that intersects and abets the growing social importance of lifestyle medicines.[8]

A recent paper by Becker is instructive for understanding how these clinical developments intersect with neoliberal theory. Becker notes what he calls a "health

---

[5]   In addition to N. S. Rose (2007), see e.g., Thacker (2005) (emphasizing the duality of biology as matter and information: "the point is that the material biological body – 'life itself' – is also the informatic body. The body materially counts only inasmuch as it is understood as information and as genetic information" (p. 86)). The canonical presentation of the "clinical gaze" is of course Foucault's (1973). Foucault delivered a lecture in Rio in 1974 that was remarkably prescient in predicting the rise of pharmaceuticals in the growth of medicine; as he wrote, "at present, medicine connects with the economy by another route. Not simply in so far as it is capable of reproducing the work force, but also in that it can directly produce wealth in that health is a need for some and a luxury for others. Health becomes a consumer object, which can be produced by pharmaceutical laboratories, doctors, etc., and consumed by both potential and actual patients. As such, it has acquired economic and market value" (2004, p. 16).

[6]   For the pathological characteristics of BRCA mutation breast cancer, see Cao, Huang, and Shao (2017), §3.3.

[7]   *Cf.* also Boenink (2010)(describing this as a "cascade" model of disease, where biomarkers predict rather than indicate the onset of disease) and Reid (2017)(arguing that the underlying model of disease is shifting, from a "pathophysiological" version based on visual evidence to a presymptomatic one based on risk).

[8]   The general move is to treat a "healthy" lifestyle as an investment in one's future self. Sharing fitness data with friends is one version; sex-tracking apps (Lupton, 2015) are another. Workplace employee wellness programs (Hull and Pasquale, 2018) are a third.

paradox," which is that the rise in lifestyle medicine seems to correlate with a rise in health-damaging behavior such as a decline in the overall exercise rate. He resolves the paradox by suggesting that people focus on drug development; young people expect future medical advances to be able to address future problems caused by their current behaviors. He then speculates that "perhaps that helps explain the acceleration in weight gain among teenagers that began about 1980" (2007, p. 402). Becker's construal of medical behavior as amenable to this sort of economic description exemplifies the extension of economic analysis into all areas of life that is characteristic of neoliberalism (see Chapter 2). That said, his analysis both seems *ad hoc* and to ignore obvious, easier explanations like hyperbolic discounting of the future. Additionally, it individualizes medicine by downplaying structural reasons why some individuals might be prone to poor health decisions. For example, Becker is silent about questions of food availability or job-related activity levels.

The broader trends identified here – both toward the neoliberalization of health policy and the development of an actuarial agency specific to it – can be brought into specific focus by taking genetic testing for HBOC as an extended study. The more granular analysis of HBOC screening also enables one to see the importance of patent availability to the emergence of neoliberal health policy and its attendant form of subjectivity. In what follows, I will look at three aspects of the emergence of this testing: the way it operationalizes risk as an indicator of disease, differences between testing regimes in the United States and the Netherlands, and the tendency of American testing practice to separate from public policy frameworks. The takeaway is that contingent features of the US system that separate patients from otherwise stabilizing policy or familial contexts serve to heighten the difficulties associated with actuarial agency. It is against this background that I will then trace litigation around the testing in the following section.

5.1.2 *Genetic Risk*

As suggested earlier, the immediate impact of personalized genomic medicine is the personalization of medical risk. It is important to underscore the difference between the emerging, genomic-based model of medicine and its predecessor. Consider the different ways they generate problems of "overdiagnosis," i.e., when a disease is correctly identified according to the criteria of that model, but it is not one that would ever be clinically significant. Overdiagnosis is not a problem of sensitivity (missing disease that meets diagnostic criteria) or specificity (identifying something as meeting diagnostic criteria that it does not actually meet). Rather, overdiagnosis is a problem in the adequacy of the disease model itself.

Consider first recent work assessing the efficacy of mammography screening. A controversial 2012 study (Bleyer and Welch, 2012) suggested that mammography has been responsible for relatively little of the reduction in breast cancer mortality, and that up to nearly a third of breast cancers detected by mammography are in fact overdiagnoses. Patients are typically encouraged to begin treatment for tumors detected by screening, so overdiagnoses subject patients to unnecessary treatment that is difficult, invasive, and potentially risky. A follow-up paper four years later (which produced similar results) underlined that visual detection of a tumor is of limited utility, since its biological and genetic characteristics are more relevant to prognosis than its size (Welch et al., 2016). The risk is not just that the visualization technology forces clinicians to use tumor size as a proxy for information that has a much greater clinical value, but that the gaze classifies as dangerous tumors things that are not.

Referring to these studies, Lynette Reid (2017) notes that autopsy studies confirm that most people have numerous "indolent" tumors when they die. Those tumors would have potentially been detected by screening, but did not become clinically significant during the patient's life. The possibility of overdiagnosis means that a decision to treat is a risk assessment hobbled by a particular blind spot: Although it is theoretically possible to estimate the prevalence of screening-based overdiagnosis at a population level, it is impossible to know if a given cancer, once treated, represented an overdiagnosis (L. Davies et al., 2018). Further, this problem of overdiagnosis would persist even if one assumed a "perfect" screening test that was 100 percent sensitive and specific. Indeed, Reid cites several studies to the effect that such a screening test would be clinically near useless, as the vast majority of the tumors it detected would never be clinically relevant. The problem of overdiagnosis confirms what genetic screening indicates: for many diseases, the clinical gaze risks collapsing under the weight of advances in screening visualization technologies.

Genetic testing requires that one consider information that is both presymptomatic and prior to the emergence of visual evidence to discover disease.[9] For example, the BRCA1/2 mutation disrupts gene repair, making it less reliable, increasing the odds of a mutation occurring. BRCA1/2 carriers have a cumulative breast cancer risk of roughly 72 percent to age 80, and BRCA1 carriers have a 44 percent cumulative ovarian cancer risk by that age (17 percent for BRCA2) (Kuchenbaecker et al., 2017).[10] Both are orders of magnitude higher than population baselines, and present these (potentially) presymptomatic patients with significant clinical management questions, especially around ovarian cancer, for which detection is very difficult (as a result, it has a very high mortality rate) but for which prophylactic surgery causes infertility. Screening detects cancer risk before cancer

---

[9] For the sake of simplicity, I am treating the models as ideal types; in actual practice, of course, various combinations are possible. For example, a patient with a known genetic risk can receive more frequent screening, since the mutation is evidence that a clinically significant tumor is more likely to develop. Conversely, a tumor detected during screening can be tested to determine its genetic type, in order to better plan treatment.

[10] This is consistent with earlier work finding that, depending on how one analyzes the data, BRCA1/2 mutation carriers are at a cumulative breast cancer risk in the 50–60 percent range by age 70, and an ovarian cancer risk in the 18–50 percent range (Stoppa-Lyonnet, 2016).

occurs, but precisely because it assigns to risk category, it also presents what one might conceptualize as its own problem of overdiagnosis because many of those with heightened genetic risk will never develop disease (Oke, 2018).

Although there are beginning to be clinical implications for treatment of BRCA1/2 induced cancers, the primary emphasis has been on risk stratification and strategies for risk management. The most significant decision a carrier faces is whether to undergo prophylactic mastectomy (associated with lower breast cancer risk) or salpingo-oophorectomy (associated with lower breast and ovarian cancer risk, as well as lower mortality from either form of cancer) (Domchek et al., 2010).[11] This is only the beginning of the decisions, however. Armed with knowledge of her mutation, a patient can proceed to analyze other risk management strategies, for example, when to start screening, what kind of screening to undergo, and how to factor the risks of false-positive results (Lowry et al., 2012). The mutation also has implications for childbearing, as it is heritable, and so a decision to have children is a decision to possibly pass on an increased cancer risk to them. It also raises the question of whether childbearing should be done via *in vitro* fertilization, so that embryos could be tested for the mutation and only those which did not inherit selected for implantation (Dekeuwer and Bateman, 2013).

The likely proliferation of such genetic tests in the future suggests that the overall result will be a differentiation and individualization of insecurity. Someone who tests positive for the BRCA1 mutation and who undergoes prophylactic, risk-reducing salpingo-oophorectomy appears to reduce her ovarian cancer risk by 70–85 percent (Domchek et al., 2010), and in this sense the testing enables a reassuring preventative strategy for some patients. Even in what appears to be a straightforward case, however, the calculations can be complicated. There are potential health risks to inducing premature menopause, and the timing of surgery matters for those risks (Domchek et al., 2010). So too, one study found that the survival benefits of prophylactic mastectomy for BRCA mutation carriers rapidly decreased with age; at age 25, the procedure increased the probability of being alive at age 80 by nearly 9 percent, but by age 50, the survival benefit had declined to 2.8 percent (Giannakeas and Narod, 2018).

Some of the difficulties here are presumably due to a lack of accumulated data, and better prediction will become possible with more evidence. A greater issue is that genetic mutations account for a relatively small portion of cancer risk. For that reason, a negative BRCA test can be nearly meaningless, unless the patient was known to be at high risk for inheriting the mutation. In other words, although BRCA carriers are likely to get either breast or ovarian cancers in their lifetimes, the

[11] In what follows, I consider only women as BRCA carriers. Men can also carry the mutation, and male carriers are at significantly increased risk for male breast cancer and prostate cancer; they are also at elevated risk for melanoma and pancreatic cancer. However, the vast majority of the research and discussion of the BRCA mutation exclusively considers HBOC as it affects women.

BRCA1/2 mutations only account for 5–10 percent of all breast cancer cases, and only about 20–25 percent of *hereditary* breast cancers.[12]

The situation with other cancers is currently even less informative. Here the problem is that, unless a given risk factor accounts for a sufficiently large percentage of those who develop a given condition, the presence of the risk factor has little prognostic value in individual cases, even if it indicates that members of a population are collectively at elevated risk (Ware, 2006). For example, one's baseline, lifetime risk of developing pancreatic cancer is about 1.5 percent. Among risk factors, the most important are age (two-thirds of patients are at least 65, and almost none under 45) and smoking (which accounts for 20–30 percent of cases).[13] Familial cases – where pancreatic cancer affects one or more first-degree relatives – account for somewhere between 4–10 percent of all cases. (This and the following data are from Matsubayashi et al., 2017.) The data, however, is currently quite inconclusive. First, one first-degree relative with pancreatic cancer puts one's odds ratio at 1.5–1.7 of relative risk. But this adds up to a 2.5 percent total risk at most. It is true that one's odds ratio goes up dramatically with increasing numbers of affected relatives; those with three or more affected relatives have a 32-fold increase in their risk, but such highly affected families are very rare. Not only that, a pathogenic germline mutation has been proven in only about 20 percent of familial cases. In this context, it is very difficult to know what to do with a negative genetic test, even in cases where there is a family history. A positive genetic test also offers relatively little clinical guidance, unless there is a strong family history. Put differently, in this case the family history is currently a much better guide to risk than the genetic test, and even familial history provides little guidance except in extreme cases. All of this is supported by research that strongly suggests that the majority of cancer risk is tied to the number of times the relevant cells have divided – i.e., to a spontaneous mutation or other replication error.[14]

These forward-looking genetic tests encourage thinking in highly complex statistical terms, and away from causal diagnoses. The risk profile that emerges is heavily influenced by antecedent decisions ranging from how to calibrate test sensitivity and specificity to how to understand variations of unknown clinical significance (VUCS). It also necessarily represents a decision to make a certain number of errors. A test which is 99 percent sensitive will miss the mutation 1 percent of the time, which means that it will miss ten carriers for every thousand patients screened. High

---

[12] As reported by the American Cancer Society (www.cancer.gov/about-cancer/causes-prevention/genetics/brca-fact-sheet, visited July 2017), citing Easton (1999) and Campeau, Foulkes, and Tischkowitz (2008).

[13] This data is from the American Cancer Association; see: www.cancer.org/cancer/pancreatic-cancer/about/key-statistics.html (visited July 2017).

[14] These results are admittedly controversial; the point was to emphasize that heredity and environment do not account for most cancer risk. For the original studies, see Tomasetti, Li, and Vogelstein (2017), Tomasetti and Vogelstein (2015). For come commentary, see Nowak and Waclaw (2017).

sensitivity generally represents a trade-off for lower specificity, and so the 99 percent sensitive test is also likely to generate a nontrivial number of false positives.

This way of thinking about the error rate, as recent work in legal theory has shown, sharply conflicts with juridical thinking. In a pair of recent papers, David Enoch, Levi Spectre, and Talia Fisher (Enoch and Fisher, 2015; Enoch, Spectre, and Fisher, 2012) compare statistically based, probabilistic reasoning with juridical. They lead with a classic scenario about a blue bus that causes harm of some sort. In that case, we have two kinds of evidence about liability. One is an eyewitness, deemed to be 70 percent reliable (in other words, they are correct in identifying things 70 percent of the time), who says the bus belongs to the Blue Bus Company; and the other is the information that 70 percent of the buses that could be in the area are owned by the Blue Bus Company. So the question: Do we find Blue Bus liable? The intuition is that most people would find against the company in the case of the witness, but would strongly hesitate to find liability based on the statistical evidence alone, even though the two kinds of evidence are, at first glance, epistemically equivalent.

Enoch et al. suggest that the reason for this divergence in intuition is that sensitivity (in a slightly different sense than used before) matters to us epistemologically. A knowledge claim is said to be sensitive, in their sense, if a counterfactual might change the outcome.[15] In other words, in the case of the witness, had they said that the bus was not blue, we would probably not blame Blue Bus. But in the case of the statistics, there is no such moment and no place to even locate a counterfactual. We know that sometimes we will be wrong in such cases. Indeed, we could be wrong repeatedly and still assert the truth that Blue Bus owns 70 percent of the buses in the area. If we are wrong in the witness case, on the other hand, we tend to demand explanation for what happened.

Myriad reports its test to be more than 99 percent sensitive, though the CDC puts the number at 98.2 percent, with a 95 percent confidence interval that the test's accuracy is between 90.3 and 99.9 percent.[16] That means that it will miss about anywhere from 1 in 10 to 1 in 1000 cases in which the person carries the mutation, with a best guess of about 1 in 50 missed cases. Myriad also says that the test is 100 percent specific. The CDC repeats the number, but both cautions that data are limited and that the 95% CI is from 80 to 100 percent (so, although quite unlikely, the test could deliver a false-positive rate of up to one in five). This is action-guiding evidence; recall that BRCA1/2 carriers often opt for prophylactic surgery for their own benefit, or to avoid having children to whom they might pass the gene.[17]

[15] Formally: "S's belief that p is sensitive = df. Had it not been the case that p, S would (most probably) not have believed that p." (2012, p. 204).

[16] www.cdc.gov/genomics/gtesting/file/print/fbr/bcanaval.pdf.

[17] Domchek et al. (2010) describe risk-reducing surgery as common. A recent South Korean study found that 46.3 percent of studied BRCA mutation carriers underwent risk-reducing salpingo-oophorectomy when it was covered by national health insurance (Lee et al., 2019). A Danish

Our epistemic situation is not going to improve; current testing is considerably more complex and generally involves testing for multiple genes. The more genes that are tested, the more likely VUCS are to be found. Indeed, concern about the inevitability of discovering unknown variants dates back more than a decade (Kohane, Masys, and Altman, 2006). As one recent analysis put it, "the more genomic data is generated, the greater is the uncertainty about the clinical meaning of this data ... Increasingly, we will be the recipients of data that we did not anticipate or, perhaps, even seek to know. Accordingly, we will be in the uncomfortable position of reacting to that data on the basis of an immature and incomplete understanding of what that data mean" (P. P. Yu, Vose, and Hayes, 2015). In a manner the effect of which is similar to that of digital rights management, there is no one to hold accountable for an erroneous test result or even an erroneous prediction as to what will happen; those are simply architected into the system.

5.1.3 Family Values: US versus Dutch Testing Regimes

Since the BRCA1/2 mutation is hereditary, clinical practices are profoundly implicated by normative and social understandings of family. Recent work comparing American and Dutch testing practices underscores this point.[18] The differences between the practices also allow one to underscore the extent to which the US model pushes in a more neoliberal direction than its Dutch counterpart. A healthy woman in the Netherlands who wishes to be tested for the BRCA mutation must, among other things, complete a detailed questionnaire that includes considerable medical information about all of her first- and second-degree relatives. Since privacy laws prevent geneticists' contacting these family members, the woman must do so herself. If she is unable to do so, the geneticist will generally refuse to offer the test, offering instead more frequent breast and ovarian screening. As Marianne Boenink notes, this practice is normatively significant in two ways. On the one hand, it both presupposes and works to create an ideal of "intensive, open, communicative, harmonious and cooperative relations," to the point that women who do not already have such family contacts "are actively counseled to restore contact and advised how to approach their relatives" (2011, p. 1797). On the other hand, it assigns a high value to accuracy in testing, and attempts to eliminate ambiguity in interpreting test results.

study found that 75 percent of women had the procedure within ten years of testing, though the number was much smaller for those without children (Skytte et al., 2010) (also reporting earlier research showing long-term uptake rates of 29–70 percent).

[18] The rapid development of clinical practices in oncology, in genetic screening, and around the BRCA1/2 mutations means that the picture sketched here should be considered a snapshot, specific to a particular historical moment. However, even as such, it indicates the point. As I note below, Myriad's online promotional materials are considerably more accurate and informative now than the first time I looked at them, in 2011.

The Dutch effort to contextualize test results and minimize ambiguity emerges clearly in comparison to the American system. Most women who receive BRCA1/2 testing in the United States do not have breast cancer, a figure that represents a reversal of the situation in 2000, when a majority who received the test were cancer patients (Guo et al., 2017). Women in the United States who are concerned about their hereditary cancer risk can receive direct-to-consumer advertising, and are invited by testing companies like Myriad to press their doctors to order testing. Myriad maintains a complex website that aims to help patients determine whether they are at risk for hereditary cancers associated with the BRCA1/2 mutation. As of this writing, Myriad's website claims to integrate family history into risk assessment, but there is no evidence that family history serves the same gatekeeping function it does in the Netherlands. The site also repeatedly emphasizes that those with positive test results can do a range of potentially beneficial things ranging from increased monitoring to risk-reducing medicines and surgeries.

The juxtaposition with the Dutch model is striking. The ambiguity presented in the Dutch situation, ambiguity sufficient for geneticists to refuse to provide the test, is here presented as a form of empowerment. As of December 2018, the patient-oriented site suggests that those with relatives who have cancer – "even a cousin or other third-degree relative" – have a possible genetic mutation in the family.[19] The ambiguity in a negative result against which Dutch clinical practice warns is missing from the general testing FAQ page, buried in a "negative results" brochure, which says that "your test has given you some helpful information but it is still best to manage your cancer risks based on your personal and family history."[20] Boenink notes that family members are conspicuously absent from the American version she studied, at two levels. First, "the American client is supposed to be able to handle test results on her own, independently from her family" (2011, p. 1798). That is, the American client is constructed as an "independent, autonomous individual who is capable of finding and making sense of information about genetic risk and predictive testing" (2011, p. 1798). Second, the American family is constructed "as a set of biologically related individuals (figuring in the pedigree), rather than as an active social unit" (2011, p. 1798).[21]

[19] https://mysupport360.com/testing/about/ (accessed December 2018, and on file with author).
[20] At https://mysupport360.com/genetic-testing/testing-results/ (visited June 2017; brochure on file with author). I was unable to generate an explanation of "no mutation detected" in December 2018; that button linked to a brochure for those who had been found to carry the mutation. I replicate the 2017 page out of charity. The current Myriad site is considerably more sophisticated than it was in 2011, as well as more accurate. The 2011 version, for example, said of a negative result that "a negative result does not mean that you have no risk for developing cancer," while the website as a whole made it difficult to find the information that only about 10 percent of breast cancer risk is hereditary (on file with author). This information is on the front of the current website, which also includes a quiz that will advise whether an individual should consider testing.
[21] Evidence of this is that one study of American women who had received genetic counseling and who tested positive for the mutation generally reported that result to parents and sisters.

The result is a medicalization of post-test social support. Recent work suggests that American women rely heavily on clinicians (whom they often find uninformed, and who can be sources of great frustration) and genetic counselors, but less on families, friends, or social networks, for help in managing a positive test result (M. Dean and Davidson, 2018). At the core of managing this risk is a feeling of inevitability. Patients tend to receive evidence that they carry the mutation as indicating that they will develop cancer, not that they have an elevated risk of doing so. Most of those interviewed in one study elected prophylactic surgery (Marleah Dean, 2016). Social support networks also broaden onto the Internet. The socially isolated American patient is part of what gives rise to support and advocacy groups for certain diseases, such as "Facing Our Risk of Cancer Empowered" (FORCE), from which the subjects of the previous two studies were recruited. Paul Rabinow's forecast of two decades ago was prescient, as he noted that we will likely see "the formation of new group and individual identities and practices arising out of these new truths ... Such groups will have medical specialists, laboratories, narratives, traditions, and a heavy panoply of pastoral keepers to help them experience, share, intervene, and 'understand' their fate" (1996, p. 102).

None of this is necessarily to endorse the apparent Dutch model of the family, but it is to note the stark contrast. That contrast can be demonstrated concretely here in the trade-off between autonomy and uncertainty. An American woman, presumed to be an autonomous instance of *homo economicus*, wishing to maximize investments in her health, is portrayed as a rational consumer and calculator of radically indeterminate information, even as the evidence suggests that this presumption is not quite accurate.[22] As Boenink puts it:

> American practice is prone to present clients with ambiguous test results that are difficult to interpret. However, Myriad hardly provides support to make sense of such results, nor does it inform clients of ways to improve the quality of the test result (for example by testing diseased relatives first). So, even though American practice does not confront the client with difficult requests with regard to her family, it is likely to increase rather than decrease uncertainty regarding the future.
>
> (Boenink, 2011, p. 1798)

In other words, the differences in individual patient experience and in the construction of patients as actuarial agents are also reflected in the larger social policies of different countries.

On the other hand, they were much less likely to report positive results to male relatives, or to report uninformative results to anyone (Vadaparampil et al., 2012). This construction may be warranted: A 2004 CDC study found that 96 percent of respondents thought that family history was important to their personal health, but only 30 percent had collected information to construct such a family history. See Baer et al. (2010).

[22] In this sense, one might complain that the Dutch practice is "paternalistic." As Bernstein notes, however, the presence of a medical professional as a gatekeeper can equally be said to be autonomy enhancing by allowing more informed choices (2010, p. 11 n40).

5.1.4 *Separation from Policy*

Although the use of the test is increasing, and the US Preventative Services Task Force (USPSTF) established guidelines for recommending BRCA-testing in 2005, survey results from a few years after the guidelines were issued indicated that relatively few clinicians recommended the test based on those guidelines (Bellcross et al., 2011). Less than one in five surveyed clinicians correctly identified all of the survey's scenarios as low or increased risk; almost half recommended the test to "any adult woman with any family history of breast cancer" – a scenario specifically contemplated and rejected as warranting testing by the USPSTF guidelines. It would be tempting to identify this as a case of overtesting, but that does not seem to have been the case either. A third of physicians aware of BRCA testing, and one quarter of those who had ordered it, failed to identify the two scenarios most associated with the presence of a BRCA mutation.

This evidence is difficult to interpret, and may indicate a learning curve that clinical practices will, over time, correct. However, more recent evidence suggests that clinical practice remains behind the science. One study of breast cancer patients and their interactions with surgeons found that a quarter of surgeons who had a high volume of patients with breast cancer managed patients with variations of unknown clinical significance the same as those with BRCA1/2. Among low volume surgeons, that number rose to half (Kurian et al., 2017). Many patients with VUCS underwent surgery despite the lack of evidence supporting the procedure in such situations. The same survey found that up to a third of patients (and a quarter of high-risk patients) only received genetic testing *after* surgery (Kurian et al., 2017). According to another study, less than 20 percent of newly diagnosed patients meeting clinical criteria for testing had it, and most never discussed it with their doctors (Childers et al. 2017). Then again, the testing criteria may themselves not be particularly helpful. A 2018 study found no statistically significant difference in the percentage of mutation carriers between patients who met National Comprehensive Cancer Network screening criteria and those who did not (Bankhead, 2018).

Similar results were obtained at the level of patients. One 2010 study found that only half of patients at the highest risk of familial cancer had even heard of genetic testing, and only 15 percent of those had discussed it with a physician (Baer et al., 2010, p. 722). Awareness of testing is much higher now, due in part to the "Angelina Jolie effect," but awareness still differed widely among population groups. The 2010 study found that awareness of genetic testing among the general population was positively correlated with a personal history of cancer, education level, and living with a partner or spouse, and negatively correlated with being a current smoker, having poor self-rating health, or living in the South (p. 719). Subsequent research indicated that nonwhite patients were less likely to know about testing (Mai et al., 2014). The additional layer of insurance coverage makes matters even more complicated. Currently, ACA (Affordable Care Act)-compliant healthcare plans are required to cover USPSTF-recommended genetic testing without cost sharing. In practice, availability of "preventative" testing can be complicated by such factors as when the test is conducted; BRCA-testing a cancer patient can be considered "diagnostic" and not "preventative." More significantly, the coverage of testing does not necessarily translate into the availability of risk-reducing treatments like prophylactic surgery. As a result, many patients will be in a position of knowing they have a genetic risk but being unable to afford to do anything about it.[23]

In sum, what seems instead to be happening, at least on the basis of this evidence, is a separation of testing practices from any structural policy; only part of this separation is attributable to a lag between science and clinical practice. What policies are in place may be of limited guidance, and practitioners are often uncertain how to implement them in any case. In such a context, it is not surprising that many patients – at least those who can afford it – would resort to self-help, a strategy abetted by the rise of direct-to-consumer (DTC) marketing. DTC testing services – including those for breast cancer – present a radicalization of the actuarial tendencies seen in the BRCA testing and have been treated as a matter of some urgency by bioethicists. The primary issue here is that whatever clinical contexts that patients might have had in the case of BRCA testing are almost completely absent from these DTC testing services. Gaia Bernstein (2010) also notes that DTC tests are typically sold as a bundled package, meaning that patients are not free to select which ones they want. This lack of context renders the entire process one of greatly increased anxiety and uncertainty. As one discussion (Surbone, 2011) notes, there is little oversight of these practices, which trade upon the public's fear of cancer and limited understanding of genetics. Potentially disturbing outcomes include inappropriate referrals, misinterpretation of results, excessive anxiety about positives, false reassurances about negatives, and even the confusion between diagnostic genetic variants and surrogate genetic markers (which account for very little risk). As Bernstein (2010) notes, people are not very good at interpreting probabilities in general; they also tend to overestimate the importance of genetics relative to lifestyle and other causes of disease. These problems are magnified on DTC websites, which are generally designed to persuade as much as they are to inform, and which trade on an image of medical legitimacy and social narratives of empowerment and individualized responsibility (Schaper and Schicktanz, 2018). It is perhaps not surprising that one recent study found that, although evidence supports the proposition that clinical genetics counseling leads to better knowledge of genetics and

---

[23] See Prince (2015). As she concludes: "Genomic technologies and the ability to test asymptomatic individuals for adult-onset conditions have created a liminal state, between cultural and bureaucratic concepts of health and illness. These individuals are not experiencing symptoms, but due to genetic or genomic testing, know that they are at increased risk of a genetic condition or disease. Testing thus creates a kind of iatrogenic condition: a no man's land at odds [with a] US healthcare system that is rooted in treatment, not prevention."

greater personal control, DTC consumers reported lower levels of confidence in their ability to use genetic information after getting tested (Carere et al., 2016).[24]

The case of 23andMe.com is instructive. In 2013, the FDA sent an exasperated letter ordering the company to stop marketing its Personal Genome Service (PGS), which it claimed came under its regulatory authority insofar as the PGS is "intended for use in the diagnosis of disease or other conditions or in the cure, mitigation, treatment, or prevention of disease, or is intended to affect the structure or function of the body."[25] The FDA detailed its own efforts to "help" 23andMe come into compliance, and the company's apparent failure to take any of the suggested steps. The concern – well documented – was that consumers are poor judges of complicated, risk-based medical information, and 23andMe was therefore putting them at risk. The FDA specifically expressed concern about BRCA testing. The FDA then began relaxing its enforcement. By late 2017, the website was back online, advertising testing for "genetic health risks," including for late-onset Alzheimer's disease and Parkinson's Disease; for "carrier status" for conditions like cystic fibrosis; and how "genes play a role" in lifestyle decisions like "genetic weight" and lactose intolerance. All were marked as meeting FDA requirements. In early 2018, the FDA authorized 23andMe to test for some (but not all) BRCA mutations associated with cancer risk, though with some limitations and requirements for contextualizing information (Caryn Rabin, 2018).

5.2 THE *MYRIAD* LITIGATION

The first paper identifying the BRCA mutation and associating it with breast cancer was published in 1990.[26] In 1991, Marc Skolnick of the University of Utah began work trying to sequence the gene, using information from a database on Mormon families that Skolnick had been developing since the 1970s and cross-linking that database with the Utah Cancer Registry. Skolnick founded Myriad Genetics in 1991, obtaining funding from Eli Lily. In 1994, Myriad filed patent applications on the gene and its mutations prior to publishing its results in *Science* later that year. Over the next few years, Myriad solidified its patent portfolio around the BRCA gene, obtained patents for diagnostic tests, opened testing facilities, built a network of referring providers, and attempted to stop potential competitors by means of cease and desist letters. Myriad's business practices sat uneasily with the cancer research

---

[24] The authors caution that this evidence is difficult, and suggest that it probably indicates that the onslaught of information caused consumers to be better aware of their own limitations. Still, they underperformed on questions about whether most genetic disorders were caused by a single gene, suggesting the importance of counseling services.
[25] For the letter, see: www.fda.gov/ICECI/EnforcementActions/WarningLetters/2013/ucm376296.htm.
[26] This paragraph is based on the account in Gold and Carbone (2010). For radium and insulin, see the discussion in Chapter 2, which is based on Hemmungs Wirtén (2015) (for radium) and Cassier and Sinding (2008) (insulin).

community and, unlike the controversial patents around radium and insulin of the previous century, were not buttressed by public stewardship arguments.

Myriad's patents were eventually challenged in court, and a byzantine infringement litigation ensued. The initial district opinion invalidated all of Myriad's contested patents on summary judgment.[27] The Federal Circuit reversed in part, holding that isolated genetic fragments (both DNA and cDNA) were patentable, as were assays to find cancer-treating drugs. The Court of Appeals also affirmed that method claims about comparing or analyzing DNA sequences were unpatentable. On appeal, the Supreme Court first vacated and remanded the decision back to the appeals court for reconsideration in light of the Court's recent *Mayo* v. *Prometheus* (2012) decision.[28] On remand the Federal Circuit produced the same result.[29] On appeal, the Supreme Court agreed to hear the case, but only on the question of whether isolated human gene fragments are patentable, refusing to hear either a question about the compatibility of the Federal Circuit's opinion with Myriad's method claims or a question about who had standing to sue Myriad. The Supreme Court then unanimously ruled that isolated human genetic sequences were not patentable, although cDNA, produced from but not identical to mRNA, was patentable.

The patentability of isolated genetic fragments is important for at least two reasons. First, as the previous section indicates, the commercialization of testing services enabled by patentability has been a significant component and driver of the emergence of neoliberal genomic medicine. Although the Supreme Court invalidated the practice, and current science has moved away from testing isolated fragments, their presumed patentability during the 2000s both drove research in the field and allowed Myriad to establish a significant first-mover advantage that it has used to solidify its position in both the HBOC and other genetic screening markets. Second, the details of the litigation, and its eventual resolution by the Supreme Court, provide an excellent opportunity to see how different understandings of power drive different ways of conceptualizing the issues in the case.

5.2.1 *Myriad at Trial: It's Not That Different*

Lab-created life forms have been patentable for over a generation. The Supreme Court's first foray into this area was Diamond v. Chakrabarty (1980), which concerned the patentability of a lab-created, single-celled organism. *Chakrabarty*, which was decided in 1980, actually dates to 1972, and the development of a novel bacterium that was capable of breaking down many of the chemicals in crude oil. The Patent Examiner allowed claims both for the method of generating the bacteria

---

[27] *AMP* v. *USPTO* (S.D.N.Y. 2010), 702 F. Supp. 2d 181.
[28] *AMP* v. *Myriad* (2012), 566 U.S. 902. For *Mayo*, see the discussion later in this chapter.
[29] *AMP* v. *Myriad* (2012), 689 F.3d 1303.

and for techniques for delivering it, but denied that a bacterium could be patentable subject matter, since, as a living organism, it was a "product of nature." As the Supreme Court emphasized, the case was a narrow one of statutory interpretation. Did Chakrabarty's bacterium fall within the scope of patent-eligible subject matter? The statute reads:

Whoever invents or discovers any new and useful process, machine, manufacture, or composition of matter, or any new and useful improvement thereof, may obtain a patent therefor, subject to the conditions and requirements of this title (35 U.S.C. §101).

In a 5–4 decision, the Court applied a broad reading of "manufacture" to conclude that the bacterium is "plainly" patentable, since the "claim is not to a hitherto unknown natural phenomenon, but to a nonnaturally occurring manufacture or composition of matter – a product of human ingenuity" (*Chakrabarty*, p. 309).

The dissent proposed that the legislative history of two other statues – the Plant Patent Act of 1930 and the Plant Variety Protection Act of 1970 – indicated that Congress had considered extending patent protection to living organisms or even to bacteria, but had either implicitly (in the 1930 Act) or explicitly (with respect to bacteria, in 1970) refused to do so. The opinion debates both of these points; what I want to emphasize here is that neither the opinion nor the dissent debate the essential theoretical point, which is that living organisms can be the products of a manufacturing process. Since *Chakrabarty*, numerous living organisms have in fact become the subject of patent claims, with everything from varieties of pesticide-resistant plants to mice disposed to cancer. Indeed, it is probably not a stretch to say that *Chakrabarty* was a significant factor in creating the biotech industry as we know it today.

At the same time, however, one should emphasize that nothing about the *Chakrabarty* decision should be surprising. Once one accepts the principal point – that the bacteria in question do not exist in nature and cannot come to exist in nature without human intervention – the conclusion follows almost inevitably. The real issue emerges when the patented object's separation from nature is ambiguous, as is the case with isolated genetic fragments. In nature, these fragments only occur *in situ* as part of longer genetic sequences, and so they only exist as fragments as a result of human intervention. The question, then, is whether the act of removing them changes them enough that they qualify as "inventions" in a patent-eligible sense: Is the fragment the "same" as it was when *in situ*?

How one answers that question depends significantly on what one thinks the fragment is: Is it information, physical matter, or some sort of hybrid entity? The PTO and biotech industry had assumed that isolated fragments were patentable, and the appellate court in *Myriad* estimated that the PTO had issued 2,645 patents claiming "isolated DNA" in the preceding twenty-nine years, and the agency had issued rule guidelines in 2001 affirming that isolated DNA was patent-eligible

(*Myriad (Fed. Cir.)*, p. 1333). The *Myriad* district court relied on *Chakrabarty* to throw all of this in question, concluding that DNA fragments are not "markedly different" from DNA sequences in nature, and that the useful part of the fragment was the same as that found in nature.

The status of the fragment is not in any way obvious, and so the outcome of the case also hinges substantially on how one understands the kind of power expressed in IP, as that tends to coincide with a particular understanding of what the fragment is. A neoliberal biopolitics straightforwardly seems to support patentability, insofar as doing so encourages innovation by allowing those who isolate genetic code to capture the economic benefits of doing so. As long as the isolated fragments were somehow different from things found in nature, the ingenuity required to create those fragments ought to be rewarded; the view of IP provides a nudge for reading the fragment as sufficiently different to be patentable. A public biopolitics will tend to view the fragments as part of nature, and say that they are external to the invention process such that whatever benefits accrue from their isolation should not be amenable to capture by patents. For someone inclined to view patents this way, normative concerns about monopolies and entry barriers, here in the form of a worry about enclosing nature to future innovative work, will loom large. Here, the fragment may seem to be the same as its counterpart in nature. Finally, for someone inclined to view patents in terms of juridical rights, questions about what metaphysical changes in genetic code are cognizable will be less important than the correct application of judicial standards such as *de minimis* levels of novelty, as well as various limiting standards borrowed from real property law. As in the hip-hop sampling cases, the juridical question is not whether something has changed in a metaphysical sense, but whether it has changed *enough* to matter legally.

In the *Myriad* district opinion, Judge Sweet follows a juridical model, and his rejection of subject-matter patentability for isolated genetic sequences centers on two elements, both of which can be seen as efforts to impose juridical standards on the unruly biopolitical questions presented. The first is that analysis should look not just at differences between the material under review and its naturally occurring counterpart, but an "on the whole" analysis of the claimed invention. The second is to reject Myriad's claim that the functional differences between isolated DNA and naturally occurring DNA amount, on the whole, to a sufficient difference. His reasoning is essentially that the function of DNA both in isolation and naturally is the same. For example, "the cited utility of the isolated DNA as a primer or probe is primarily a function of the nucleotide sequence identity between native and isolated BRCA1/2 DNA" and "were the isolated *BRCA1/2* sequences different in any significant way, the entire point of their use – the production of BRCA1/2 proteins – would be undermined" (*Myriad (SDNY)*, p. 231). Accordingly:

> While the absence of proteins and other nucleotide sequences is currently required for DNA to be useful for the cited purposes, the purification of native DNA does not

alter its essential characteristic – its nucleotide sequence – that is defined by nature and central to both its biological function within the cell and its utility as a research tool in the lab. The requirement that the DNA used be "isolated" is ultimately a technological limitation to the use of DNA in this fashion, and a time may come when the use of DNA for molecular and diagnostic purposes may not require such purification. The nucleotide sequence, however, is the defining characteristic of the isolated DNA that will always be required to provide the sequence-specific targeting and protein coding ability that allows isolated DNA to be used for the various applications cited by Myriad. For these reasons, the use of isolated DNA for the various purposes cited by Myriad does not establish the existence of differences "in kind" between native and isolated DNA that would establish the subject matter patentability of what is otherwise a product of nature.

(Myriad (SDNY), pp. 231–232)

That is, it does not matter where the instructions are executed; they are the same instructions. This emphasis on their informatic component, when combined with a search for substantial differences, leads Judge Sweet to argue that isolated gene sequences should fail patentability because they are too similar to products of nature.

5.2.2 Myriad on Appeal: The Metaphysics of Difference

On appeal, the Federal Circuit reversed, focusing on the determination of the DNA not just as information but as embodied information. In so doing, the court addressed the case biopolitically. As it summarizes, "the [district] court relied on the fact that, unlike other biological molecules, DNAs are the 'physical embodiment of information,' and that this information is not only preserved in the claimed isolated DNA molecules, but also essential to their utility as molecular tools" (*Myriad (Fed. Cir.)*, p. 1317). Genetic sequences can be viewed both as information and as objects. How does one understand this duality in terms of patents?

The *Myriad* appellate decision resolves this issue by declaring that genetic sequences are patentable, even as they are understood informatically, as long as one simultaneously concludes that the information necessarily occurs in an embodied form. On the one hand, the argument emphasizes that the object status of information depends on the matter in which it is instantiated. On the other hand, it considers and then rejects a view according to which visualization can serve as a proxy for determining if information depends on the matter in which it is instantiated. Together, these reasons suggest that the (re)presentation of data is an act that produces a new object. The opinion rejects precisely the arguments Judge Sweet found persuasive:

The district court disparaged the patent eligibility of isolated DNA molecules because their genetic function is to transmit information. We disagree, as it is the distinctive nature of DNA molecules as isolated compositions of matter that

determines their patent eligibility rather than their physiological use or benefit ...
The claimed isolated DNA molecules are distinct from their natural existence as
portions of larger entities, and their informational content is irrelevant to that fact.
We recognize that biologists may think of molecules in terms of their uses, but
genes are in fact materials having a chemical nature and, as such, are best
described in patents by their structures rather than their functions. In fact, many
different materials may have the same function (e.g., aspirin, ibuprofen, and
naproxen).

(Myriad (Fed. Cir.), p. 1330)

As I will note later, the comparison to over-the-counter painkillers inadvertently
suggests the real limitation of the functional argument: It is unclear why marking
this particular function as essential renders other functional differences irrelevant.
After all, aspirin and ibuprofen both function by blocking the production of prosta-
glandins, but they do so differently, and have other effects which are different.

The court's language about similarity and difference is a proxy for a theoretical
distinction: All of the *value* lies in the content of the information, but the *information itself* is part of an object, and changes if the object surrounding it changes.
This distinction between the value of the information and the information itself in
turn allows the court to reject a strategy that emphasizes the more abstractly
understood informational character of the genetic code. As Katherine Hayles
(1999) and other scholars have reminded us, this is good metaphysics: The idea of
disembodied information, popularized by the growth of the Internet, is a myth. It is
also good neoliberal biopolitics because allowing the patentability of the genetic
sequence allows the internalization of that value, which would otherwise remain an
externality.

In the first oral argument, the government produced a test designed to separate
the information and the vehicle bearing it. According to this "magic microscope"
test, "if an imaginary microscope could focus in on the claimed DNA molecule as it
exists in the human body, the claim covers ineligible subject matter" (*Myriad (Fed.
Cir.)*, p. 1326). If Judge Sweet focuses on informational similarity, the magic
microscope test attempts to achieve an analogous result with a focus on visual
similarity. That is, the microscope attempts to keep the focus on the "chemical
nature" of the material in question, and to then provide a standard for showing that it
is the same. Given the logic of the information/value distinction, the court is bound
to reject this attempt at separation. Hence "the ability to visualize a DNA molecule
through a microscope, or by any other means, when it is bonded to other genetic
material, is worlds apart from possessing an isolated DNA molecule that is in hand
and usable. It is the difference between knowledge of nature and reducing a portion
of nature to concrete form, the latter activity being what the patent laws seek to
encourage and protect" (*Myriad (Fed. Cir.)*, p. 1331). Visualizing something does not
change it.

If the court's reasoning expresses biopolitics readily, it has difficulty precisely around questions of traditional juridical standards. This difficulty can be presented in the form of a dilemma. On one horn of the dilemma is the problem that if every isolation of something is constitutive of a new object, then virtually everything becomes patentable. Judge Sweet alluded to this risk in the district opinion, suggesting that, under Myriad's proposed logic, "it is difficult to discern how any invention could fail the test" since "there will almost inevitably be some identifiable differences between a claimed invention and a product of nature" (*Myriad (SDNY)*, p. 229). This is precisely why he attempted to focus on the "claimed invention as a whole," as noted earlier. The problem with that solution, as evidenced by the painkiller analogy, is that the proposed criterion for "sufficiently distinct" comes across as completely arbitrary.

The other horn of the dilemma is the problem that if one does not insist on treating all isolations as patentable, the choice of criteria for deciding which ones qualify also risks being wholly arbitrary. One needs some criterion for knowing when a candidate object can be taken as a humanly created artifact, as opposed to a mere natural occurrence. The government proposed visibility as a negative criterion: If I can see the same thing in nature, then a proposed object is not an artifact. The Court immediately detects the problem with this argument. The selection of visibility is entirely *ad hoc*; essential differences may well be invisible and have to do with the "structure" of the thing in question or to limitations imposed by the representing technology. However, the endpoint of that line of thinking is also not satisfactory, as there may always be something unrepresented in the object and the original to which it is being compared, such that the lack of represented difference does not prove that there is no difference. One still needs to know what kind of difference is important. Why, in other words, does chemical structure present the essence of something considered as an invention?

An example of this difficulty is raised by the dissent. If removing the DNA changes it, then why does removing a leaf from a tree not produce an analogous change? The majority replies that "snapping a leaf from a tree is a physical separation, easily done by anyone. Creating a new chemical entity is the work of human transformation, requiring skill, knowledge, and effort." The "skill, knowledge and effort" standard, however, itself seems wholly *ad hoc*. This becomes clear when the opinion rejects the dissent's analogy to removing a kidney:

> A kidney is an organ, not a well-defined composition of matter or an article of manufacture specified by §101. No one could confuse extensive research needed to locate, identify, and isolate a gene with the extraction of an organ from a body. One is what patents are intended to stimulate research on and hence are properly patent eligible, and the other, while obviously essential to human wellbeing, is not what patents are understood to cover under the patent statute.

(Myriad (Fed. Cir.), p. 1332)

But there can be no question that successful "isolation" of a kidney requires "skill, knowledge, and effort," as well as, presumably, "extensive research" at some point, even if the technique is standard now. The argument thus risks reducing to the idea that only whatever is currently at the cutting edge of research is patentable.

Both horns of the dilemma relate to the dual status of genetic code as object and information. Both horns of the dilemma also risk the imposition of seemingly arbitrary judicial criteria. This point is worth underscoring, because it highlights the biopolitical nature of the questions involved. In other words, it illustrates sharply the extent to which life processes themselves are becoming part of economic, social, and legal processes. The situation is analogous to the status of those on life support in persistent vegetative state, whose status as "living" or "dead" is as much a matter of political resolution as it is a natural one.[30] Litigation as to what constitutes nature – "life itself" – and what constitutes invention must be settled, with tremendous stakes for a significant portion of the economy.

5.2.3 *The Supreme Court's* Myriad *Decision*

In 2013, The Supreme Court unanimously ruled that Myriad could patent cDNA – a sequence of nucleotides generated from naturally occurring mRNA (cDNA contains only the coding exons found in the gene *in situ*, and not the noncoding introns) – but could not claim a patent on the isolated genetic sequence itself.[31] The Court proposed that "Myriad's principal contribution was uncovering the precise location and genetic sequence of the BRCA1 and BRCA2 genes within chromosomes 17 and 13" and then proceeded to address the question of whether "this renders the genes patentable" (*Myriad*, p. 2116). The Court produced three arguments to answer in the negative. First, relying on *Funk Brothers Seed Co. v. Kalo Inoculant Co.* (1948), the Court reasoned that Myriad's claim fell within the "law of nature" exception to patentability. On this argument, Myriad had *found* the BRCA gene mutations, but had not invented anything. *Funk* concerned a patent on a novel mixture of bacterial supplements designed to facilitate nitrogen fixing by legumes. Different legumes used different bacteria, and they had previously been sold separately, as it had been assumed that they mutually inhibited one another. Bond had discovered a set that did not do so, and so was able to produce a single product that could be used on multiple legumes. The Court begins by underlining that "the qualities of these bacteria, like the heat of the sun, electricity, or the qualities of metals, are … manifestations of laws of nature, free to all men and reserved

---

[30] One should note that statistical regularity allows gene patentability to escape an even more fundamental arbitrariness. That is, as the Supreme Court noted, "technically, there is no 'typical' gene because nucleotide sequences vary between individuals, sometimes dramatically" (*Myriad*, p. 2112). Both the normal and deviant sequences are statistical representations.

[31] The Court declined to revisit any other aspects of the case, allowing the lower court rejection of diagnostic patents to stand.

exclusively to none." The successful aggregation of these bacteria present "no more than the discovery of some of the handiwork of nature" and as such not patentable since "each species has the same effect it always had." As a result, the product amounted to "hardly more than an advance in the packaging" of the bacteria. (*Funk Bros.*, p. 131)

Second, the Court made similarly quick dispatch of the argument that the act of removing the nucleotides chemically altered them and therefore rendered them new. Pointing out that Myriad was interested in the information contained in the nucleotide, the Court pointed out that Myriad's reasoning would allow a competitor to avoid infringing on Myriad's patents by isolating the BRCA sequence plus one more nucleotide. Since the patent was awarded to a specific chemical composition, the competitor would escape infringement by virtue of having made something different. This argument points to the same problem of arbitrariness noted earlier: Treating all isolations as patentable makes everything patentable. Concluding that Myriad would resist this outcome on the grounds that it was the information contained in the nucleotide that the company was interested in, the Court concluded that the information in the isolated sequence was the same as that found in nature, and so was also subject-matter ineligible. Finally, the Court argued that there was no sufficient reason in this case to defer to the erroneous PTO practice of awarding patents to isolated genetic sequences, even if the practice had been a longstanding one.

This was the entire opinion, with the addition of a few caveats that it was not to be taken to deny patents on other aspects of the genetic testing process or the techniques for developing tests, and that the Court was not expressing an opinion on whether cDNA satisfied other standards for patent eligibility beyond §101. Still, the opinion harbors a significant and obvious difficulty in that the Court used competing logics in resolving the eligibility of isolated DNA and of cDNA. If the difference between the cDNA and the isolated DNA is that the former contains only coding exons, and the latter also contains noncoding "junk" introns, then it would seem that the information contained in both is identical.[32] Indeed, the Court's argument here seems rather difficult: "cDNA retains the naturally occurring exons of DNA, but it is distinct from the DNA from which it was derived. As a result, cDNA is not a 'product of nature' and is patent eligible under §101, except insofar as very short series of DNA may have no intervening introns to remove when creating cDNA. In that situation, a short strand of cDNA may be indistinguishable from natural DNA" (*Myriad*, p. 2119). In other words, the Court invokes the material differences between DNA and cDNA to grant patent eligibility to the latter, but uses the informatic identity between DNA *in situ* and isolated DNA to deny patent eligibility

---

[32] There may of course turn out to be an informatic distinction as well, since introns appear to be important in regulating gene expression. In other words, deleting them might be problematic. See Shaul (2017) for a recent survey.

to isolated DNA. The case thus leaves a significant question hanging: When is the criterion for novelty physical, and when is it informatic?

Dan Burk put this point particularly strongly, suggesting that the opinion was "at best incoherent," because:

> One is ... forced to conclude that molecules that differ structurally from a native molecule are both excluded from and included within patentable matter, while molecules with the same coding information as a native molecule are *also* both excluded from and included within patentable subject matter.

(2014, pp. 507–508)

There is also a wide potential impact to the decision, as "pharmaceutical and other chemical developers routinely extract useful organic molecules from a variety of native sources," and these molecules contain no coding sequences. This means that "depending on whether one believes that structure or information is the determining criterion in *Myriad*, it is difficult, and perhaps impossible, to fathom how Justice Thomas's reasoning is to be applied to the patent eligibility of such novel chemicals" (2014, p. 509). One problem with the *Myriad* decision is the lack of "a coherent theory as to why the differences in certain molecular characteristics should be overlooked in favor of the similarities in other characteristics" (2014, p. 516).

It seems to me that the Court is struggling to apply juridical understandings of power to the case of gene patenting, but in the service of a public biopolitical concern about excessive enclosure. This happens in at least two ways. First, struggling with the need to look at both the informatic and material aspects of DNA, the Court was attempting, if somewhat incoherently, to articulate a doctrine according to which the chemical composition had to change "enough" to override the informatic similarity. Even if it is not clear where the line is, it would arguably distinguish the case of extracted DNA sequences, which were modified only as much as necessary to extract them from an organism, as opposed to cDNA, which is missing all of the supposedly irrelevant introns. Such a result would align patent jurisprudence not just with precedent about mixing things, but with aspects of copyright, where some *de minimis* level of originality – and not just hard work – was declared by the Court to be requisite for copyright eligibility in *Feist* (1991), and which has figured prominently in more current litigation surrounding hip-hop sampling.

Second, the Court is assuming a sharp nature/art distinction of the sort that no longer makes sense in modern biology, given the importance of the material/informatic duality. As Bruno Latour and Donna Haraway both suggested some time ago, modern science is characterized by hybrid or cyborg entities that blur this distinction.[33] The move into a post-Fordist economy complicates the distinction yet

---

[33] See Haraway (1991) and Latour (1993). The original Aristotelian distinction was under considerable pressure in the seventeenth century; I discuss this point at length in the context of Thomas Hobbes in (2009b, pp. 25–34).

further when applied to patents. At noted earlier, statutory law defines patentable subject matter as "new and useful processes, machines, compositions or matter, or articles of manufacture" (35 U.S.C. §101). The schema works better in an industrial setting than a post-industrial one because all of these patentable things tended to occur in certain objects that could be claimed as patentable. As Burk notes, "products, at least to the extent that they constitute objects, are inherent in the concept of process ... Making and using entail some type of object: some *thing* is made, and some *thing* is used. In classic industrial setting, the substrates of the process were fairly apparent, and extant in what is now §101; machines and materials visibly interacted as inputs generating outputs" (2014, p. 527).

With the rise of immaterial goods and a post-Fordist economy, however, it is increasingly difficult to point to discrete things either at the level of product or process, and the ability to characterize immaterial goods informatically suggests that they could be understood as either thing or process. The computer software cases exemplify the problem, since "software defines a set of physical relationships that may model other relationships" and "software routinely collapses the usually comfortable distance between symbolic expression and physical instantiation, concomitantly collapsing the distance between laws of nature and their material substrates" (Burk, 2014, p. 529). These cases, however, are inconsistent and repeat many of the same problems; the work-around is usually in the claims-drafting process, where applicants emphasize the physical machines that are to run their software. Of course, such a strategy usually makes little sense from a computer science or coding standpoint.

On Burk's view, however, the conceptual confusion goes even deeper. Even if we could successfully distinguish processes and products, or laws of nature from their application, the more basic "laws of nature" exclusion itself is problematic because it fails to understand the interpretive work of science. Court decisions routinely cite Newton's laws, for example. However, those laws meet the criteria established in *Mayo* insofar as "a Newton or an Einstein constructs a model that entails the qualities or characteristics of the universe, but is not a quality or characteristic of the universe" (2014, p. 519) Evidence for this point is that Newton's laws have of course turned out limited in scope to certain macro-level measurements.

He concludes that what is really going on in those cases, taken as part of the "laws of nature" doctrine, is a judicial attempt to set the limits of what patents can cover:

> One might conclude that the jurisprudence of "laws of nature" is intended to push patentees toward narrower, more specific claims on tangible instantiations. This policy of maintaining fundamental access to critical constructs is probably correct, and is perhaps the most sensible reading of the process subject matter cases ... Excluding conceptual inventions from patent eligibility pushes exclusivity further downstream to the stage of finished products, requiring narrower claims on

concrete implementations, rather than allowing conceptual patents early in the development of a technology. This rationale makes far more sense than to claim that certain ideas are off-limits to the patent system because they are not the product of human invention.

(2014, p. 535)

Generally, "the degree of abstraction serves as a rough metric of the sort of claim breadth likely to preempt future uses" (2014, p. 540). The preemption doctrine suggested here is well known from real property law (if your property blocks the only access to a public beach, expect to be required to allow a pass-through of some sort), and has been suggested before in the context of gene patenting (Kane, 2004, 2011). Burk's construal of the opinion pushes it in the direction of the underlying public biopolitics, and away from the Court's effort at bright juridical lines. In moving away from the metaphysical question as to whether something "is" natural, it also tends to reopen questions about the monopoly power of patent owners. Forcing narrower claims would serve to increase the potential number of products in a given market. Something like a preemption doctrine would serve to limit the ability of patent owners to create entry barriers to new competitors, and might be viewed as akin to restraints on the ability of patent owners to restrict access to nonpatented products by way of tying arrangements.

5.2.4 *What Happens after* Myriad?: *Entrenching Actuarial Agency*

Myriad imposed a juridical limit on the patentability of life itself. It also may not make a difference. There are, indeed, at least two broad ways in which *Myriad* might even push medicine in an even more biopolitical direction. As with the case of trademark disparagement, the application of juridical rules may serve to limit public biopolitics more than it limits neoliberalism. The first way, which would tend to promote a neoliberal version of biopolitics, has to do with its indirect promotion of actuarial agency. The second, which is characteristic of biopolitical regimes generally, is about the promotion of administrative regulation. Narrowly, the use of isolated genetic sequences in testing was becoming scientifically obsolete by the time of the decision, and analysis published immediately before the decision suggested that almost no matter what it said, it would be of limited impact (Offit et al., 2013). One effect was the rapid development of price competition in the genetic testing market, with the result that the cost for testing dropped from over $3,000 in 2013 to nearly $250 in 2017. At the same time, Myriad retained its position as a dominant market player, largely because the presumption of patentability under which it had operated allowed it to accumulate the best dataset of BRCA mutation tests and test results. Myriad's initial monopoly, in other words, allowed it to construct a substantial first-mover advantage, which it was able to use as an entry barrier to competitors. That is, the monopoly allowed both higher pricing and the creation of entry barriers; absent that monopoly, the price quickly dropped, but the entry barriers remained.

More significantly, the complexity of genetic risk assessment is rapidly increasing with the advance of the technologies behind it. Not only are genes more or less penetrant, but "the risk of cancer at a given site may be elevated by mutations in one of a number of different genes, and a mutation in a particular gene often increases risk for more than one type of cancer" (Domchek et al., 2013). Genetic panels are now often multiplex, with multiple sequences tested in parallel, a "qualitatively different" procedure from serial testing, and one that vastly increases the complexity of results. Recent research indicates that two-thirds of women with breast cancer who receive genetic screening now get multiple-gene sequencing, rather than only BRCA1/2 sequencing. In 2013, by contrast, that number was only 25 percent (Kurian et al., 2018). Allison Kurian, the lead author of the study, suggests that, as a result of *Myriad*, testing for multiple genes is now cheaper than it used to be for BRCA1/2 alone (Ingram, 2018). In this sense, while the pre-*Myriad* regime encouraged the development of testing, and *Myriad* prevented the internalization of all the gains from the BRCA1/2 sequence, it nevertheless made the move to individualized risk even more prominent. The specific timing of the patentability of isolated genetic fragments served as a ladder that Myriad no longer needs.

In this regard, what happened after the *Myriad* decision is not a surprise. Although the decision relied on informatic similarity to reject gene patenting, it endorsed the patentability of cDNA. As long as introns continue to be irrelevant to genetic testing, cDNA is the functional equivalent of DNA for informatic purposes. *Myriad* thus encouraged a key component of a clinical regime of more patented DNA tests that attempt to produce a risk profile for developing various conditions. In that sense, even though it invoked juridical standards to impose limits on subject matter patentability, it further entrenched a world where patent law, at least in the case of medicine, is a dispositive of neoliberal biopower.

The second broad way that *Myriad* (and other recent §101 cases) might inadvertently serve to further the biopoliticization of IP is through an indirect promotion of administrative regulation over property law. Indeed, as I will discuss, the Court in the 2018 *Oil States* decision endorsed a narrow application of administrative procedure to assess claims against patent validity. In this context, as Anne Laakmann notes, the ambiguity created around subject-matter eligibility by *Myriad* and the other §101 cases may push firms to eschew juridical IP claims, relying instead on trade secrecy. The case thus risks undermining its own defense of the public domain, since trade secrets both lack the publication requirement associated with patents and can potentially last much, much longer. In the absence of patent protection, or ambiguity over what is protected, "inventors of new algorithms for interrogating and interpreting data may turn to secrecy as a means to appropriate the value of patent-ineligible discoveries" (2016, p. 145). This, in turn, creates incentives to create new regulatory policy to encourage the dissemination and publication of such information. Again, Laakmann: "in areas in which patent eligibility is uncertain, the regulatory system can be structured to create alternative incentives for innovators to generate and disclose information resources" (2016, p. 156). To be sure, such policies have not been enacted as of this writing. However, Laakmann makes the case that they would be efficient in the absence of property rights, and perhaps even administratively superior to property rights. As I will note in Chapter 6, the absence of property rights does not entail the absence of politics and there is no reason to expect that innovators will cease to attempt to internalize as many of the gains of their research as possible. The absence of property as a governmental strategy might in this case result in its replacement by administration.

At the same time, the particular structure of administrative regulation in the United States favors a neoliberal model of biopolitics. Evidence for this is that Myriad's primary problems did not occur in the privatized US healthcare system, where both a regulatory focus on individual patient outcomes and a general acceptance of various strategies of risk segmentation and differential bearing of risk are widely accepted. The problems instead occurred in countries with strong public health programs, such as Canada and France. Gold and Carbone suggest that this was the fundamental problem underlying Myriad's difficulties in these countries: Although critics of the company would cite legal issues, those criticisms "miss a more fundamental tension: that between commercialization practices and the administration of public health care systems" (2010, p. 41).

These public health agencies were charged with seeing to the best overall public health, given the expectation that the BRCA test was at the leading edge of a wave of expected and expensive new genetic tests. Integrating these tests into the larger picture of public health was important, and administrators insisted on their own prerogative in negotiating and setting these priorities. Thus, Gold and Carbone suggest that a "focus on legal rights is misleading since when legal rights conflicted with business and governmental norms and with institutional structures, it was the set of legal rights that were of least significance" (2010, p. 41).

The core problem is that, as noted earlier, the payers in the United States are individuals who will have varying degrees of insurance coverage, both for the test and any follow-up treatment. Although the ACA instituted a degree of health-system quasi-policy into the mix, it still leaves considerable variability as to what sorts of treatments patients can access (Prince, 2015). On the other hand, "outside the US, the purchasers of the test were not, for the most part, individual patients, but publicly administered health systems" (2010, p. 43). Particularly in Canada, regulatory and public health agencies had difficulty in reconciling Myriad's insistence on the adoption of its own (expensive) gold-standard test to the exclusion of others, when the agencies needed instead to find "the most effective overall combination of tests and counseling to detect and treat breast cancer" (2010, p. 44). This sense of a collective, integrated policy goal is largely absent from the US system. For example, research into the US system has expressed concern that the *de facto* US public policy of privatizing health education and health services provision might lead vulnerable populations receiving DTC marketing for the BRCA test to then ignore more important public health messages, like the need for traditional screening (Schillinger and Dohan, 2008). As one paper comparing the US and European experiences put it, "in a context in which consumers have to take on more and more responsibility for their own health, it is understandable that there is an increased interest in do-it-yourself testing schemes. The organization of the public healthcare system in Europe may be less stimulating in that respect" (Borry and Howard, 2008, pp. 14–15). Myriad did not seek to understand how to position itself in countries with strong public health programs, where administering the test had to be understood in the context of public health objectives, and not as a function of consumer demand.

5.3 THE SUPREME COURT VERSUS NEOLIBERAL PATENTS

The preceding discussion of the *Myriad* litigation is intended to underscore the complexity of the relations between patents on the one hand and subjectivity and the economy on the other. It is also intended to highlight the different ways that different models of IP as juridical, public biopolitical, or neoliberal biopolitical generate different readings of the same issue. In *Myriad*, the Supreme Court decided against patent eligibility, somewhat incoherently attempting to do so on juridical grounds. The present section looks at two further kinds of efforts by the Supreme Court to press back against the logic of neoliberal patenting. In the first part, I contextualize the *Myriad* decision in the context of other recent cases attempting to restrict subject matter eligibility. In the second part, I look at a recent decision on patent exhaustion, the primary logic of which, I will argue, is grounded in the Court's rejection of one application of Chicago school antitrust doctrine.

5.3.1 *Narrowing Patent Eligibility Juridically*

Beyond *Myriad*, the Supreme Court has been trying to restrict patent rights for over a decade now, even if its decisions have not always been greeted as models of clarity. In *Bilski* v. *Kappos* (2010), the Court ruled in a divided 5-4 opinion that a claimed business method failed subject-matter patentability by virtue of being an abstract idea. Justice Kennedy's opinion for the Court ruled somewhat narrowly on these grounds. In a concurrence, Justice Stevens (joined by Ginsburg, Breyer, and Sotomayor) argued at length that it would have been better simply to reject business methods patents. Not only are business method patents historically dubious, allowing them would also be bad for competition: They are unnecessary for innovation, close off the "basic tools of commercial work" (*Illinois Tool Works*, p. 653), and would leave business people under constant threat of litigation for even

quotidian decisions.[34] The basic contours of subject matter eligibility and its exceptions date to 1853, in which the Supreme Court ruled in *LeRoy* v. *Tatham* that "a
principle is not patentable" (*Tatham*, p. 175).[35] These recent opinions might collectively be read as an effort to reassert the basic parameters of that decision, as *Bilski*
inaugurated something of a pattern. Here I will show how these cases invoke
juridical standards in the service of promoting a biopolitics governed by public
interest.

In *Mayo v. Prometheus* (2012), the Court – this time unanimously – further specified
the abstract ideas exclusion in a case about drug dosing. Earlier precedent distinguished between unpatentable abstract ideas and their potentially patentable "application." In *Mayo*, the claimed patents "purport to apply natural laws describing the
relationships between the concentration in the blood of certain thiopurine metabolites
and the likelihood that the drug dosage will be ineffective or induce harmful side-
effects" (*Mayo*, p. 1294). In other words, different patients respond differently to the
drugs in question, and the procedures in question assisted doctors in titrating the drugs
based on metabolite levels present in a patient's blood after an initial dose. The Court
concluded that this application did not satisfy §101 eligibility. It first ruled that the
claimed processes did little more than state the laws of nature and direct doctors to
apply them; it then expressed a worry about the excessive enclosure of nature and the
potential effects that would have on innovation. The first arguments exhibit juridical
reason; the second present what I have been calling a public biopolitics.

Let us consider the juridical aspects of the opinion first. According to the second
prong of the so-called machine or transformation test, something can satisfy patent
eligibility if it transforms an article from one state to another. The Court rejected the
analysis of the Federal Circuit, according to which:

> In addition to these natural correlations, the claimed processes specify the steps of
> (1) "administering a [thiopurine] drug" to a patient and (2) "determining the
> [resulting metabolite] level." These steps, it explained, involve the transformation
> of the human body or of blood taken from the body. Thus, the patents satisfied the
> Circuit's "machine or transformation test," which the court thought sufficient to
> "confine the patent monopoly within rather definite bounds," thereby bringing the
> claims into compliance with §101.
>
> (*Mayo*, p. 1296)

---

[34] *Bilski* was the Court's first foray into §101 since 1981, and the analysis was sufficiently murky that
two prominent patent academics argued that §101 subject-matter patentability analysis be
avoided when any other means of challenging a patent were available, showing empirically
that patents challenged on §101 grounds were usually challenged on other grounds as well. As
they conclude, "under the circumstances, it is best not to try to map the swampy terrain of
§ 101 in any great detail. Whenever possible, we argue, try something else: just avoid it"
(Crouch and Merges, 2010, p. 1691).

[35] For the argument that the basic contours of the patent system were set in the nineteenth
century, see Reilly (2018).

It is worth noting that the appellate court's reasoning was very similar to what it later produced in *Myriad*: Here, taking the blood from the body and measuring it constitutes a transformation of the blood, and administering drugs to the body change the body. This line of reasoning is flatly rejected by the Supreme Court, which argues instead for the need for juridical principle. This distinction is perhaps most clearly expressed in two places. The first is when the Court considers Prometheus' claim that removal of the blood transforms it. In response, Justice Breyer suggests for the Court that the claimed removal transformation was irrelevant insofar as this "step could be satisfied without transforming the blood, should science develop a totally different system for determining metabolite levels that did not involve such a transformation." In other words, the current status of scientific processes is irrelevant to the legal principles of patentability. The second is when the Court rejects an argument in a government brief that §101 be interpreted very broadly (and the patents perhaps rejected on other grounds); the Court objects that this "would make the 'law of nature' exception to §101 patentability a dead letter" (*Mayo*, p. 1303).

When considering the application question, Justice Breyer first notes that the claims in question recite laws of nature, i.e., the "relationships between concentrations of certain metabolites in the blood and the likelihood that a dosage of a thiopurine drug will prove ineffective or cause harm" (*Mayo*, p. 1296). To be patentable as an application of the law of nature, the claim needs to do more than "recite a law of nature and then add the instruction 'apply the law'" (*Mayo*, p. 1297).[36] The claims in question, Breyer reasons, do little more than that:

> Beyond picking out the relevant audience, namely those who administer doses of thiopurine drugs, the claim simply tells doctors to: (1) measure (somehow) the current level of the relevant metabolite, (2) use particular (unpatentable) laws of nature (which the claim sets forth) to calculate the current toxicity/inefficacy limits, and (3) reconsider the drug dosage in light of the law. These instructions add nothing specific to the laws of nature other than what is well-understood, routine, conventional activity, previously engaged in by those in the field. And since they are steps that must be taken in order to apply the laws in question, the effect is simply to tell doctors to apply the law somehow when treating their patients.
>
> (*Mayo*, pp. 1299–1300)

---

[36] Breyer adduces the following examples by way of explanation: "Einstein, we assume, could not have patented his famous law by claiming a process consisting of simply telling linear accelerator operators to refer to the law to determine how much energy an amount of mass has produced (or vice versa). Nor could Archimedes have secured a patent for his famous principle of flotation by claiming a process consisting of simply telling boat builders to refer to that principle in order to determine whether an object will float" (*Mayo*, p. 1297). The logic recalls *Funk Bros.* insofar as that decision also relied on treating the novel use or arrangement of natural processes as noninventive, insofar as the processes did the same thing in the claimed invention as they did outside it.

Breyer did not invoke the term, but the standard is essentially that there is a *de minimis* floor below which the concept of "application" has no meaning, and that Prometheus fails to clear that bar.[37]

The 2014 *Alice* v. *CLS Bank* decision (again, unanimously) affirmed this line of reasoning, arguing that "the mere recitation of a generic computer cannot transform a patent-ineligible abstract idea into a patent-eligible invention." *Alice* is important, both because it has been highly influential and because it shows that the problem of §101 patent eligibility is a larger problem for the information economy than just biotechnology. In *Alice*, the Court invalidated as an abstract idea a scheme for mitigating "settlement risk, *i.e.*, the risk that only one party to an agreed-upon financial exchange will satisfy its obligation. In particular, the patent claims are designed to facilitate the exchange of financial obligations between two parties by using a computer system as a third-party intermediary." The court reasoned that the claims were directed to "the abstract idea of intermediated settlement" and that they "merely require generic computer implementation," thereby "fail[ing] to transform that abstract idea into a patent-eligible invention." They thus failed to meet the standards for subject-matter eligibility articulated in *Myriad* and *Mayo* (*Alice*, p. 2349). Citing *Mayo*'s rejection of "apply it," the Court here rejects stating an abstract idea while adding the words "apply it with a computer" (*Alice*, p. 2350). As with *Feist*'s search for originality in copyright, the Court here searches for an "inventive concept" that is "sufficient to assure that the patent in practice amounts to significantly more than a patent upon the [ineligible concept] itself" (*Alice*, p. 2355). That juridical search in turn is motivated by a concern about avoiding preemption, the enclosure of abstract ideas, which are a "basic tool" of scientific work. In other words, the assumption is that monopoly in such cases is bad for innovation, and whether monopolies can be efficient is not a concern the court emphasizes.

Alice favorably cites (*Alice*, p. 2354) both *Bilski* and a pair of mid-nineteenth century cases, *O'Reilly* v. *Morse* (1854) and *LeRoy* v. *Tatham* (1853). *Mayo* had similarly cited the trio of cases (*Myriad* oddly cited none of them). *O'Reilly* concerned the printing mechanism in telegraph machinery, and is particularly helpful in seeing the context. In it, the Supreme Court invalidated a claim by Samuel Morse to (in Justice Taney's words) "every improvement where the motive power is the electrical or galvanic current, and the result is the marking or printing [of] intelligible characters, signs, or letters at a distance" (*O'Reilly*, p. 112). Taney adds that "if this claim can be maintained, it matters not by what process or machinery the result is accomplished" (p. 113). An independent and different way

---

[37] This is not to say that the resulting "inventive concept" standard is successful, merely that this appears to be what the Court is attempting to do. For a collection of critiques of "inventive concept," see Taylor (2019). It seems important here to recognize that the juridical standard is in the service of limiting the enclosure of nature.

to get to the letters, even if superior, would be covered, and "the inventor could not use it, nor the public have the benefit of it, without the permission of the patentee" (*O'Reilly*, p. 113). In short, the patent eligibility cases, following a genealogy that the Court invokes fairly consistently, and following a logic similar to the "public franchise" language we will see in *Oil States*, underscores that the public is the focus of the basis for patents.

With respect to effects on future innovation, the *Mayo* court concludes by making a biopolitical claim by looking at public policy and the risk of foreclosing future invention. In so doing, it cites scholarship by notable patent scholars whose work is informed by law and economics, notably a paper by Mark Lemley (and others) (Lemley et al., 2011), as well as the canonical book by Landes and Posner on *The Economic Structure of Intellectual Property Law*. The concern with enclosure, as noted in the introductory section, expresses an anxiety about blurring the boundaries between art and nature, and is precisely the way that a concern over monopoly power would manifest itself in this context. As I noted earlier, Dan Burk (2014) has suggested that the concern about excessive patentability and enclosure is one way of providing a coherent reading to cases like *Myriad* and the invocation of subject-matter eligibility, one that minimizes the somewhat difficult juridical determinations as to what constitutes nature or application. Burk (2016) suggests that the *Alice* test has proven to be difficult, and the Federal Circuit has issued both opinions that would tend to substantially restrict patentability using it, and ones that would offer a wider scope. In particular, it is difficult to conceptualize a criterion to decide when something is too abstract to satisfy criteria for patentability. He underscores again that concern about preemption that could provide a unifying thread to a more coherent review process. In any case, the Federal Circuit seems to be using the *Alice* test as a mechanism for restricting patent eligibility; in 2017, only four of fifty-eight patents challenged under §101 were upheld by the court; in each of the three precedential cases, the court found that the claims in question were not directed to abstract ideas (Ouellette, 2018).[38]

5.3.2 *Patent Exhaustion*

In 2017, the Supreme Court ruled in *Impression Products* v. *Lexmark International* that the sale of a patented product "exhausts" the patent holder's claim to derive patent revenue from that particular article, at least as a matter of patent law. A brief background is in order. Printer toners are like razor blades: companies charge

---

[38] It is worth noting that the pattern of limiting patentability applies to more than just §101. For example, the unanimous *KSR* v. *Teleflex* (2007) expressed similar skepticism about obviousness (§103 of the statute). *Teleflex* evidences similar concern about the public utility of patents; thus awarding patents to innovation that would likely occur in "the ordinary course without real innovation retards progress and may, in the case of patents combining previously known elements, deprive prior inventions of their value or utility" (*Teleflex*, p. 419).

extravagant prices for the toner without which their printers will not operate, while selling the printer itself fairly cheaply. Such a strategy creates secondary markets in toner, either in third-party cartridges that are designed to be compatible with the printer or in strategies for refilling used cartridges. Naturally, printer companies hate these secondary markets, and so engage in all sorts of strategies to suppress them. They warn consumers that using nonproprietary cartridges will cause poor print quality and void their warranty. They design their devices to try to detect off-brand toner, and refuse to operate if it is installed. They also litigate, although those efforts often fail. For example, in 2004, the Sixth Circuit ruled that efforts to circumvent a cartridge-detection system did not violate copyright law.[39]

In *Impression Products*, Lexmark had sued a manufacturer of aftermarket ink cartridges, which obtained used cartridges from either overseas markets or from consumers who had emptied them. The manufacturer then refilled and sold them. Lexmark argued that its exclusive rights should extend to the resold cartridges. In ruling against Lexmark, the Supreme Court relied primarily on what it took to be settled common law on property alienation: When you sell something, you don't get to derive revenue from subsequent sales.[40] If Lexmark wanted to try to extend its patent rights, the company could contractually forbid users to give their spent cartridges to companies like Impression, for example, but that would be a matter of contract law, not property. Patents, the court declared, are a species of property, and patent rights are exhausted – i.e., end – when the patented product is sold.

The opinion is brief and nearly unanimous. Here is Justice Roberts:

> This case presents two questions about the scope of the patent exhaustion doctrine: First, whether a patentee that sells an item under an express restriction on the purchaser's right to reuse or resell the product may enforce that restriction through an infringement lawsuit. And second whether a patentee exhausts its patent rights by selling its product outside the United States, where American patent laws do not apply. We conclude that a patentee's decision to sell a product exhausts all of its patent rights in that item, regardless of any restrictions the patentee purports to impose or the location of the sale.
>
> (*Impression Products*, p. 1529)

In immediate reaction, the decision was hailed as a victory for consumers (Roberts, 2017). It also aligns patent exhaustion jurisprudence – which is entirely a judicial artifact – more closely with statutory copyright first-sale doctrine.

Impression Products clearly established a juridical bright line on patent exhaustion. What is less evident from the opinion is that it pushes back against neoliberal orthodoxy on the topic, as promulgated by Chicago-style law and economics. As noted in Chapter 2, law and economics drops the aversion to monopolies

---

[39] See *Lexmark International, Inc.* v. *Static Control Components, Inc.* 387 F.3d (2004).
[40] For criticism of this reading of the common law, see Hovenkamp (2018).

characteristic of public biopolitics. Shortly after the *Impression Products* decision was announced, Herbert Hovenkamp, a leading patent scholar, pronounced judgment on behalf of contemporary antitrust doctrine: The decision was a poor one because it "stated what amounts to a *per se* rule," such that "no further inquiry is made into the patentee's market power, anticompetitive effects, or other types of harms, whether enforcement of the condition is socially costly or valuable, or has a positive or negative impact on innovation" (2018, p. 515). The inquiries that Hovenkamp wanted to see are precisely the ones that have become central to law-and-economics-based antitrust litigation; as noted in the discussion of neoliberal theory, precisely this opposition to *per se* judicial rules substantially motivated the Chicago reconception of monopoly. *Per se* rules were to be replaced with empirical and evidence-based "rules of reason" designed to require a showing of actual market harm, and not just its presumption. The problem with *Impression Products*, in other words, is that it failed to use Chicago antitrust theory in assessing patent exhaustion; moreover "no good reason exists why the appropriate rule for patent policy" on alienation "should be any different than the rule for antitrust policy" (2018, p. 538).

Post-sale restraints on patents are typically, and were in this case, vertical insofar as they operate between a seller and buyer rather than between sellers. Hovenkamp argues that "decades of litigation under the antitrust laws has concluded that vertical restrictions should be treated more benignly than horizontal agreements involving competitors" and that they are appropriately assessed by rule of reason analysis (2018, p. 517). Specifically, tying agreements such as the one overturned in *Impression Products* are by "general although not unanimous consensus among antitrust economists" thought both to increase output and to be consumer welfare enhancing, "perhaps by a wide margin" (2018, p. 518). Hovenkamp then cites two consumer-welfare-enhancing effects – a decrease in the price of printers and increased welfare for low-intensity users; this is to be balanced against the reduction in welfare for high-intensity users (2018, p. 518).

The difference between pre- and post-Chicago views of antitrust law as it applies to patent exhaustion is notable in two areas Hovenkamp cites. The first has to do with restricting downstream uses of a patented product. In *U.S. v. Univis Lens* (1942), the Supreme Court overturned on both exhaustion and antitrust grounds a provision requiring a minimum price on downstream products made with a patented product. In distinction from this, the Federal Circuit had more recently been using patent exhaustion doctrine to distinguish unconditional from conditional sale of patented things. Patent rights were exhausted by an unconditioned sale of a patented thing, but downstream usage restrictions could be enforced when "the limiting condition was clear and simultaneous with (or announced prior to) the sale" (Hovenkamp, 2018, p. 527). The Supreme Court did not rule on patent exhaustion again until 2008, in a case that was "insufficiently clear about the condition requirement" that *Impression Products* finally rejected (p. 532). In this sense, *Impression Products* was more like the 1942 decision than either the 2008 case or current practice.

The second area is patent misuse. Also in 1942, the Supreme Court had ruled in *Morton Salt v. Suppiger*. Morton and Suppiger both sold unpatented salt tablets used in canning food, and Suppiger also owned the rights to a machine for depositing the tablets. Suppiger had filed an infringement claim against a similar machine made by Morton, but the decision revolved around Suppiger's practice of leasing its machines to commercial canners on the condition that they purchase salt tablets only from Suppiger. The Court based its decision on the anticompetitive nature of the tie on the salt tablet market, emphasizing the "public interest" behind patent policy. It concluded that:

> Where the patent is used as a means of restraining competition with the patentee's sale of an unpatented product, the successful prosecution of an infringement suit, even against one who is not a competitor in such sale, is a powerful aid to the maintenance of the attempted monopoly of the unpatented article, and is thus a contributing factor in thwarting the public policy underlying the grant of the patent.

(*Suppiger*, p. 493)

That is, Suppiger's use of the patent to facilitate anticompetitive behavior in the salt tablet market rendered the patent on the depositing machine unenforceable. In 1944, in the first of the Court's *Mercoid* decisions, Justice Jackson had written for the Court that "the fact that the patentee has the power to refuse a license does not enable him to enlarge the monopoly of the patent by the expedient of attaching conditions to its use." He underscored that it is "the public interest which is dominant in the patent system" and that "the patent is a privilege. But it is a privilege which is conditioned by a public purpose" (*Mercoid*, pp. 665–666). This use of concerns about monopoly to emphasize the public nature of pre-neoliberal IP should by now be familiar.

Decisions such as *Mercoid* were also a substantial part of the impetus for the 1952 patent reform legislation, one aspect of which was to protect patent rights from antimonopoly-based patent-misuse decisions (Taylor, 2019). Indeed, the appellate decision that *Impression Products* overturned made specific reference to these cases, noting that Congress had acted both in 1952 and 1988 to restrict patent misuse doctrine (*Lexmark v. Impression*, p. 749 n11). As recently as 2006, the Supreme Court distanced itself from *Mercoid* and other earlier decisions, noting that "this Court's strong disapproval of tying arrangements has substantially diminished." Thus, as someone trained in recent antitrust theory would expect, "rather than relying on assumptions, in its more recent opinions the Court has required a showing of market power in the tying product" (*Jungersen*, p. 35).

Impression Products ignored *Illinois Tool Works* and distinguished the older cases on the (somewhat shaky) grounds that they were not actually about the patent right, but were about sales that violated antitrust laws of the time. *Impression Products* also, probably because the case did not quite fit, ignored the 1988 Act, and was thereby also able to ignore both considerations of market power and conditional sales that would be more familiar to empirically driven neoclassical antitrust analysis. In both downstream restrictions and patent misuse, what happened between 1942 and now, and what makes the logic of *Impression Products* seem anomalous, was the incorporation of antitrust law into Chicago law and economics, and the presumptive parallel between post-sale enforcement of patent restrictions and questions of vertical integration.

In short, the significance of *Impression Products* lies less, perhaps, in the price of toner cartridges, and more in the Supreme Court's rejection of a specific theory of antitrust. In this regard, the case recalls (but does not cite) *FTC v. Actavis* (2013) decided four years earlier. *Actavis* is important in this context because the Court explicitly rejects Chicago school orthodoxy on antitrust. In *Activis*, the Court invalidated what had become a fairly common practice, at least within the pharmaceutical industry, so-called pay-to-delay. Essentially, patent holders would settle with potential generic manufacturers: The generic manufacturers would drop claims against the patent's viability in return for a substantial payment and an agreed-upon delay in entering the market. The gist of Justice Breyer's opinion is that these settlements were being used to shut down challenges to the patent's validity, challenges that had been encouraged by the 1984 Hatch-Waxman Act. In so doing, the settlements could be subject to antitrust regulation, since they potentially stifled competition. The issue was whether the dictum that patent holders could do anything within the scope of their patent monopoly could extend to buying-out efforts to question the legitimacy of that monopoly. Breyer's answer was that they could not.

Writing in dissent, Chief Justice Roberts explicitly endorses the Chicago school's framing of the relation between monopoly and competition: "the majority invokes 'pro-competitive antitrust policies,' but misses the basic point that patent laws promote consumer interests in a different way, by providing protection against competition" (*Actavis*, p. 174). He then cites Hovenkamp, Janis, Lemley, and Leslie's *Intellectual Property and Antitrust* for the proposition that "patent policy encompasses a set of judgments about the proper trade-off between competition and the incentive to innovate over the long run" (qt. *Actavis*, p. 174). In other words, IP is a matter of dynamic efficiency, the promotion of which trumps static considerations about market competitiveness, on the theory that consumer welfare will thereby be benefitted more.

Despite the citation, Hovenkamp (2015, p. 328) argues at length that *Actavis* reached the right result. For Hovenkamp, Roberts' argument is compromised by an overreliance on the question of what is "within the scope" of the patent, and the use of that question to shield patentholders from scrutiny. Just as an ordinary property claim does not license all behavior on the property, the presence of a valid patent claim should not exempt the patentholder from all scrutiny. The conceptual core of Hovenkamp's position is to focus on competitiveness and the potential of pay-to-delay settlements to reduce competition. Hovenkamp points out that, because the entry of a generic reduces drug prices so sharply, the total revenue from a patented drug that is sold exclusively by the patentee until the end of the patent duration is likely higher than the total revenue from the patented drug and a single generic competitor, as contemplated by the Hatch-Waxman Act. In that situation, the patentee and potential competitor have an incentive to divide that surplus between themselves; the competitor agrees not to go to market until the patent would expire anyway, and they settle on a payment based on their estimate of the strength of the patent. Because Hatch-Waxman prohibits any other challenges to the patent, the settlement protects the revenue from the patent from future challenges. The result is a guaranteed delay in the introduction of generics and a guaranteed reduction in challenges to dubious patents. Allowing such schemes is thus anticompetitive.[41] This competition-oriented argument is the sort of thing that pre-Chicago antitrust law favored, though Hovenkamp's analysis of market incentives moves beyond earlier application of *per se* rules.

The counterargument, implied by Roberts, is that the monopolies generated by patents are necessary for innovation, and that greater dynamic efficiency is more important than whatever static inefficiency is caused by a decrease in competition. As noted earlier, this should be easily recognizable neoliberal theory. Hovenkamp addresses the argument by way of an analysis of expected returns on pharmaceutical innovation. Citing evidence that patented drugs face rapidly diminishing market value due to the emergence of competing "me too" drugs, he suggests that the value added by pay-to-delay represents an extension on the return to the patent beyond what the patentee would have expected under ordinary conditions. Certainly Hovenkamp's position does not retreat from the general proposition that antitrust law should concern itself with consumer welfare. The tendency of patents to generate me-too drugs, for example, might be efficient from a consumer welfare standpoint, but it can readily be seen to be a problem for *social* welfare insofar as it diverts resources away from undertreated diseases like malaria and into things like multiple remedies for erectile dysfunction. That broader question does not enter the analysis here. The analysis does, however, emphasize the extent to which "competition" can be important even to consumer welfare, against a default position that patents, because putatively pro-innovation, are for that reason pro-consumer welfare.

5.4 ARE PATENTS PROPERTY?

The 2011 America Invents Act specifies that the validity of patents, in terms of whether they meet conditions of patentability (utility, nonobviousness, and

---

[41] "Congress did not foresee that this situation creates an opportunity that is well known in the history of collusion: sharing the monopoly profit is a better outcome for the cartel players, no matter how little or how much each of them produces. The only trick is to make the cartel legal" (2015, pp. 522–523). Tim Wu (2013) also endorses *Actavis* as good competition policy.

novelty), could be challenged on the basis of prior art through an administrative *inter partes* review (IPR). The process, though quite procedurally elaborate, can result in patent revocation and is conducted entirely within the administrative apparatus of the PTO. The IPR procedure marked a significant elevation of agency power in post-issuance patent review. For its part, the Constitution establishes that "the judicial Power of the United States, shall be vested in one supreme Court, and in such inferior Courts as the Congress may from time to time ordain and establish" (Art. III, §1). *Oil States* v. *Greene* (2018) accordingly challenged whether the government could revoke a patent without going through the courts, given that patents are property. The case thus presented a direct, rights-based juridical challenge to an attempt to deal with patents biopolitically on efficiency grounds.

The answer to the challenge, delivered in a 7-2 opinion by Justice Thomas, is that the review process is constitutional. The basic argument of the opinion is that patents are not private property so much as they are a public franchise, and as such are not the sort of thing the Constitution is talking about when it says property claims have to run through the judicial branch. As Thomas argues, "[T]he decision to *grant* a patent is a matter involving public rights – specifically, the grant of a public franchise" (*Oil States*, p. 1373, emphasis original). As nineteenth-century case law establishes, a patent "take[s] from the public rights of immense value, and bestow[s] them upon the patentee" (*Oil States*, p. 1373), by granting a right of exclusion (traditionally the core of property). It does so to incentivize invention. It then follows logically that the decision to remove a patent is also a matter of public franchise. Thomas cites a 1966 ruling that administrative review covers the "issuance of patents whose effects are to remove existent knowledge from the public domain" (*Oil States*, p. 1374). In other words, if the patent does not cover something novel, it takes knowledge that was available to the public and privatizes it.

In this way, the opinion exemplifies public biopolitics in the pre-neoliberal version. It does not quote Mill, but could easily have done so. As I noted in Chapter 2, Mill justifies the departure from *laissez-faire* on the grounds that inventions are of tremendous public value, but require nurturing by the state. Similar instances of justified state intervention include public funding of things like universities (Mill, 1965, p. 968). He also explains what happens in terms of a publicly granted patent license: "this is not making the commodity dear for [the inventor's] benefit, but merely postponing a part of the increased cheapness which the public owe to the inventor, in order to compensate and reward him for the service" (p. 928). The point is not to internalize externalities for the sake of the inventor. At I noted, this sense of knowledge as a public good is specific to modern liberalism.

In a very brief concurrence, Justices Breyer, Ginsburg, and Sotomayor push things much further, and suggest that other types of property claims might also be adjudicated by administrative means. Thus, "the conclusion that *inter partes* review is a matter involving public rights is sufficient to show that it violates neither Article III nor the Seventh Amendment. But the Court's opinion should not be read to say that matters involving private rights may never be adjudicated other than by Article III courts, say, sometimes by agencies" (*Oil States*, p. 1379). In its expansiveness, the concurrence makes evident that Justice Thomas' opinion is also supportive of the administrative state. Justice Thomas does go to considerable trouble to argue that the ruling only applies to Article III determinations, and does not reach questions such as whether patents are property for purposes of the Fifth Amendment's Takings Clause. The opinion also notes that the ability of losers in an *inter partes* review to appeal to the Federal Circuit tempers the reach of the opinion. That said, and as a contrast to the dissent shows, the ruling presents a clear endorsement of the biopolitical state. It is also not the only case where the Court has rejected traditional juridical remedies in favor of one more tailored to economic efficiency. For example, *eBay* v. *MercExchange* (2006), allowed – in a break with practice dating to the 1800s – relief to expand beyond injunctions.

In dissent, Justice Gorsuch argues that patents are property, that they represent considerable economic investment (even in getting the invention patented, never mind the cost of developing it), and that the framers would have had it no other way. The dissent frames the question as one of juridical rights. At least two interesting subplots emerge from it: First, Gorsuch is fully aware that he is fighting public biopolitics and the concern for efficiency with juridical rights. He directly says that the efficiency of the administrative review does not justify rights violations ("economy supplies no license for ignoring these – often vitally inefficient – protections" (*Oil States*, p. 1380)). He also says that subverting judicial independence allows "powerful interests" and "armies of lobbyists and lawyers to influence (and even capture) politically accountable bureaucracies" (*Oil States*, p. 1381). This is the rights-based view of limits on governmental power, cashed out through a strong view of separation of powers in the US Constitution.[42] As Gorsuch puts it, "the framers went to great lengths to guarantee a degree of judicial independence for future generations" (*Oil States*, p. 1380).

The split between biopolitical and juridical reasoning rests precisely on how the patent right is conceptualized. Where Justice Thomas frames it in terms of a public franchise, Gorsuch views it as something held by individuals. Thus, "until recently, most everyone considered an issued patent a personal right – no less than a home or farm – that the federal government could revoke only with the concurrence of independent judges" (*Oil States*, p. 1380). He argues that at the time of the Constitution, "only courts could hear patent challenges in England" and that "if facts were

---

[42] Gorsuch seems less concerned about the cost of inefficient litigation; there is a bit of a rosy view of the judicial process. This rosy view has also prevented serious review of fair use in copyright, which requires litigating; only defendants with means can afford a fair use defense. Others have to fold.

in dispute, the matter first had to proceed in the law courts" (*Oil States*, p. 1381). The majority debates him, claiming that the English system allowed privy courts to invalidate patents, that the framers had to know this, and that they were the 18c analogue of the administrative review under question. Gorsuch responds that the privy courts had stopped doing so by the mid-1700s. The debate over the original meaning of the patent right is an artifact of Thomas' and Gorsuch's originalist approaches to constitutional interpretation, and is of less interest here than the sharply contrasting views of power they invoke.

Gorsuch also implicitly accuses the majority of invoking a view of executive authority as arbitrary, deciding where and to whom the law applies. As he writes, "because the job of issuing invention patents traditionally belonged to the Executive, the Court proceeds to argue, the job of revoking them can be left there too. But that doesn't follow. Just because you give a gift doesn't mean you forever enjoy the right to reclaim it" (*Oil States*, p. 1385). This is striking: If Gorsuch thinks his analogy is doing theoretical work, and not just rhetorical, patents are like grace in one sense – they can be bestowed according to a logic which is irrelevant to the juridical validity of their bestowing. Once bestowed, they become juridical rights that cannot be revoked without juridical process. Not only that, juridical process, on this reading, must be done in Courts, and not in other agencies, even if they construct an adversarial procedure. The accusation against the majority is that it vests arbitrary power of decision into the executive. Again, this is a core challenge to the administrative state: Is it rational? There are various checks and balances built in to deter arbitrary agency decision-making, including in the present instance, but Gorsuch's dissent reaches one of the core philosophical differences about the relative merits of rights-based versus biopolitical views of governance.

The majority appears to be less interested in the basis for limiting patent rights than the fact that they are limited. In this sense, *Oil States* fits neatly into the recent line of cases pushing back against patent rights. It is also willing to attempt somewhat of a tightrope walk to do so, reminiscent of Thomas' efforts in *Myriad* to rule that isolated gene fragments were not patentable, but that lab-produced cDNA was. At the same time, *Oil States* is a moment in a larger battle over the scope of the administrative state. That is, even as *Oil States* will serve to continue the evolution of patent law in biopolitical directions, it is also enmeshed in larger legal battles over the relative merits of biopolitics – in both its public and neoliberal guises – and more traditional views of juridical power.

5.5 CONCLUSION

This chapter has traced what one might call, in broad terms, the difficult intersection of the assumptions and dispositives of a neoliberal economic order premised on internalizing the values of intangible goods, on the one hand, and the traditional assumptions of patent law, on the other. It puts into stark relief the ways in which neoliberal biopolitics differs from its public variety. The cases tracked here occupy a liminal space between an ambivalent endorsement of the appurtenances of the administrative state, a partial endorsement of the Chicago reformulation of antitrust doctrine, and a return to more juridical principles as a mechanism to limit patentability, particularly when the economic order presses toward patenting increasingly intangible goods, or goods that would traditionally have been considered off-limits as part of nature. The current situation also has a sense of déjà vu to it, as the Court's efforts to rein in patents has been met by both doctrinal confusion and calls for legislative reform aimed at both clarifying and increasing the range of what can be patented. At least one commentator (Taylor, 2019) has compared the situation today with the 1940s, when the Court was aggressively applying antirust rules to limit patents in cases like *Suppiger* and *Mercoid*.

Whatever the merits of the comparison, it seems important in the present context to note two differences between then and now. First, *Impression Products* notwithstanding, the Court today has not adopted the antimonopoly fervor of the New Deal court. In areas outside patents, Chicago-school orthodoxy on antitrust is dominant. In the context of patents, cases like *Illinois Tool Works* indicate the Court's willingness to accept things like tying arrangements, and cases like *eBay* suggest a willingness to apply market-based analysis, at least in some instances, even in areas where juridical rules like injunctions have been the norm. Even *Impression Products* tries to distance itself from the antitrust laws of the 1940s. Second, the rising economic importance of immaterial goods that blur traditional boundaries between nature and invention, or abstract ideas and invention, explored here in the context of biotechnology, provide the terrain for current theoretically-challenging patent disputes. Put simply, things like computer software and lab-created life forms did not exist in the 1940s.

As with copyright and trademark, then, trends in contemporary capitalism are important in framing developments in IP. These trends are part of the general neoliberalization of the economy, and are reflected across a range of theoretical and doctrinal issues. In the case of patents, it is striking the extent to which the Court's §101 jurisprudence resists a neoliberal understanding of the patent power. Instead, the Court seems to be using a variety of strategies in defense of a nature that remains barred to internalization. It is unclear the extent to which this resistance will prove successful, and the implications of Court resistance for the sorts of subjectification encouraged by innovation in fields like biomedicine also remain unclear. The Court has tempered its general acceptance of a stronger view of IP with a direct refusal to embrace aspects of Chicago antitrust doctrine in some patent cases. Still, the Court has also embraced the administrative state in *inter partes* review, a key component of biopolitical governmentality more generally. The sum of these developments suggests that Court jurisprudence is conflicted and internally inconsistent, not because it is confused, but because its conceptualization of the patents is simultaneously pulled by more than one view of power.

6

Conclusion: Politics Was Already in the Way

Put most briefly, this book has argued three things. First, intellectual property (IP) is a form of power. By that I mean that it exists in and through specific institutional, political, and social contexts, and influences the behavior of people in various ways, with varying degrees of coercion attached. Second, the nature of this power has been shifting, particularly in the last thirty years or so. If one divides modern forms of power into an admittedly rough schema, it is possible to adumbrate juridical, public biopolitical, and neoliberal biopolitical variants. Although no form of power as socially diffuse and culturally fundamental as IP will monolithically transition from univocally expressing one form of power to another, it is possible to observe a marked shift in IP law in the direction of neoliberal biopower. This shift is evident in the increasing adoption of individualizing, market-driven provisions grounded in a Demsetzian understanding of property driven by the internalization of (public-facing) externalities. From the attempt to patent isolated genetic fragments to efforts to protect brands as themselves commodities, IP law has increasingly insinuated itself into the everyday lives of individuals, nudging them to understand themselves as market actors at all times, rewarding producers who produce for market exploitation and consumers who interact with cultural products as though they were so produced.

Third, we can see that IP law, as other forms of power, is also legible as a process of subjectification, which is to say that it is in the business of making people. The blockhead model of creativity and correlative passive consumer, the brand conscious individual envisioned by regimes like trademark dilution, and the actuarial agent of contemporary biomedicine are all examples of the kinds of individuals imagined by neoliberal biopower and encouraged by its expression in intellectual property policy. These are contingent forms, as the contrast with the Mertonian scientist, the sampling artist who sees appropriation as creation, and the artist who sees in a Louis Vuitton bag a powerful symbol for cultural critique indicate. So too, individuals do not naturally approach music as consumers and resist being forced to do so by DRM technologies. It takes effort to persuade scientists that they should treat their research process as governed by the standards of *homo economicus* and artists that they should pay for access to culturally important symbols.

One result of these theses is that they make it possible to underscore that the relation between IP and the kinds of power it expresses is a not a necessary one. This is not to say that the relation is arbitrary in the sense that it is random; there are very good reasons to do with larger social and political processes that help to explain the history of why IP law is what it is today. The intellectual property regime we have is the product of the interaction between political struggles and the models of power they express. That also means that there is no law of nature that says we need to have intellectual property at all; more importantly, there is no law of nature that says that we need to have the kind of intellectual property that we do. There are different logics of power at work in different IP regimes; that our current regime is lurching towards a neoliberal logic does not mean that others are not possible. Indeed, juridical power and public biopower underlie much of the resistance to the neoliberalization of IP.

To the extent that this result is correct, it has implications for how we understand both Foucauldian narratives of power and intellectual property. In the case of the former, it is important to emphasize two points. On the one hand, the sort of genealogical work on neoliberalism initiated by Foucault in the *Birth of Biopolitics* lectures is important, but demands further research. At one level, forty years of neoliberalization allows one to broaden our understanding of how the basic moves of extending economic analysis into all social realms and reconceptualizing individuals as entrepreneurs of themselves generates new forms of power and new forms of subjectivation. The decline of Fordism, or rather its replacement in Western economies by what is variously called by terms such as cognitive capitalism or immaterial labor, has enabled more markets to extend their reach into areas outside the factory and into cognitive and emotional processes. This extension is mirrored by the emergence of new sites for subjectivity, for example, by managing oneself as an assemblage of carefully curated brand identities. At another level, the further development of neoliberalism allows one to see additional areas where it has departed significantly from classical liberalism. The rise of Chicago law and economics is underplayed in many accounts of neoliberalism, as is the revision of antitrust doctrine. To the extent that this study has contributed to these genealogies, it has succeeded.

On the other hand, both Foucault and many appropriations of Foucault underemphasize the importance of legal institutions. Foucault's thesis that juridical power has been supplanted (or perhaps supplemented) by something else, be it biopower or governmentality or neoliberalism, has often led to the uncritical conflation of juridical power and legal institutions. A careful reading of Foucault, at least in his better moments, suggests that he did not intend this conflation, and that his tendency to downplay legislation and legal action is misguided. In any case, as

I hope the preceding discussion has demonstrated, courts and other legal institutions remain vital sites for the expression and articulation of power today. Not only that, they are sites where different understandings of power can be and are contested. Like any other social institution, courts are sites for both the articulation of power and resistance to it. The present study of IP represents, in a way, an easy case for the thesis, because IP is entirely a creation of law. However, law remains a vital site for understanding the operation of power in a variety of other fields, and genealogical work in them needs to pay careful attention to legal institutions. As the case of the Worldwide Church of God with which I opened indicates, even such deeply personal phenomena as religious experience can be mediated by legal institutions in unexpected ways.

In terms of understanding IP, the most important result of this study is that it is useful to understand IP as a kind of power. Further, it is important to understand power in differential terms, as operating according to different logics. This has several implications. First, criticisms of IP that address primarily its quantity or decry it as a form of power only tell part of the story. It is true that there is "more" IP law now than in the past, measured both in terms of its extension into new areas and its intensity in the areas that it does cover. That argument is important, but it does not say why that quantitative increase in IP is either bad or good. Indeed, it runs the risk of defaulting to a position that the alternative to too much IP is no IP. It might be the case that no IP would be good, but such claims often seem tethered to the idea that a world without IP would be a world without the imbrication of power relations into cultural production.

A second implication is that we have no reason to assume that such a world without power could ever be the case, and many reasons to think that it would not. Cultural production inevitably involves power relations. This point is harder to see than it should be because neoliberalism is depoliticizing, hiding its political economy behind a veneer of internalization and consumer preferences.[1] An excessive focus on markets makes us forget why the spaces outside of markets matter; or, as Hardt and Negri memorably put it, "private property makes us stupid" (2004, p. 188). This is particularly clear in the way that DRM deflects responsibility for the control it exerts over users onto supposedly neutral technological platforms rather than those who insist on their presence, as I argued in Chapter 3 on copyright. In such an environment, it is too easy to fail to recognize the extent to which IP necessarily

---

[1] Of the many books advancing this thesis, it seems to me that Wendy Brown (see, e.g., 2005, 2015) and Phillip Mirowski (e.g., 2011, 2013) are among the clearest. See also Sell (2003) (documenting the extent to which current IP policy is the product of rent-seeking maneuvering by pharmaceutical executives). As I noted in the introduction, a number of recent studies emphasize that the economic relations of IP are actually power relations: see, e.g., Craig (2019), Goodrich et al. (2013), Tehranian (2012), as well as earlier work such as Coombe (1998). More specific studies are cited in reference to the cases I discuss.

embodies political relations, and the extent to which its absence will also embody political relations.

The inference from the absence of IP to the absence of power is without foundation.[2] Research into so-called low-IP zones – areas of cultural production where IP law is unavailable or has been rejected by the relevant actors – shows that there are a range of alternatives to IP, but that all of them involve complex relations of power, whether that power is exercised through social norms, market pressures, architectural features, or direct physical coercion.[3] This research is fascinating and valuable precisely because it helps us to imagine a world with different kinds of social relations around intellectual goods. These relations can, but do not necessarily have to, rely on social norms. For one, IP law itself interacts in complicated ways with social norms, especially when transgression of property is itself a form of critique. Hip-hop sampling is a prominent example in a constellation of often (but not necessarily) critical practices that functions critically precisely when it is at the margins of legality.[4] Indeed, if one's goal is innovation, social norms can work to dampen innovation by siloing creativity into narrow channels, away from the benefits of cross-fertilization (Bair & Pedraza-Fariña, 2018). In any case, social norms matter when it comes to our relations to intellectual goods, and how they make us as people.

Research into Wikipedia and global influenza surveillance and vaccine preparation underscores that low-IP zones can also rely on institutional and legal structures other than IP to succeed. Here, law and organization manage many of the problems of scale that commons-governed regimes otherwise face when the social networks in which they are embedded are not particularly tight-knit (Hoffman & Mehra, 2009; Kapczynski, 2017). These studies are also closely aligned with work offering market-based, economic accounts of innovation that do not reduce to neoliberalism, and with research into the ways commons-based access can function as a governance strategy.[5] In all of these cases, the biopolitics of IP is allowed to be understood in a more public way and without neoliberal commitments while not devolving into assumptions that no forms of regulation or power will be operative other than "free" markets.

---

[2] I am certainly not making a new point. For example, Lessig makes it in *Code* (2006 [originally 1999]), where he criticizes libertarian theorists for treating cyberspace as unregulable. The empirical research cited here allows a more nuanced understanding, however. See also, e.g., Julie E. Cohen (2012) (arguing that liberalism's understanding of power and rights leads it to misunderstand subjectivity).

[3] I am following Lessig (1998) in listing these four kinds of regulation; there may be more. For the low-IP zones, see, e.g., Raustiala & Sprigman (2012); Rosenblatt (2011).

[4] Other examples include fan fiction. For the importance of transgressing property to critique, see Peñalver & Katyal (2010); for expression and critique, see Katyal (2006b). On the difficulty of stable property regimes emerging when social norms are fluid, see Fitzpatrick (2006).

[5] In the context of information, most prominently in the work of Yochai Benkler; see, e.g., 2000, 2002, 2006. See also Kapczynski (2012).

As this suggests, and more broadly, the argument here underscores two further points about IP. First, the cultural and economic arguments need to be understood together in terms of a larger, public biopolitics of innovation. In that space, more traditionally "political" questions are important to foreground. For example, even where "negative spaces" of IP exist, there is a risk that they would immediately be appropriated by cultural elites or market actors. This is the force of Anupam Chander and Madhavi Sunder's (2004) warning against the "romance of the public domain." To locate something in the public domain means that it is free for everyone to use. In the case of indigenous people in particular, this can have disastrous results, as it not only reinscribes the idea that indigenous people are objects of knowledge but not producers, but also potentially opens up their entire cultural production to expropriation by Western multinationals. At the same time, as Hemmungs Wirtén (2008) points out, the original English commons land use regimes were fundamentally regimes designed to manage around poverty under feudalism. Any return to public biopolitics or a different understanding of property cannot be a return either to poverty or to feudalism.

That said, the governance of English commons areas was one that was willing to prioritize static efficiencies over dynamic ones. The absolute Demsetzian priority of dynamic efficiency, no matter the cost in static terms, is one that a public biopolitics would put on the table. In so doing, it would make intelligible claims to human capabilities outside of market gains. These sorts of immediately political frameworks are the sort imagined by capabilities theorists, and they would enable difficult questions about (for example) the relative priority of patent-incentivized pharmaceutical or genomic innovation, on the one hand, and more broad-based public health initiatives or the development of medicines targeting diseases that predominantly affect the poor, on the other. The neoliberal model of IP simply ignores these as political questions, defusing them behind a façade of supposedly politically neutral, economically based theory.

Shortly after introducing vocabulary around biopower, Foucault began to speak in detail about governance strategies.[6] Setting aside terminological questions, Foucault's shift in emphasis underscores that questions about power and intellectual goods can also be explored as issues of governance. Here, there is considerable work dedicated to understanding how intellectual goods might be understood as part of a "cultural commons" and how different governance strategies function in such contexts.[7] As I noted in Chapter 2, this work builds on and supplements work that

---

[6] The roughly contemporary *Society must be Defended* lectures (2003) [1975–6] and *History of Sexuality I* (1988a) [1976] were followed by the *Security, Territory, Population* lecture course that pursued "governmentality" (2007) [1977]. For a detailed account of Foucault's intellectual trajectory during this period, see Elden (2016).

[7] This work has been pursued most vigorously by Madison, Frischmann, and Strandburg. For the initial schematic, see (2010); for a revision, see (2017) This literature builds on the work of Elinor Ostrom; see, e.g., Hess & Ostrom (2003).

attempts to understand how resources can be produced and managed in the absence of property regimes, or when property regimes are only part of that governance. It also specifically attempts to recover a sense in which the politics of IP can be seen as public, as against the neoliberal privatization of the current internalization model.[8]

Any consideration of the relevant economic, cultural, or norm-based strategies for encouraging innovation needs to consider the kinds of people envisioned by those strategies. I have made the case here that neoliberal biopolitics envisions all inter-actions in market terms, and all interactions with IP as market transactions. It accordingly models, and works to encourage people to understand themselves as, instances of *homo economicus*. This is evident across a diverse array of examples, from the effort to nudge university researchers in terms very different from those of traditional scientific norms to the blockhead model of creativity central to the standard copyright narrative. It is also evident in the ways that trademark and branding culture interact to encourage individuals to fashion their identities in relation to corporate brands, or the ways that patents and biotechnology interact to produce actuarial medical subjects. Classical liberalism operates with a more cabined economic subject, one who is also considered a member of a semi-autonomous civil society or public sphere.[9]

Recovering a sense of politics as the intersection and struggle of different under-standings of power, as implemented through different governance strategies, is important to moving beyond the neoliberal reduction of society to economics. Foucault closes his *Birth of Biopolitics* lectures by making precisely this point:

> In the modern world, in the world we have known since the nineteenth century, a series of governmental rationalities overlap, lean on each other, challenge each other, and struggle with each other: art of government according to truth, art of government according to the rationality of the sovereign state; and art of government according to the rationality of the governed themselves. And it is all these different arts of government, all these different types of ways of calculating, rationalizing, and regulating the art of government which, overlapping each other, broadly speaking constitute the object of political debate from the nineteenth century. What is politics, in the end, if not both the interplay of these different arts of government with their different reference points and the debate to which these different arts of government give rise? It seems to me that it is here that politics is born.
>
> (2008, p. 313)

---

[8] One difficulty is the tension between "common" and "public"; they are not equivalent regimes, as commons regimes imply some degree of governance in a way that "public" does not. This point is pursued in the final chapter of Hemmungs Wirtén (2008). See also Kapszynski (2014), noting the oddness of treating (public) infrastructural and commons regimes as straightfor-wardly analogous. On this problem as refracted through the distinction between property and contract, see later.

[9] If it is clear that classical liberalism is different, it is not clear that it is better, as much feminist, race theory, and postcolonial literature has argued extensively. Concerns about justice and expropriation need to be central to any future revisioning of IP.

To translate: The politics of IP is manifest in the interplay of rationalities of juridical power, public biopolitics, and neoliberal biopolitics.

Viewing IP through the logics of biopower also has implications for critique insofar as it underscores that some things that appear opposed to neoliberal IP are, at another level, fundamentally aligned with it. For example, distributed or DIY biology presents itself as anti-institutional and anti-IP. At the same time, it adopts much of the same rhetoric of open markets championed by Silicon Valley, and it actively encourages participants to understand themselves in the very same entrepreneurial terms encouraged by other forms of neoliberalism. It also positions technology as something consumed, and one's status as a medical patient as a private matter (for this critique, see Delfanti, 2017). So too, the university uptake of distributed biotech further encourages university faculty to model themselves as *homo economicus*, and not *homo scientificus*, continuing the trajectory enabled by allowing university patents. Desai (2015) criticizes search-cost criticisms of trademark expansion on similar grounds, arguing that they fail to undermine the Chicago school theory of antitrust that actually subtends recent trademark expansion.

To be sure, this is a neoliberalism modeled on Hayek and not on Bork, as it is opposed in principle to monopolies and large corporations. But insofar as it emphasizes such fundamental neoliberal tenants as the centrality of innovation, a faith in markets as instruments of both efficiency and justice, and a model of personhood modeled on the business entrepreneur, the opposition to IP seems from this point of view to be less important than the ways it shares a view of power. The critique of IP from distributed biology and the search-cost critique of dilution both restage an important but internecine struggle between the early neoliberal emphasis on markets and the later view that monopolies can be more efficient drivers of innovation, and that this dynamic efficiency outweighs whatever static inefficiencies might be involved. One immediate implication, as evidenced in work that attempts to recuperate Kenneth Arrow's part of the Demsetz–Arrow debate, is that attention to static inefficiencies is important, and that static inefficiency can be an important counterweight to claims about future innovation.

A second implication is that the Chicago school endorsement of monopolies has been an important factor in allowing the expansion and individualization of IP, and work opposed to that expansion needs to attend to the underlying tolerance for monopolies. The Supreme Court took a step in this direction in its *Impression Products* patent exhaustion decision, but the idea that monopolies are likely efficient and the underlying theory that social welfare can be reduced to consumer welfare is central to the structure of hegemonic articulations of neoliberal IP. This is behind, for example, the urge to protect brand trademarks even when there is no market competition: Consumers are said to be better off, even if they pay more, when affective attachment to brands is encouraged and then monetized. So, too, it undergirds the copyright regime's tendency to reduce all interactions with cultural goods into market-based consumption such that welfare could be maximized by regulating interaction-as-consumption. As Rebecca Tushnet put the point, "the greatest trick the content industry ever pulled was getting people to believe that readers and listeners are 'consumers,' as if they swallowed speech like candy" (Tushnet, 2004, p. 566n145).

If strategies that oppose expansionist IP need to be viewed in terms of their relation to neoliberal proprietization, the converse also holds. Strategies to oppose neoliberalism may very well attempt to use IP and to wrest it from neoliberalism. This strategy is prominently on display in indigenous efforts to use geographic indicators to protect culturally specific practices of production. The potential risks and benefits of such a strategy are apparent. On the one hand, it can successfully return power to local producers and communities, using Western affective attachments to "native authenticity" to extract added value from consumers in distant markets. On the other hand, it risks entrenching local elites at the expense of producers, while simultaneously risking producing a homogenization and commodification of the very local practices it was designed to protect. In the case of copyright, more expansive views of free speech and authorship, views that would push back against the ability of rightsholders to profit from all downstream, derivative works, would carve out more space for cultural interaction that was not governed by the logic of consumer-oriented consumption.

The Supreme Court has ventured into this territory repeatedly in the case of patents, and with mixed results. It has substantially narrowed the scope of subject-matter eligibility, and there is some evidence that the Federal Circuit's implementation of that narrowing is moving toward an implicit effort to prevent excessive enclosure of nature (Burk, 2016). Still, the *Myriad* litigation shows both that there are numerous ways to pursue such a strategy, and that timing matters: The presumptive legitimacy of patents on isolated gene fragments both gave *Myriad* a dominant first-mover advantage in the market for BRCA testing, and allowed the development of genomic sequencing technologies that do not rely on isolated genetic fragments. In that sense, the legal issues that *Myriad* adjudicated become a ladder that the development of genomic medicine and the actuarial agency it brings with it no longer require. So too, when the Supreme Court struck down statutory restrictions on trademark registration for disparaging speech on Free Speech grounds, the effect may have been to remove one of the few policy-based impediments to the further expansion of branding culture.

***

IP is poised to be tremendously important, both economically and culturally, into the foreseeable future. At the same time, as a legal regime, IP is situated in broader economic and cultural contexts. In particular, IP is currently under pressure from opposite directions. On the one hand, as noted earlier, various forms of opposition rooted in what might be called public biopolitics are applying pressure to make IP more public, and less restrictive. From the point of view of the models of power developed here, these pressures articulate concerns based either in the public or even in terms of the rights of individual subjects.

On the other hand, there is a sense in which the Demsetzian logic of neoliberal IP tends towards supplanting IP on neoliberal grounds. After all, as Hemmungs Wirtén (2015) reminds us, IP still is a public right in the sense that claiming IP still requires publication. Trade secrets impose no such publication requirement (and they last forever, barring theft), and so more completely reflect an ethos of privatization. Indeed, as noted in Chapter 5, in areas where the Courts have restricted patent eligibility, commentators have suggested that corporations are likely to rely on trade secrets to achieve similar results.[10] Similarly, as trademark moves from protecting markets to protecting brands, then not just trade secrets, but other aspects of contract law, such as nondisclosure agreements, become increasingly important as strategies to protect proprietary interests. After all, a substantial part of Mattel's efforts to shut down competitors to its Barbie line revolved around contract provisions, not trademark (Lobel, 2018). In 1996, President Obama signed the Defend Trade Secrets Act, which for the first time created a federal action for trade secret misappropriation, which had previously relied on state law.

However, the history of trade secrets has been an outsider to IP. First, as noted earlier, IP requires the disclosure of information and trade secrecy requires hiding it. In addition, as Robert Bone argues, a trade secret action is "based at its core on the breach of relationally specific duties. The majority of trade secret cases involve disloyal employees who use or disclose their employers' secrets in violation of a duty of confidence stemming from the employer–employee relationship" (1998, p. 244). Trade secret law has thus historically tended to align with contract without reducing to it, as there can still be liability without a contract.

The reliance on contract or unfair business practices generates a different genealogy when one considers trade secrets as an expression of power. Robert Bone (1998) suggests that the nineteenth century basically conceptualized it as property in a secret (defined as information over which one has obtained exclusive control), with trespass happening when someone violates the secret. The question then became how to know if someone had illegitimate access to the secret (rather than having, for example, discovered it independently). The law then relied on standards imported from areas such as contract. The advent of legal realism pulled the rug out from under this formalistic view of property as exclusive possession, and so trade secret law no longer serves any function beyond what areas like contract can provide.

In other words, although trade secrets have long been recognized as part of innovation policy, the have tended to operate as private law. In this context, Mark

[10] On this see especially Laakmann (2016).

Lemley (2008) argues that trade secret law could usefully be reconceptualized as intellectual property, precisely because a properly constructed trade secret law could actually encourage disclosure of information, and serve the IP goal of disseminating innovation, and not just encouraging innovation itself. His primary argument is that, in the absence of well-defined trade secret protection that provides a workable standard of "reasonable" efforts to protect information, companies will tend to inefficiently over-invest in secrecy, using walls, fences, and other elaborate techniques for keeping information under wraps. They will also be inefficiently unwilling to disclose information under any circumstances where there is not already a contract in place, since they will be unable to rely on extracontractual standards of privity. Reconceptualizing trade secrets as IP, then, would be good for public biopolitics, given that one also views IP as a form of public biopolitics. In the status quo, as I indicated in the discussion of gene patents, a move to a combination of administration and trade secrets may well result in a further privatization of innovation.[11]

These pressures guarantee both that IP is not going anywhere soon, and that it is going to remain controversial. That IP can be viewed as an expression of power and that the kinds of power IP expresses is contingent nonetheless suggests a way forward. We should ask ourselves what kind of social relations, power allocations, and subjects we want, and frame some basic questions about IP on that basis. There is no reason that IP has to be a dispositive of neoliberal biopower, no matter how much large corporations try to convince us of this. I would like to close by suggesting two ways forward that this implies.

First, there is space for a renovated public biopolitics. The word "innovation" currently does far too much work, and often serves to paper over a number of important questions not just the relative merits of static and dynamic efficiency, but more fundamental questions about what all this innovation is for. That is, the tendency to default to the word "innovation" matters because it impedes work not just on whether more innovation is necessarily good in itself (or the related question of the relative weights one should assign to static and dynamic efficiency), but what kinds of innovation are better or worse. There is an analogy here to how earlier neoliberal theory tended to discuss "preferences:" Their satisfaction was an unquestioned good. As Will Davies (2012) has argued, more recent neoliberal thought has tended to recognize that not all preferences are substantively equal. Similarly, not all innovation is obviously substantively equal.

---

[11] A genealogy of trade secrets and the accompanying modern contract form, and their role in innovation, is well beyond the scope of this study. However, as capitalism increasingly relies on "innovation" as its primary measure of new value, we can expect the continuing proliferation and intensification of strategies to internalize the rewards of innovative activities. In this sense, the genealogy of neoliberal IP presented here represents part of a larger story that has yet to be told.

Even as late as the New Deal, when one can see the beginnings of a more expansive theory of IP, that expansion was tempered by concern for monopolies as well as by other, deliberate efforts to promote the public good. This "core role of debates over citizenship" receded in the post-war period (Wilf, 2008, p. 206). That is, although economic and social concerns were directly linked, there was no neoliberal reduction of the social to the economic. By many metrics, the public biopolitics version of IP did (or would do) significantly better than the current one. However, the social shift to what autonomists call the "complete subsumption" of markets into social relations suggests that a simple return to public biopolitics will not just be difficult to effect, but difficult to imagine. Much of the extension of property and other market relations into all aspects of life envisioned by theorists such as Becker has already happened. As theorists such as Rosemary Coombe (1998) and Jack Balkin (2004) have noted, theories that rely on distinctions between political and cultural, or commercial and noncommercial, speech are increasingly problematic, and a responsible approach to its regulation through IP will begin with that acknowledgment, and with an acknowledgment that awareness of contingent relations of social power is essential. This is the lesson of examples like the use and reappropriation of ethnic slurs in trademark, or of hip-hop sampling in copyright. In other words, the blurring of traditionally public and market spaces does not mean that there are no resources available to consider how positive externalities might be retained for the public.

Many of these would not require radical doctrinal changes in the law in question. Recognizing the public interest in university research into patented inventions, independent of any latent "commercial" interest in that research, would be a start. In the case of trademark, Rochelle Cooper Dreyfuss (1990) argues that when a brand name carries sufficiently important, socially expressive meaning, uses of it that convey that meaning outside of a brand-signaling context ought to be protected. For example, Nadia Plesner would be able to use the image of a Luis Vuitton bag to promote awareness of famine in Darfur (Katyal, 2015). Such a move would protect a public good that was not reducible to market terms. Similarly, one could extend parody defenses in copyright to cases where the work in question is being used to parody something else, at least in cases where the work in question can serve metaphorically; for example, Mickey Mouse might stand in for a certain image of mainstream, 1950s culture. Along the same lines, fair use might be extended to categories like fan fiction, or the concept of "derivative work" could be more narrowly defined by, or even replaced with, something that focused more on social value (Julie E. Cohen, 2007, p. 1204) . Finally, even if the anticircumvention provisions of the copyright act are here to stay, legislation codifying the "right to tinker" or the various exemptions that currently require renewal through the Copyright Office would serve to stabilize and secure the ability of users to interact with copyrighted material on their own terms.

Some of these reforms might occur outside of IP. For example, ensuring adequate, nonmarket funding for university research would help to ensure that university scientists need not style themselves as members of *homo economicus* (Strandburg, 2005). Looking at other incentive structures such as races or prizes could incentivize research into diseases that afflict those who cannot afford new drugs (Kapczynski, 2012). Tim Wu (2012) has suggested that market structure matters as much or more than IP for innovation, and so antitrust policy could be strengthened to reduce entry barriers to innovation. Resurrecting moribund doctrines like copyright and patent misuse would be one way into this. More radically, emphasis on measures of welfare other than GDP could help to reframe the broader question of what it means to promote the arts and sciences (Chon, 2006; Sunder, 2012). It is entirely possible that inefficiency is a good that needs to be encouraged sometimes, precisely because it creates a space for subjectification (Frischmann & Selinger, 2018). All of these would push back, with varying degrees of intensity, against the tendency of neoliberalization to, in Wendy Brown's (2015) apt phrasing, undo the *demos*.

A second intriguing possibility is to reimagine what property looks like, and how we understand it. In particular, is there a way to imagine intellectual property as expressing a different kind of power, one that is more attentive to issues of wealth distribution, social justice, and other urgent concerns? As Naomi Mezey (2007) points out, the core of what she calls the "paradox of cultural property" is a disconnect between the fluidity of cultural formations, boundaries, and meanings, on the one hand, and the fixity of property rights, on the other. There is however no necessary reason why cultural and legal understandings of ownership need to take the form they do in current IP law. In other words, neoliberal views of IP themselves are cultural formations, subject to the same possible changes as the cultures of which they are a part. One version of this reimagination is in the recognition that exclusionary property regimes can be situated in a continuum of governance strategies. More fundamentally, property can be imagined in political and social terms, as techniques for stewardship over important resources or strategies to promote social interaction.[12] As the New Jersey Supreme Court bluntly put it in a real property case, "property rights serve human values. They are recognized to that end, and are limited by it" (*Shack*, p. 303).[13] The point echoes concerns about the public benefit of knowledge that IP incentivizes, especially as that suggests the need to be wary of the effects of IP monopolies on markets. At the same time, in its affirmation of the rights of migrant farm workers to access medical care and a policy to promote that access, the case underscores that the values promoted by property need not be economic.

As Carol Rose has repeatedly noted, when we imagine property relations, we imagine ourselves, and so the stories we tell ourselves about property matter.[14] These are fundamentally stories about socialization and social ordering; as she puts it,

---

[12] For governance, see H. Smith (2002); for stewardship, see Carpenter et al. (2009).
[13] I thank Madhavi Sunder for reminding me of the importance of *Shack*.
[14] The following makes particular use of C. M. Rose (1990, 1999, 2005, 2006).

"property is one of the most sociable institutions that human beings have created, depending as it does on mutual forbearance and on the recognition of and respect for the claims of others" (2005, p. 1019). The point of course is to notice that there are different visions of this sociality, and different understandings of the relations and institutions of power that undergird and operationalize that vision. The neoliberal narrative about internalization of externalities articulates one such vision. It is not the only possible story about property, and as the presence of both public biopolitical and juridical narratives indicates, it is not even the only story that has actually been told about IP. It is of relatively recent invention, dating to the rise of the law and economics movement more generally. As a vision of sociality, it has tended to occlude the public biopolitics of modern liberalism that IP initially tended to express.

Although the narrative about internalizing externalities is specific, it also tends to repeat a more general cultural narrative according to which exclusivity is imagined as an ideal form, and utilitarian calculations are used to claim that this distribution is just because it is welfare promoting in a general sense. Thus, at its inception, IP was understood using the tools of classic liberalism, with an emphasis on public benefits and a distrust of monopolies. Liberalism emerged hand in hand with *laissez-faire* capitalism and colonialism, and so a straightforward return to the political economy of the mid-nineteenth century is clearly problematic today. Attention to how new forms of social value can be created needs to be accompanied by attention to how other forms of social value can be nurtured. As the contours and limitations of the various biopolitical understandings of IP become clear, we need to become more intentional about how we situate our own imaginings of property and ownership in terms of those understandings of power. It is time to get clear about what IP is for, so that we can tell a better story about it.

Works Cited

Aaker, D. A. (1991). *Managing Brand Equity: Capitalizing on the Value of a Brand Name*. New York: Free Press.

(2011). *Brand Relevance: Making Competitors Irrelevant*. San Francisco: Jossey-Bass.

Alice Corp. v. CLS Bank Int'l, 134 U.S. 2347 (2014).

Amoore, L. (2004). Risk, Reward and Discipline at Work. *Economy and Society*, 33(2), 174–196. doi:10.1080/0308514041001677111.

AMP v. Myriad, 689 F.3d 1303 (Fed. Cir. 2012).

AMP v. Myriad, 133 S. Ct. 2107 (2013).

AMP v. USPTO, 702 F. Supp. 2d 181 (S.D.N.Y. 2010).

Anten, T. (2006). Self-Disparaging Trademarks and Social Change: Factoring the Reappropriation of Slurs into Section 2(a) of the Lanham Act. *Columbia Law Review*, 106(2), 388–434.

Armstrong, H. W. (1985). *Mystery of the Ages*. Retrieved from www.thetrumpet.com/literature/books_and_booklets/730.

Arrow, K. (1962). Economic Welfare and the Allocation of Resources for Invention. In *The Rate and Direction of Inventive Activity: Economic and Social Factors* (pp. 609–626). Princeton: Princeton University Press.

Arvidsson, A. (2004). On the "Pre-History of the Panoptic Sort": Mobility in Market Research. *Surveillance and Society*, 1(4), 456–474.

Aufderheide, P., Milosevic, T., & Bello, B. (2015). The Impact of Copyright Permissions Culture on the US Visual Arts Community: The Consequences of Fear of Fair Uuse. *New Media & Society* 18(9), 2012–2027. doi:10.1177/1461444815575018.

Baer, H. J., Brawarsky, P., Murray, M. F., & Haas, J. S. (2010). Familial Risk of Cancer and Knowledge and Use of Genetic Testing. *Journal of General Internal Medicine*, 25(7), 717–724. doi:10.1007/s11606-010-1334-9

Bair, S., & Pedraza-Fariña, L. (2018). Anti-Innovation Norms. *Northwestern Law Review*.

Baker, J. B. (2007). Beyond Schumpeter vs. Arrow: How Antitrust Fosters Innovation. *Antitrust Law Journal*, 74(3), 575–602.

Balkin, J. M. (2004). Digital Speech and Democratic Culture: A Theory of Freedom of Expression for the Information Society. *New York University Law Review*, 79(1), 1–55.

Bankhead, C. (2018, May 7). Genetic Test Criteria Often Miss Breast Cancer Risk. *MedPage Today*. Retrieved from www.medpagetoday.com/meetingcoverage/additionalmeetings/72742.

Barrett, B. (2015). Keurig's My K-Cup Retreat Shows We Can Beat DRM. *Wired*. Retrieved from www.wired.com/2015/05/keurig-k-cup-drm/

Barron, A. (2010). Copyright Infringement, "Free-Riding" and the Lifeworld. In L. Bentley, J. Davis, & J. C. Ginsburg (Eds.), *Copyright and Piracy: An Interdisciplinary Critique* (pp. 93–127). Cambridge: Cambridge University Press.

Bartow, A. (2015). The Gender of Trademarks and Luxury Branding. In H. Sun, B. Beebe, & M. Sunder (Eds.), *The Luxury Economy and Intellectual Property* (pp. 145–170). New York: Oxford University Press.

Becker, G. S. (1995). The Economic Approach to Human Behavior. In R. Febrero & P. S. Schwartz (Eds.), *The Essence of Becker* (pp. 3–17). Stanford: Stanford University Press.

(2007). Health as Human Capital: Synthesis and Extensions. *Oxford Economic Papers*, 59(3), 379–410. doi:10.1093/oep/gpm020.

Beebe, B. (2008). The Semiotic Account of Trademark Doctrine and Trademark Culture. In G. B. Dinwoodie & M. D. Janis (Eds.), *Trademark Law and Theory: A Handbook of Contemporary Research* (pp. 42–62). Cheltenham: Edward Elgar Publishers.

(2010). Intellectual Property Law and the Sumptuary Code. *Harvard Law Review*, 123, 809–889.

(2014). The Suppressed Misappropriation Origins of Trademark Antidilution Law: The Landgericht Elberfeld's *Odol* Opinion and Frank Schechter's "The Rational Basis of Trademark Protection". In J. C. Ginsburg & R. C. Dreyfuss (Eds.), *Intellectual Property at the Edge: The Contested Contours of IP* (pp. 59–80). Cambridge: Cambridge University Press.

Bell, A., & Parchomovsky, G. (2005). A Theory of Property. *Cornell Law Review*, 90, 531–615.

Bellcross, C. A., Kolor, K., Goddard, K. A., Coates, R. J., Reyes, M., & Khoury, M. J. (2011). Awareness and Utilization of BRCA1/2 Testing among U.S. Primary Care Physicians. *American Journal of Preventive Medicine*, 40(1), 61–66. doi:10.1016/j.amepre.2010.09.027.

Benkler, Y. (2000). An Unhurried View of Private Ordering in Information Transactions. *Vanderbilt Law Review*, 53, 2063–2080. doi:10.1162/DAED_a_00121.

(2002). Coase's Penguin, or, Linux and the Nature of the Firm. *Yale Law Journal*, 112, 370–446.

(2006). *The Wealth of Networks: How Social Production Transforms Markets and Freedom*. New Haven: Yale University Press.

Benkler, Y., & Nissenbaum, H. (2006). Commons-Based Peer Production and Virtue. *Journal of Political Philosophy*, 14(4), 394–419. doi:10.1111/j.1467-9760.2006.00235.x.

Berardi, F. (2009). *The Soul at Work: From Alienation to Autonomy* (F. Cadel & G. Mecchia., Trans. J. E. Smith Ed.). Los Angeles: Semiotext(e).

Berlinguer, G. (2004). Bioethics, Health, and Inequality. *Lancet*, 364(9439), 1086–1091. doi:10.1016/s0140-6736(04)17066-9.

Bernstein, G. (2010). Direct-to-Consumer Genetic Testing: Gatekeeping the Production of Genetic Information. *UMKC Law Review*, 79(2), 1–12.

Bessière, J. (2002). Local Development and Heritage: Traditional Food and Cuisine as Tourist Attractions in Rural Areas. *Sociologia Ruralis*, 38(1), 21–34. doi:10.1111/1467-9523.00061.

Biebricher, T. (2014). Sovereignty, Norms, and Exception in Neoliberalism. *qui parle*, 23(1), 77–107.

Bilski v. *Kappos*, 561 U.S. 593 (2010).

Binkley, S. (2009). The Work of Neoliberal Governmentality: Temporality and Ethical Substance in the Tale of Two Dads. *Foucault Studies*, 6, 60–78.

(2014). *Happiness as Enterprise: An Essay on Neoliberal Life*. Albany: State University of New York Press.

Blewett, R. A. (1995). Property Rights as a Cause of the Tragedy of the Commons: Institutional Change and the Pastoral Maasai of Kenya. *Eastern Economic Journal*, 21(4), 477–490.

Bleyer, A., & Welch, H. G. (2012). Effect of Three Decades of Screening Mammography on Breast-Cancer Incidence. *New England Journal of Medicine*, 367(21), 1998–2005. doi: doi:10.1056/NEJMoa1206809.

Bloom, A. (2012). Speaking "Truth" to Biopower. *Southwestern University Law Review*, 41, 241–252.

Bode, K. (2018). Once Again, Activists Must Beg the Government to Preserve the Right to Repair. *vIce.com*. Retrieved from https://motherboard.vice.com/en_us/article/mbxzyv/dmca-1201-exemptions.

Boenink, M. (2010). Molecular Medicine and Concepts of Disease: The Ethical Value of a Conceptual Analysis of Emerging Biomedical Technologies. *Medicine, Health Care and Philosophy*, 13(1), 11–23. doi:10.1007/s11019-009-9223-x.

(2011). Unambiguous Test Results or Individual Independence? The Role of Clients and Families in Predictive BRCA-Testing in the Netherlands Compared to the USA. *Social Science & Medicine*, 72(11), 1793–1801. doi:10.1016/j.socscimed.2010.06.011.

Bone, R. G. (1998). A New Look at Trade Secret Law: Doctrine in Search of Justification. *California Law Review*, 86, 241–313.

(2008). Schechter's Ideas in Historical Context and Dilution's Rocky Road. *Santa Clara Computer and High Technology Law Journal*, 24, 469–506.

Borgmann, A. (1995). The Moral Significance of Material Culture. In A. Feenberg & A. Hannay (Eds.), *Technology and the Politics of Knowledge* (pp. 85–93). Indianapolis: Indiana University Press.

(2010). Reality and Technology. *Cambridge Journal of Economics*, 34(1), 27–35. doi:10.1093/cje/bep021 10.1093/cje/ben055.

Bork, R. H. (1993). *The Antitrust Paradox: A Policy at War with Itself*. New York: MacMillan.

Borry, P., & Howard, H. (2008). DTC Genetic Services: A Look across the Pond. *American Journal of Bioethics*, 8(6), 14–16. doi:10.1080/15265160802248252.

Boyle, J. (1997). *Shamans, Software and Spleens: Law and the Construction of the Information Society*. Cambridge: Harvard University Press.

(2000). Cruel, Mean, or Lavish? Economic Analysis, Price Discrimination, and Digital Intellectual Property. *Vanderbilt Law Review*, 53, 2007–2039.

(2008). *The Public Domain: Enclosing the Commons of the Mind*. New Haven: Yale University Press.

Bridgeport Music v. Dimension Films, 410 F.3d 792 (2005).

Brïdson, K., & Evans, J. (2004). The Secret to a Fashion Advantage is Brand Orientation. *International Journal of Retail & Distribution Management*, 32(8), 403–411. doi: doi:10.1108/09590550410546223.

Bronk, R. (2013). Hayek on the Wisdom of Prices: A Reassessment. *Erasmus Journal for Philosophy and Economics*, 6(1), 82–107.

Brown, M. F. (2003). *Who Owns Native Culture?* Cambridge: Harvard University Press.

Brown, W. (2005). Neoliberalism and the End of Liberal Democracy. In *Edgework: Critical Essays on Knowledge and Politics* (pp. 37–59). Princeton: Princeton University Press.

(2006). *Regulating Aversion: Tolerance in the Age of Identity and Empire*. Princeton: Princeton University Press.

(2015). *Undoing the Demos: Neoliberalism's Stealth Revolution*. New York: Zone Books.

Bryant, R. L. (2013). Branding Natural Resources: Science, Violence and Marketing in the Making of Teak. *Transactions of the Institute of British Geographers*, 38(4), 517–530. doi:10.1111/tran.12006.

Buck, D., Getz, C., & Guthman, J. (1997). From Farm to Table: The Organic Vegetable Commodity Chain of Northern California. *Sociologia Ruralis*, 37(1), 3–20. doi:10.1111/1467-9523.00033.

Bugos, G. E., & Kevles, D. J. (1992). Plants as Intellectual Property: American Practice, Law, and Policy in World Context. *Osiris, 2nd series* 7, 74–104.

Burk, D. L. (2014). The Curious Incident of the Supreme Court in *Myriad Genetics*. *Notre Dame Law Review*, 90(2), 505–542.

(2016). Beyond Abstraction: Applying the Brakes to Runaway Patent Ineligibility. *Journal of Law and the Biosciences*, 3(3), 697–703. doi:10.1093/jlb/lsw055.

Burk, D. L., & Gillespie, T. (2006). Autonomy and Morality in DRM and Anti-Circumvention Law. *tripleC*, 4(2), 239-245.

Busch, L., & Tanaka, K. (1996). Rites of Passage: Constructing Quality in a Commodity Subsector. *Science, Technology & Human Values*, 21(1), 3–27. doi:10.1177/016224399602100101.

Callon, M. (1998). Introduction: The Embeddedness of Economic Markets in Economics. In M. Callon (Ed.), *The Laws of the Markets* (pp. 1–58). Oxford: Blackwell.

Callon, M., Méadel, C., & Rabeharisoa, V. (2002). The Economy of Qualities. *Economy and Society*, 31(2), 194–217.

Camargo, R., & Ried, N. (2016). Towards a Genealogy of Pharmacological Practice. *Medicine, Health Care and Philosophy*, 19(1), 85–94. doi:10.1007/s11019-015-9648-3.

Campeau, P. M., Foulkes, W. D., & Tischkowitz, M. D. (2008). Hereditary Breast Cancer: New Genetic Developments, New Therapeutic Avenues. *Human Genetics*, 124(1), 31–42. doi:10.1007/s00439-008-0529-1.

Cao, A., Huang, L., & Shao, Z. (2017). The Preventive Intervention of Hereditary Breast Cancer. In E. Song & H. Hu (Eds.), *Translational Research in Breast Cancer: Biomarker Diagnosis, Targeted Therapies and Approaches to Precision Medicine* (pp. 41–57). Singapore: Springer Singapore.

Carere, D. A., Kraft, P., Kaphingst, K. A., Roberts, J. S., & Green, R. C. (2016). Consumers Report Lower Confidence in Their Genetics Knowledge Following Direct-to-Consumer Personal Genomic Testing. *Genetic Medicine*, 18(1), 65–72. doi:10.1038/gim.2015.34.

Carpenter, K. A., Katyal, S. K., & Riley, A. R. (2009). In Defense of Property. *Yale Law Journal*, 118, 1022–1125.

Caryn Rabin, R. (2018, March 6). F.D.A. Approves First Home Testing for Three Breast Cancer Mutations, With Caveats. *New York Times*. Retrieved from www.nytimes.com/2018/03/06/well/fda-brca-home-testing.html.

Cassier, M., & Sinding, C. (2008). 'Patenting in the Public Interest:' Administration of Insulin Patents by the University of Toronto. *History and Technology*, 24(2), 153–171. doi:10.1080/07341510701810948.

Cervellon, M.-C. (2012). Victoria's Dirty Secrets. *Journal of Advertising*, 41(4), 133–145. doi:10.1080/00913367.2012.10672462.

Chander, A., & Sunder, M. (2004). The Romance of the Public Domain. *California Law Review*, 92, 1331–1373.

Cheng, E. K. (2006). Structural Laws and the Puzzle of Regulating Behavior. *Northwestern University Law Review*, 100, 655–717.

Childers, C. P., Childers, K. K., Maggard-Gibbons, M., & Macinko, J. (2017). National Estimates of Genetic Testing in Women with a History of Breast or Ovarian Cancer. *Journal of Clinical Oncology*, 35(34), 3800–3806. doi:10.1200/jco.2017.73.6314.

Chon, M. (2006). Intellectual Property and the Development Divide. *Cardozo Law Review*, 27, 2814–2904.

Citron, D. K. (2014). *Hate Crimes in Cyberspace*. Cambridge: Harvard University Press.

Clark, A. (2003). *Natural-Born Cyborgs: Minds, Technologies, and the Future of Human Intelligence*. Oxford; New York: Oxford University Press.

Cochoy, F. (2002). *Une sociologie du packaging, ou l'âne de Buridan face au marché*. Paris: Presses Universitaires de France.

Cohen, F. S. (1932). The Subject Matter of Ethical Science. *International Journal of Ethics*, 42(4), 397–418.

   (1935). Transcendental Nonsense and the Functional Approach. *Columbia Law Review*, 35(6), 809–849.

Cohen, J. E. (1998). Lochner in Cyberspace: The New Economic Orthodoxy of 'Rights Management'. *Michigan Law Review*, 97, 462–563.

   (2007). Creativity and Culture in Copyright Theory. *University of California, Davis Law Review*, 40, 1151–1205.

   (2012). *Configuring the Networked Self: Law, Code, and the Play of Everyday Practice*. New Haven: Yale University Press.

Collier, S. J. (2009). Topologies of Power: Foucault's Analysis of Political Government beyond 'Governmentality'. *Theory, Culture & Society*, 26, 78–108.

Coombe, R. J. (1998). *The Cultural Life of Intellectual Properties: Authorship, Appropriation, and the Law*. Durham: Duke University Press.

Cooper, M. (2008). *Life as Surplus: Biotechnology and Capitalism in the Neoliberal Era*. Seattle: University of Washington Press.

Craig, C. J. (2019). Critical Copyright Law and the Politics of 'IP'. In E. Christodoulidis, R. Dukes, & M. Goldoni (Eds.), *Research Handbook on Critical Legal Theory* forthcoming. Cheltenham: Edward Elgar.

Crouch, D., & Merges, R. P. (2010). Operating Efficiently Post-*Bilski* by Ordering Patent Doctrine Decision-making. *Berkeley Technology Law Journal*, 25, 1673–1692.

Davies, L., Petitti, D. B., Martin, L., Woo, M., & Lin, J. S. (2018). Defining, Estimating, and Communicating Overdiagnosis in Cancer Screening. *Annals of Internal Medicine*, 169(1), 36–43. doi:10.7326/M18-0694.

Davies, W. (2011). The Political Economy of Unhappiness. *New Left Review*, 71(Sept-Oct), 65–80.

   (2012). The Emerging Neocommunitarianism. *The Political Quarterly*, 83(4), 767–776. doi: doi:10.1111/j.1467-923X.2012.02354.x.

   (2014). *The Limits of Neoliberalism: Authority, Sovereignty and the Logic of Competition*. London: Sage.

Dean, M. (2016). "It's Not if I Get Cancer, It's When I Get Cancer": BRCA-Positive Patients' (un)certain Health Experiences Regarding Hereditary Breast and Ovarian Cancer Risk. *Social Science & Medicine*, 163, 21–27. doi:http://dx.doi.org/10.1016/j.socscimed.2016.06.039.

Dean, M., & Davidson, L. G. (2016). Previvors' Uncertainty Management Strategies for Hereditary Breast and Ovarian Cancer. *Health Communication*, 33(2), 122–130. doi:10.1080/10410236.2016.1250187.

Dean, O. (2006). Copyright in the Courts: The Return of the Lion. *WIPO Magazine*, (April). Retrieved from www.wipo.int/wipo_magazine/en/2006/02/article_0006.html.

Dekeuwer, C., & Bateman, S. (2013). Much More than a Gene: Hereditary Breast and Ovarian Cancer, Reproductive Choices and Family Life. *Medicine, Health Care, and Philosophy, 16*(2), 231–244. doi:10.1007/s11019-011-9361-9

Delfanti, A. (2017). Distributed Biotechnology. In D. Tyfield, R. Lave, S. Randalls, & C. Thorpe (Eds.), *The Routledge Handbook of the Political Economy of Science,* 237–48. New York: Routledge.

Demsetz, H. (1967). Toward a Theory of Property Rights. *The American Economic Review, 57*(2), 347–359.

(1969). Information and Efficiency: Another Viewpoint. *The Journal of Law & Economics,* 12(1), 1–22.

(1970). The Private Production of Public Goods. *The Journal of Law & Economics,* 13(2), 293–306.

(2008). *From Economic Man to Economic System: Essays on Human Behavior and the Institutions of Capitalism.* Cambridge; New York: Cambridge University Press.

Desai, D. R. (2012). From Trademarks to Brands. *Florida Law Review, 64,* 981–1044.

(2015). The Chicago School Trap in Trademark: The Co-Evolution of Corporate, Antitrust, and Trademark Law. *Cardozo Law Review, 37,* 551–620.

Deselnicu, O. C., Costanigro, M., Souza-Monteiro, D. M., & Thilmany McFadden, D. (2013). A Meta-Analysis of Geographical Indication Food Valuation Studies: What Drives the Premium for Origin-Based Labels? *Journal of Agricultural and Resource Economics, 38*(2), 204–219.

Diamond v. Chakrabarty, 447 U.S. 303 (1980).

Dilts, A. (2011). From 'Entrepreneur of the Self' to 'Care of the Self:' Neo-liberal Governmentality and Foucault's Ethics. *Foucault Studies,* 12(October), 130–146.

Domchek, S. M., Bradbury, A., Garber, J. E., Offit, K., & Robson, M. E. (2013). Multiplex Genetic Testing for Cancer Susceptibility: Out on the High Wire Without a Net? *Journal of Clinical Oncology,* 31(10), 1267–1270. doi:10.1200/jco.2012.46.9403

Domchek, S. M., Friebel, T. M., Singer, C. F. et al. (2010). Association of Risk-Reducing Surgery in BRCA1 or BRCA2 Mutation Carriers with Cancer Risk and Mortality. JAMA, 304(9), 967–975. doi:10.1001/jama.2010.1237

Dourish, P. (2001). *Where the Action Is: The Foundations of Embodied Interaction.* Cambridge: MIT Press.

Dreyfuss, R. C. (1990). Expressive Genericity: Trademarks as Language in the Pepsi Generation. *Notre Dame Law Review, 65,* 397–424.

(2002). Commodifying Collaborative Research. In N. Elkin-Koren & N. W. Netanel (Eds.), *The Commodification of Information* (pp. 397–413). The Hague: Kluwer.

Easton, D. F. (1999). How Many More Breast Cancer Predisposition Genes are There? *Breast Cancer Research,* 1(1), 14–17.

Elden, S. (2016). *Foucault's Last Decade.* Cambridge: Polity.

Eldred v. Ashcroft, 537 U.S. 186 (2003).

Elkin-Koren, N. (2002). It's All About Control: Rethinking Copyright in the New Information Landscape. In N. Elkin-Koren & N. W. Netanel (Eds.), *The Commodification of Information* (pp. 79–106). The Hague: Kluwer.

Enoch, D., & Fisher, T. (2015). Sense and "Sensitivity:" Epistemic and Instrumental Approaches to Statistical Evidence. *Stanford Law Review, 67,* 557–611.

Enoch, D., Spectre, L., & Fisher, T. (2012). Statistical Evidence, Sensitivity, and the Legal Value of Knowledge. *Philosophy & Public Affairs,* 40(3), 197–224. doi:10.1111/papa.12000.

Epstein, R. (2002). The Allocation of the Commons: Parking on Public Roads. *The Journal of Legal Studies,* 31(S2), S515–S544. doi:10.1086/342023

Ewald, F. (1990). Norms, Discipline, and the Law. *Representations*, (30), 138–161. doi:10.2307/2928449

Fallon, R. H., Jr. (1994). Two Senses of Autonomy. *Stanford Law Review*, 46, 875–905.

Fennell, L. A. (2012). Lumpy Property. *University of Pennsylvania Law Review*, 160, 1955–1993.

Finch, A., Evans, G., & Narod, S. A. (2012). BRCA Carriers, Prophylactic Salpingo-Oophorectomy and Menopause: Clinical Management Considerations and Recommendations. *Womens Health (Lond Engl)*, 8(5), 543–555. doi:10.2217/whe.12.41

Fitzpatrick, D. (2006). Evolution and Chaos in Property Rights Systems: The Third World Tragedy of Contested Access. *Yale Law Journal*, 115, 996–1048.

Flurry, S. (2006). *Raising the Ruins*. Retrieved from www.thetrumpet.com/literature/books_and_booklets/967.

Foster, R. J. (2007). The Work of the New Economy: Consumers, Brands, and Value Creation. *Cultural Anthropology*, 22, 707–731.

   (2008). Commodities, Brands, Love, and Kula. *Anthropological Theory*, 8(1), 9–25. doi:10.1177/1463499607087492.

Foucault, M. (1973). *The Birth of the Clinic: An Archaeology of Medical Perception* (A. M. S. Smith, Trans.). New York: Vintage Books.

   (1975[1977]). *Discipline and Punish: The Birth of the Prison*. New York: Pantheon Books.

   (1982). The Subject and Power. In H. L. Dreyfus & P. Rabinow (Eds.), *Michel Foucault: Beyond Structuralism and Hermeneutics* (pp. 208–226). Chicago: University of Chicago Press.

   (1984a). The Politics of Health in the Eighteenth Century (C. Porter, Trans.). In P. Rabinow (Ed.), *The Foucault Reader* (pp. 273–289). New York: Pantheon Books.

   (1984b). What is an Author? In P. Rabinow (Ed.), *The Foucault Reader* (pp. 101–120). New York: Pantheon Books.

   (1988a). *The History of Sexuality* (R. Hurley, Trans. Vol. 1). New York: Vintage Books.

   (1988b). Technologies of the Self. In L. H. Martin, H. Gutman, & P. H. Hutton (Eds.), *Technologies of the Self: A Seminar with Michel Foucault*, 16–49. Amherst: University of Massachusetts Press.

   (1994a). The Birth of Social Medicine. In J. J. Faubion (Ed.), *Power* (pp. 134–156). New York: New Press.

   (1994b). Truth and Juridical Forms. In J. J. Faubion (Ed.), *Power* (pp. 1–89). New York: New Press.

   (2003). *Society Must Be Defended: Lectures at the Collège de France, 1975–1976* (D. Macey, Trans.). New York: Picador.

   (2004). The Crisis of Medicine or the Crisis of Antimedicine. *Foucault Studies*, 1, 5–19.

   (2007). *Security, Territory, Population: Lectures at the Collège de France, 1977–1978* (G. Burchell, Trans. M. Senellart Ed.). New York: Palgrave Macmillan.

   (2008). *The Birth of Biopolitics: Lectures at the Collège de France, 1978–1979* (G. Burchell, Trans. M. Senellart Ed.). New York: Palgrave Macmillan.

   (2012). The Mesh of Power. *Viewpoint Magazine*, 2. Retrieved from www.viewpointmag.com/2012/09/12/the-mesh-of-power/.

Freidberg, S. (2004). *French Beans and Food Scares: Culture and Commerce in an Anxious Age*. New York: Oxford University Press.

Frischmann, B. M. (2007). Evaluating the Demsetzian Trend in Copyright Law. *Review of Law & Economics*, 3, 649–677).

Frischmann, B. M., & Lemley, M. A. (2006). Spillovers. *Columbia Law Review*, 100, 101–143.

Frischmann, B. M., & Selinger, E. (2018). *Re-Engineering Humanity*. Cambridge and New York: Cambridge University Press.

FTC v. *Actavis*, 570 U.S. 136 (2013).

Funk Brothers Seed Co. v. *Kalo Inoculant Co.*, 333 U.S. 127 (1948).

Galkina Cleary, E., Beierlein, J. M., Khanuja, N. S., McNamee, L. M., & Ledley, F. D. (2018). Contribution of NIH Funding to New Drug Approvals 2010–2016. *Proceedings of the National Academy of Sciences*, 115(10), 2329. doi:10.1073/pnas.1715368115.

Garrett, A. (2012). Knowing the Essence of the State in Spinoza's Tractatus Theologico-Politicus. *European Journal of Philosophy*, 20(1), 50–73. doi:10.1111/j.1468-0378.2012.00512.x

Giannakeas, V., & Narod, S. A. (2018). The Expected Benefit of Preventive Mastectomy on Breast Cancer Incidence and Mortality in BRCA Mutation Carriers, by Age at Mastectomy. *Breast Cancer Research and Treatment*, 167(1), 263–267. doi:10.1007/s10549-017-4476-1

Gibson, J. (2007). Risk Aversion and Rights Accretion in Intellectual Property Law. *Yale Law Journal*, 116, 882–951.

Gillespie, T. (2007). *Wired Shut: Copyright and the Shape of Digital Culture*. Cambridge: MIT Press.

(2010). The Politics of 'Platforms'. *New Media & Society*, 12(3), 347–364. doi:10.1177/1461444809342738

Gold, E. R., & Carbone, J. (2010). Myriad Genetics: In the Eye of the Policy Storm. *Genetic Medicine*, 12(1s), S39–S70.

Golder, B., & Fitzpatrick, P. (Eds.). (2010). *Foucault's Law*. London: Routledge.

(2010). *Foucault and Law*: Ashgate.

Goodrich, P., Katyal, S. K., & Tushnet, R. (2013). Critical Legal Studies in Intellectual Property and Information Law Scholarship. *Cardozo Arts & Entertainment Law Journal*, 31, 601–623.

Gordon, W. J. (2008). Moral Philosophy, Information Technology, and Copyright: The Grokster Case. In J. v. d. Hoven & J. Weckert (Eds.), *Information Technology and Moral Philosophy* (pp. 270–300). Cambridge: Cambridge University Press.

Goswami, N. (2008). Autophagia and Queer Transnationality: Compulsory Heteroimperial Masculinity in Deepa Mehta's Fire. *Signs*, 33(2), 343–369. doi:10.1086/521052

Grand Upright Music, Ltd v. *Warner Bros. Records Inc.*, 780 F. Supp. 182 (SDNY 1991).

Grimmelmann, J. (2009). The Ethical Visions of Copyright Law. *Fordham Law Review*, 77, 2005–2037.

Grodzinsky, F. S., & Tavani, H. T. (2010). Appying the 'Contextual Integrity' Model of Privacy to Personal Blogs in the Blogosphere. *International Journal of Internet Research Ethics*, 3(2), 38–47.

Guo, F., Hirth, J. M., Lin, Y. L., Richardson, G., Levine, L., Berenson, A. B., & Kuo, Y. F. (2017). Use of BRCA Mutation Test in the U.S., 2004–2014. *American Journal of Preventive Medicine*, 52(6), 702–709. doi:10.1016/j.amepre.2017.01.027

Hacking, I. (1986). Making Up People. In T. C. Heller, M. Sosna, & D. E. Welleby (Eds.), *Reconsructing Individualism: Autonomy, Individuality, and the Self in Western Thought* (pp. 222–236). Stanford: Stanford University Press.

Haraway, D. (1991). A Cyborg Manifesto: Science, Technoloy, and Socialist-Feminism in the Late Twentieth Century. In *Simians, Cyborgs, and Women: The Reinvention of Nature* (pp. 149–182). New York: Routledge.

Harcourt, B. E. (2011). *The Illusion of Free Markets*. Cambridge: Harvard University Press.

Hardt, M., & Negri, A. (2004). *Multitude: War and Democracy in the Age of Empire*. New York: Penguin.

Harvey, D. (2003). *The New Imperialism*. Oxford: Oxford University Press.

(2005). *A Brief History of Neoliberalism*. Oxford; New York: Oxford University Press.

Hayek, F. A. (1944). *The Road to Serfdom*. Chicago: University of Chicago Press.

(1948). *Individualism and Economic Order*. Chicago: University of Chicago Press.

Hayles, N. K. (1999). *How We Became Posthuman: Virtual Bodies in Cybernetics, Literature, and Informatics*. Chicago: University of Chicago Press.

Hébert, K. (2010). In Pursuit of Singular Salmon: Paradoxes of Sustainability and the Quality Commodity. *Science as Culture*, 19(4), 553–581. doi:10.1080/09505431.2010.519620

Heller, M. A. (1998). The Tragedy of the Anti-Commons: Property in the Transition from Marx to Markets. *Harvard Law Review*, 111, 621–688.

Hemmungs Wirtén, E. (2008). *Terms of Use: Negotiating the Jungle of the Intellectual Commons*. Toronto: University of Toronto Press.

(2015). The Patent and the Paper: a Few Thoughts on Late Modern Science and Intellectual Property. *Culture Unbound*, 7, 600–609.

Herz, M., & Diamantopoulos, A. (2013). Activation of Country Stereotypes: Automaticity, Consonance, and Impact. *Journal of the Academy of Marketing Science*, 41(4), 400–417. doi:10.1007/s11747-012-0318-1

Hess, C., & Ostrom, E. (2003). Ideas, Artifacts, and Facilities: Information as a Common-Pool Resource. *Law and Contemporary Problems*, 66, 111–145.

Hetcher, S. A. (2009). Hume's Penguin, or, Yochai Benkler and the Nature of Peer Production. *Vanderbilt Journal of Entertainment and Technology Law*, 11, 963–1000.

Heymann, L. A. (2005). The Birth of the Authornym: Authorship, Pseudonymity, and Trademark Law. *Notre Dame Law Review*, 80, 1377–1449.

Hobart, M. E., & Schiffman, Z. S. (1998). *Information Ages: Literacy, Numeracy and the Computer Revolution*. Baltimore: Johns Hopkins University Press.

Hobbes, T. (1971). *A Dialogue between a Philosopher and a Student of the Common Laws of England* (J. Cropsey Ed.). Chicago: University of Chicago Press.

Hoffman, D. A., & Mehra, S. K. (2009). Wikitruth through Wikiorder. *Emory Law Journal*, 59, 152–209.

hooks, b. (1999). Eating the Other. In *Black Looks: Race and Representation* (pp. 21–40). Boston: South End Press.

Hovenkamp, H. (2015). The Rule of Reason and the Scope of the Patent. *San Diego Law Review*, 52, 515–554.

(2018). Reasonable Patent Exhaustion. *Yale Journal of Regulation*, 35(2), 513–548.

Hughes, J. (2006). Champagne, Feta, and Bourbon: The Spirited Debate about Geographical Indications. *Hastings Law Journal*, 58, 299–386.

Hull, G. (2003a). Digital Copyright and the Possibility of Pure Law. *qui parle*, 14, 21–47.

(2003b). Thoughts on the Fetishization of Cyberspeech and the Turn from 'Public' to 'Private' Law. *Constellations: An International Journal of Critical and Democratic Theory*, 10(1), 113–134.

(2009a). Clearing the Rubbish: Locke, the Waste Proviso, and the Moral Justification of Intellectual Property. *Public Affairs Quarterly*, 23, 67–93.

(2009b). *Hobbes and the Making of Modern Political Thought*. London: Continuum.

(2009c). Overblocking Autonomy: The Case of Mandatory Library Filtering Software. *Continental Philosophy Review*, 42(1), 81–100. doi:10.1007/s11007-009-9097-x.

(2012). Coding the Dictatorship of 'the They:' A Phenomenological Critique of Digital Rights Management. In M. Sanders & J. J. Wisnewski (Eds.), *Ethics and Phenomenology* (pp. 197–220). Lanham, MD: Lexington Books.

(2013). Biopolitics Is Not (Primarily) about Life: On Biopolitics, Neoliberalism, and Families. *Journal of Speculative Philosophy*, 27(3), 322–335.

(2017). Equitable Relief as a Relay between Juridical and Biopower: The Case of School Desegregation. *Continental Philosophy Review*, 50(2), 225–248.

Hull, G., & Pasquale, F. (2018). Toward a Critical Theory of Corporate Wellness. *BioSocieties*, 13(1), 190–212. doi:10.1057/s41292-017-0064-1.

Hume, M., & Mills, M. (2013). Uncovering Victoria's Secret: Exploring Women's Luxury Perceptions of Intimate Apparel and Purchasing Behaviour. *Journal of Fashion Marketing and Management: An International Journal*, 17(4), 460–485. doi:10.1108/JFMM-03-2013-0020.

Hunt, A. (1992). Foucault's Expulsion of Law: Toward a Retrieval. *Law and Social Inquiry*, 17(1), 1–38.

Ilbery, B., & Kneafsey, M. (2000). Producer Constructions of Quality in Regional Speciality Food Production: A Case Study from South West England. *Journal of Rural Studies*, 16(2), 217–230. doi:https://doi.org/10.1016/S0743-0167(99)00041-8.

Illinois Tool Works Inc. v. *Independent Ink, Inc.*, 547 U.S. 28 (2006).

Impression Products v. *Lexmark International*, 137 S. Ct. 1523 (Supreme Court of the U.S. 2017).

In re Brunetti, 877 F.3d 1330 (Fed. Cir. 2017).

In re Tam, 808 F.3d 1321 (Fed. Cir. 2015).

Ingram, D. (2018, May 14). Multigene Test in Breast Ca Often Skipped Until After Surgery. *MedPage Today*.

Introna, L. D., & Nissenbaum, H. (2000). Shaping the Web: Why the Politics of Search Engines Matters. *The Information Society*, 16(3), 169-185. doi:10.1080/01972240050133634.

James, R. (2015). *Resilience & Melancholy: Pop Music, Feminism, Neoliberalism*. Alresford: Zero Books.

Jefferson, T. (1956). *The Papers of Thomas Jefferson* (Vol. 13). Princeton: Princeton University Press.

Juffer, J. (1996). A Pornographic Femininity? Telling and Selling Victoria's (Dirty) Secrets. *Social Text* (48), 27–48. doi:10.2307/466785.

Jungersen v. *Ostby & Barton Co.*, 335 U.S. 560, 335 U.S. 560 (1949).

Kane, E. M. (2004). Splitting the Gene: DNA Patents and the Genetic Code. *Tennessee Law Review*, 71, 707–767.

(2011). Patenting Genes and Genetic Methods: What's at Stake? *Journal of Business and Technology Law*, 6, 101–134.

Kapczynski, A. (2008). The Access to Knowledge Mobilization and the New Politics of Intellectual Property. *Yale Law Journal*, 117, 804–885.

(2012). The Cost of Price: Why and How to Get Beyond Intellectual Property Internalism. *UCLA Law Review*, 59, 970–1026.

(2014). Intellectual Property's Leviathan. *Law and Contemporary Problems*, 77, 131–145.

(2017). Order without Intellectual Property Law: Open Science in Influenza. *Cornell Law Review*, 102, 1539–1648.

Kary, J. H. (1999/2000). Contract Law and the Social Contract: What Legal History Can Teach Us about the Political Theory of Hobbes and Locke. *Ottawa Law Review*, 31, 73–91.

Katyal, S. K. (2006a). Performance, Property, and the Slashing of Gender in Fan Fiction. *Journal of Gender, Social Policy and the Law*, 14, 461–518.

(2006b). Semiotic Disobedience. *Washington University Law Review*, 84, 489–571.

(2010a). Stealth Marketing and Antibranding: The Love that Dare Not Speak Its Name. *Buffalo Law Review*, 58, 795–849.

(2010b). Trademark Intersectionality. *UCLA Law Review*, 57, 1601–1699.

(2015). Cosmopolitanism and the Transnational Trademark. In H. Sun, B. Beebe, & M. Sunder (Eds.), *The Luxury Economy and Intellectual Property* (pp. 309–337). New York: Oxford University Press.

Kennedy, D. (1993). The Stakes of Law, or Hale and Foucault! In *Sexy Dressing Etc.* (pp. 83–125). Cambridge: Harvard University Press.

Keyes, C. L. (1996). At the Crossroads: Rap Music and Its African Nexus. *Ethnomusicology*, 40(2), 223–248. doi:10.2307/852060.

Khan, L. M. (2018a). The Ideological Roots of America's Market Power Problem. *Yale Law Journal Forum*, 127, 960–979.

(2018b). The New Brandeis Movement: America's Antimonopoly Debate. *Journal of European Competition Law and Practice*, 9(3), 131–132.

Knopper, S. (2009). *Appetite for Self-Destruction: The Spectacular Crash of the Record Industry in the Digital Age*. New York: Free Press.

Koebler, J. (2017). Why American Farmers Are Hacking Their Tractors with Ukrainian Firmware. *Vice*. Retrieved from https://motherboard.vice.com/en_us/article/xykkkd/why-american-farmers-are-hacking-their-tractors-with-ukrainian-firmware.

Kohane, I. S., Masys, D. R., & Altman, R. B. (2006). The Incidentalome: A Threat to Genomic Medicine. *JAMA*, 296(2), 212–215. doi:10.1001/jama.296.2.212.

KSR v. *Teleflex*, 550 U.S. 398 (2007).

Kuchenbaecker, K. B., Hopper, J. L., Barnes, D. R. et al. (2017). Risks of Breast, Ovarian, and Contralateral Breast Cancer for brca1 and brca2 Mutation Carriers. *JAMA*, 317(23), 2402–2416. doi:10.1001/jama.2017.7112.

Kukla, R. (2012). "Author TBD": Radical Collaboration in Contemporary Biomedical Research. *Philosophy of Science*, 79(5), 845–858. doi:10.1086/668042.

Kurian, A. W., Li, Y., Hamilton, A. S., Ward, K. C. et al. (2017). Gaps in Incorporating Germline Genetic Testing into Treatment Decision-Making for Early-Stage Breast Cancer. *Journal of Clinical Oncology*, 35(20), 2232–2239. doi:10.1200/jco.2016.71.6480.

Kurian, A. W., Ward, K. C., Hamilton, A. S. et al. (2018). Uptake, Results, and Outcomes of Germline Multiple-Gene Sequencing after Diagnosis of Breast Cancer. *JAMA Oncology*, 4(8), 1066–1072. doi:10.1001/jamaoncol.2018.0644

Kwall, R. R. (2006). Inspiration and Innovation: The Intrinsic Dimension of the Artistic Soul. *Notre Dame Law Review*, 81, 1945–2012.

Laakmann, A. B. (2016). A Property Theory of Medical Innovation. *Jurimetrics: The Journal of Law, Science & Technology*, 56, 117–163.

Lafraniere, S. (2006, March 22). In the Jungle, the Unjust Jungle, a Small Victory. *New York Times*. Retrieved from www.nytimes.com/2006/03/22/world/africa/in-the-jungle-the-unjust-jungle-a-small-victory.html.

Landes, W. M., & Posner, R. A. (1987). Trademark Law: An Economic Perspective. *Journal of Law and Economics*, 30, 265–309.

Latour, B. (1992). Where Are the Missing Masses? The Sociology of a Few Mundane Objects. In W. E. Bijker & J. Law (Eds.), *Shaping Technology/Building Society* (pp. 225–258). Cambridge: MIT Press.

(1993). *We Have Never Been Modern* (C. Porter, Trans.).

Lawrence, T. (2011). A History of Drag Balls, Houses, and the Culture of Voguing. In S. Baker (Ed.), *Voguing and the House Ballroom Scene of New York*, 1989–92. London: Soul Jazz.

Lee, E.-G., Kang, H. J., Lim, M. C. et al. (2018). Different Patterns of Risk Reducing Decisions in Affected or Unaffected BRCA Pathogenic Variant Carriers. *Journal of Korean Cancer Association*, 51(1), 280–288. doi:10.4143/crt.2018.079

Lemley, M. A. (1997). Romantic Authorship and the Rhetoric of Property. *Texas Law Review*, 75, 873–906.

(2005). Property, Intellectual Property, and Free Riding. *Texas Law Review*, 83, 1031.

(2008). The Surprisinig Virtues of Treating Trade Secrets as IP Rights. *Stanford Law Review*, 61, 311–354.

(2015). Faith-Based Intellectual Property. *UCLA Law Review*, 62, 1328–1346.

Lemley, M. A., Risch, M., Sichelman, T., & Wagner, R. P. (2011). Life after *Bilski*. *Stanford Law Review*, 63(6), 1315–1347.

LeRoy v. Tatham, 55 U.S. 156 (1853).

Lessig, L. (1998). The New Chicago School. *The Journal of Legal Studies*, 27(S2), 661–691. doi:10.1086/468039.

(2006). *Code and Other Laws of Cyberspace, Version 2.0*. New York: Basic Books.

Levmore, S. (2002). Two Stories about the Evolution of Property Rights. *The Journal of Legal Studies*, 31(S2), S421–S451. doi:10.1086/342027.

Levy, L. (2018, December 6). The Gatekeepers of SoundCloud Rap. *Vulture*. Retrieved from www.vulture.com/2018/12/the-gatekeepers-of-soundcloud-rap.html.

Lexmark Int'l, Inc. v. *Impression Products*, 816 F.3d 721 (2016).

The Lingerie Industry Reveals Some Secrets: Growing Market Raises Questions about Self-Image. (2014). *Strategic Direction*, 30(3), 19–21. doi:10.1108/SD-02-2014-0018.

Litman, J. (2002). Electronic Commerce and Free Speech. In N. Elkin-Koren & N. W. Netanel (Eds.), *The Commodification of Information* (pp. 23–42). The Hague: Kluwer.

(2006). *Digital Copyright*. Amherst: Prometheus Books.

Lobel, O. (2018). *You Don't Own Me: How Mattel v. MGA Entertainment Exposed Barbie's Dark Side*. New York: W. W. Norton & Company.

Locke, J. (1997). *Political Essays* (M. Goldie Ed.). Cambridge: Cambridge University Press.

Long, C. (2006). Dilution. *Columbia Law Review*, 106, 1029–1078.

Loughran v. Quaker City Chocolate & Confectionery Co., 286 F. 694 (1923).

Loughran v. Quaker City Chocolate & Confectionery Co., 296 F. 822 (3rd Cir. 1924).

Lovett, F. (2010). Cultural Accommodation and Domination. *Political Theory*, 38(2), 243–267. doi:10.1177/0090591709354870.

Lowry, K. P., Lee, J. M., Kong, C. Y. et al. (2012). Annual Screening Strategies in BRCA1 and BRCA2 Gene Mutation Carriers: A Comparative Effectiveness Analysis. *Cancer*, 118(8), 2021–2030. doi:10.1002/cncr.26424.

Lubochinski, E. J. (2003). Hegel's Secret: Personality and the Housemark Cases. *Emory Law Journal*, 52, 489–514.

Lupton, D. (2015). Quantified Sex: A Critical Analysis of Sexual and Reproductive Self-Tracking Using Apps. *Culture, Health & Sexuality*, 17(4), 440–453. doi:10.1080/13691058.2014.920528.

Macaulay, T. B. (1841). Copyright. Retrieved from https://en.wikisource.org/wiki/Copyright_Law_(Macaulay).

Madison, M. J., Frischmann, B. M., & Strandburg, K. J. (2009). The University as Constructed Cultural Commons. *Washington University Journal of Law and Policy*, 30, 365–403.

(2010). Constructing Commons in the Cultural Environment. *Cornell Law Review*, 95(2010), 657–709.

Mai, P. L., Vadaparampil, S. T., Breen, N., McNeel, T. S., Wideroff, L., & Graubard, B. I. (2014). Awareness of Cancer Susceptibility Genetic Testing. *American Journal of Preventive Medicine*, 46(5), 440–448. doi:http://dx.doi.org/10.1016/j.amepre.2014.01.002.

Mansfield, B. (2003). Fish, Factory Trawlers, and Imitation Crab: The Nature of Quality in the Seafood Industry. *Journal of Rural Studies*, 19, 9–21.

Marazzi, C. (2008). *Capital and Language: From the New Economy to the War Economy*. Los Angeles; Cambridge: Semiotext(e).

Matal v. Tam, 137 S. Ct. 1744 (2017).

Mathur, P., Jain, S. P., & Maheswaran, D. (2012). Consumers' Implicit Theories about Personality Influence Their Brand Personality Judgments. *Journal of Consumer Psychology*, 22(4), 545–557. doi:http://dx.doi.org/10.1016/j.jcps.2012.01.005.

Matsubayashi, H., Takaori, K., Morizane, C. et al. (2017). Familial Pancreatic Cancer: Concept, Management, and Issues. *World Journal of Gastroenterology*, 23(6), 935–948. doi:10.3748/wjg.v23.i6.935.

Mayo v. Prometheus, 132 S. Ct. 1289 (Supreme Court of the U.S. 2012).

Menapace, L., Colson, G., Grebitus, C., & Facendola, M. (2011). Consumers' Preferences for Geographical Origin Labels: Evidence from the Canadian Olive Oil Market. *European Review of Agricultural Economics*, 38(2), 193–212. doi:10.1093/erae/jbq051.

Mercoid Corp. v. Mid-Continent Inv. Co., 320 U.S. 661 (1944).

Merges, R. P. (1993). Are You Making Fun of Me? Notes on Market Failure and the Parody Defense in Copyright. *American Intellectual Property Law Association Quarterly Journal*, 21, 305–312.

(2011). *Justifying Intellectual Property*. Cambridge: Harvard University Press.

(2017a). Against Utilitarian Fundamentalism. *[ssrn]*.

(2017b). Economics of Intellectual Property Law. In F. Parisi (Ed.), *The Oxford Handbook of Law and Economics: Volume 2: Private and Commercial Law* (pp. 200–219). Oxford: Oxford University Press.

Merrill, T. W. (1998). Property and the Right to Exclude. *Nebraska Law Review*, 77(4), 730–755.

Merrill, T. W., & Smith, H. E. (2001). What Happened to Property in Law and Economics? *Yale Law Journal*, 111, 357–398.

(2007). The Morality of Property. *William and Mary Law Review*, 48, 1849–1895.

Mezey, N. (2007). The Paradoxes of Cultural Property. *Columbia Law Review*, 107(8), 2004–2046.

Mill, J. S. (1965). *The Principles of Political Economy* (Vol. III). London: Routledge & Kegan Paul.

Miller, P., & Rose, N. (1990). Governing Economic Life. *Economy and Society*, 19(1), 1–31. doi:10.1080/03085149000000001.

Mirowski, P. (2011). *Science-Mart: Privatizing American Science*. Cambridge: Harvard University Press.

(2013). *Never Let a Serious Crisis Go to Waste: How Neoliberalism Survived the Financial Meltdown*. London: Verso.

Monsanto Chemical Co. v. Perfect Fit Products Manufacturing Co., No. 12-416, 349 F.2d 389 (2nd Cir. 1965).

Morton Salt Co. v. G. S. Suppiger Co., 314 U.S. 488 (1942).

Moseley v. V. Secret Catalogue, 537 U.S. 413 (2003).

Moseley v. Victoria's Secret Catalogue, Brief for Respondent, No. 01-1015, 537 U.S. 413 (2003).

Newman, G. E., & Dhar, R. (2014). Authenticity Is Contagious: Brand Essence and the Original Source of Production. *Journal of Marketing Research (JMR)*, 51(3), 371–386.

Nimmer, D. (2001). Copyright in the Dead Sea Scrolls: Authorship and Originality. *Houston Law Review*, 38, 1–217.

(2003). 'Fairest of them All' and other Fairy Tales of Fair Use. *Law and Contemporary Problems*, 66, 264–287.

Nowak, M. A., & Waclaw, B. (2017). Genes, Environment, and "Bad Luck". *Science*, 355(6331), 1266.

O'Reilly v. Morse, 56 U.S. 62 (1854).

Oeppen, J., & Vaupel, J. W. (2002). Broken Limits to Life Expectancy. *Science*, 296(5570), 1029.

Offit, K., Bradbury, A., Storm, C., Merz, J. F., Noonan, K. E., & Spence, R. (2013). Gene Patents and Personalized Cancer Care: Impact of the Myriad Case on Clinical Oncology. *Journal of Clinical Oncology*, 31(21), 2743–2748. doi:10.1200/jco.2013.49.7388.

Oguamanam, C. (2009). Beyond Theories: Intellectual Property Dynamics in the Global Knowledge Economy. *Wake Forest Intellectual Property Law Journal*, 9(2), 105–154.

Oil States v. Greene, 138 S. Ct. 1365 (Supreme Court of the U.S. 2018).

Oke, J. (2018). Why BRCA Screening Will Harm (Some) Women. Retrieved from https://blogs.bmj.com/bmjebmspotlight/2018/01/24/brca-screening-will-harm-women/.

Okin, S. M. (2002). Mistresses of Their Own Destiny:' Group Rights, Gender, and Realistic Rights of Exit. *Ethics*, 112, 205–230.

Oliar, D. (2006). Making Sense of the Intellectual Property Clause: Promotion of Progress as a Limitation on Congress's Intellectual Property Power. *Georgetown Law Journal*, 94, 1771–1845.

Ouellette, L. (2018). What Happened in Patent Law in the Past Year? Retrieved from https://writtendescription.blogspot.com/2018/01/what-happened-in-patent-law-in-past-year.html.

Park, J. K., & John, D. R. (2010). Got to Get You into My Life: Do Brand Personalities Rub Off on Consumers? *Journal of Consumer Research*, 37(4), 655–669. doi:10.1086/655807.

(2012). Capitalizing on Brand Personalities in Advertising: The Influence of Implicit Self-Theories on Ad Appeal Effectiveness. *Journal of Consumer Psychology*, 22(3), 424–432. doi:http://dx.doi.org/10.1016/j.jcps.2011.05.004.

Parry, B. (2008). Geographical Indications: Not all Champagne and Roses. In L. Bently, J. Davis, & J. C. Ginsburg (Eds.), *Trade Marks and Brands: An Interdisciplinary Critique*. Cambridge: Cambridge University Press.

Patry, W. (2009). *Moral Panics and the Copyright Wars*. Oxford: Oxford University Press.

Peeler, C. D. (1999). From the Providence of Kings to Copyrighted Things (and French Moral Rights). *Independent International and Comparative Law Review*, 9, 423–456.

Peñalver, E. M., & Katyal, S. K. (2010). *Property Outlaws: How Squatters, Pirates, and Protesters Improve the Law of Ownership*. New Haven: Yale University Press.

Perfect 10 v. Google, 653 F.3d 976 (9th Cir. 2011).

Perfect 10, Inc. v. Amazon.com, Inc., 508 F.3d 1146 (9th Cir. 2007).

Phili, S. (2013, May 6). Robin Thicke on that Banned Video, Collaborating with 2 Chainz and Kendrick Lamar, and His New Film. GQ. Retrieved from www.gq.com/story/robin-thicke-interview-blurred-lines-music-video-collaborating-with-2-chainz-and-kendrick-lamar-mercy.

Pike, A. (2009). Geographies of Brands and Branding. *Progress in Human Geography*, 33(5), 619–645. doi:10.1177/0309132508101601.

(2011). Placing Brands and Branding: A Socio-Spatial Biography of Newcastle Brown Ale. *Transactions of the Institute of British Geographers*, 36(2), 206–222. doi:10.1111/j.1475-5661.2011.00425.x.

(2013). Economic Geographies of Brands and Branding. *Economic Geography*, 89(4), 317–339. doi:10.1111/ecge.12017.

Posner, R. A. (2005). Intellectual Property: The Law and Economics Approach. *Journal of Economic Perspectives, 19*(2), 57–73.

Poster, M. (2001). *What's the Matter with the Internet?* Minneapolis: University of Minnesota Press.

Prince, A. E. R. (2015). Prevention for Those Who Can Pay: Insurance Reimbursement of Genetic-Based Preventive Interventions in the Liminal State between Health and Disease. *Journal of Law and the Biosciences, 2*(2), 365–395. doi:10.1093/jlb/lsv008.

Rabinow, P. (1996). Artificiality and Enlightenment: From Sociobiology to Biosociality. In *Essays on the Anthropology of Reason* (pp. 91–111). Princeton: Princeton University Press.

Rabinow, P., & Rose, N. (2006). Biopower Today. *BioSocieties, 1*, 195–217.

Rai, S. (2001, August 25). India–U.S. Fight on Basmati Rice Is Mostly Settled. *New York Times.* Retrieved from www.nytimes.com/2001/08/25/business/india-us-fight-on-basmati-rice-is-mostly-settled.html.

Raustiala, K., & Sprigman, C. (2012). *The Knockoff Economy: How Imitation Sparks Innovation.* Oxford and New York: Oxford University Press.

Reid, L. (2017). Truth or Spin? Disease Definition in Cancer Screening. *The Journal of Medicine and Philosophy: A Forum for Bioethics and Philosophy of Medicine, 42*(4), 385–404. doi:10.1093/jmp/jhx006.

Reilly, G. (2018). Our 19th Century Patent System. *IP Theory, 7*(2). Retrieved from www.repository.law.indiana.edu/ipt/vol7/iss2/3.

Richards, C. (2012, July 6). The Court Case that Changed Hip-Hop – From Public Enemy to Kanye – Forever. *Washington Post.* Retrieved from www.washingtonpost.com/opinions/the-court-case-that-changed-hip-hop–from-public-enemy-to-kanye–forever/2012/07/06/.

Riley, A. R. (2000). Recovering Collectivity: Group Rights to Intellectual Property in Indigenous Communities. *Cardozo Arts and Entertainment Law Journal, 18*, 175–225.

Roberts, J. J. (2017). Supreme Court's Printer Decision Is Good News for Retailers and Consumers. Retrieved from http://fortune.com/2017/05/30/supreme-court-printers/.

Rose, C. M. (1990). Property as Storytelling: Perspectives from Game Theory, Narrative Theory, Feminist Theory. *Yale Journal of Law & the Humanities, 2*(1), 37–57.

    (1999). Canons of Property Talk, or, Blackstone's Anxiety. *Yale Law Journal, 108*, 601–632.

    (2005). Property in all the Wrong Places. *Yale Law Journal, 114*, 991–1019.

    (2006). Introduction: Property and Language, or, the Ghost of the Fifth Panel. *Yale Journal of Law and the Humanities, 18*(1), 1–28.

Rose, M. (1993). *Authors and Owners: The Invention of Copyright.* Cambridge: Harvard University Press.

Rose, N. S. (2007). *Politics of Life Itself: Biomedicine, Power, and Subjectivity in the Twenty-First Century.* Princeton: Princeton University Press.

Rose, T. (1989). Orality and Technology: Rap Music and Afro-American Cultural Resistance. *Popular Music and Society, 13*(4), 35–44. doi:10.1080/03007768908591371.

    (1991). "Fear of a Black Planet": Rap Music and Black Cultural Politics in the 1990s. *The Journal of Negro Education, 60*(3), 276–290. doi:10.2307/2295482.

Rosenblatt, E. L. (2011). A Theory of IP's Negative Space. *Columbia Journal of Law and the Arts, 34*, 317–365.

Rust v. Sullivan, 500 U.S. 173 (Supreme Court of the U.S. 1991).

Sasso, B. (2014). Congress Passed a Cell-Phone Unlocking Bill. But It Won't Do Much. *The Atlantic.* Retrieved from www.theatlantic.com/politics/archive/2014/07/congress-passed-a-cell-phone-unlocking-bill-but-it-wont-do-much/457434/.

Schaper, M., & Schicktanz, S. (2018). Medicine, Market, and Communication: Ethical Considerations in Regard to Persuasive Communication in Direct-To-Consumer Genetic Testing Services. *BMC Medical Ethics*, 19(1), 56. doi:10.1186/s12910-018-0292-3.

Schechter, F. I. (1925). *The Historical Foundations of the Law Relating to Trade-Marks*. New York: Columbia University Press.

—— (1927). The Rational Basis of Trademark Protection. *Harvard Law Review*, 40(6), 813–833. doi:10.2307/1330367.

Schillinger, D., & Dohan, D. (2008). Genetic Testing for Vulnerable Populations: What Kinds of Communication We Need and Do Not Need. *The American Journal of Bioethics*, 8(6), 12–14. doi:10.1080/15265160802248393.

Schlozman, K. L., Verba, S., & Brady, H. E. (2011). Who Speaks? Citizen Political Voice on the Internet Commons. *Daedalus*, 140(4), 121–139. doi:10.1162/DAED_a_00119.

Schur, R. L. (2011). *Parodies of Ownership: Hip-Hop Aesthetics and Intellectual Property Law*. Ann Arbor: University of Michigan Press.

Sell, S. K. (2003). *Private Power, Public Law: The Globalization of Intellectual Property Rights*. Cambridge: Cambridge University Press.

Seltzer, W. (2010). Free Speech Unmoored in Copyright's Safe Harbor: Chilling Effects of the DMCA on the First Amendment. *Harvard Journal of Law and Technology*, 24(1), 171–232.

Senftleben, M. (2009). The Trademark Tower of Babel – Dilution Concepts in International, US and EC Trademark Law. *International Review of Intellectual Property and Competition Law*, 40(1), 45–77.

Shaul, O. (2017). How Introns Enhance Gene Expression. *The International Journal of Biochemistry & Cell Biology*, 91, 145–155. doi:https://doi.org/10.1016/j.biocel .2017.06.016.

Shiva, V. (1999). *Biopiracy: The Plunder of Nature and Knowledge*. Boston: South End Press.

Silbey, J. (2008). The Mythical Beginnings of Intellectual Property. *George Mason Law Review*, 15, 319–379.

—— (2014). *The Eureka Myth: Creators, Innovators, and Everyday Intellectual Property*. Stanford: Stanford University Press.

Simon, J. (2002). Taking Risks: Extreme Sports and the Embrace of Risk in Advanced Liberal Societies. In T. Baker & J. Simon (Eds.), *Embracing Risk: The Changing Culture of Insurance and Responsibility* (pp. 177–208). Chicago: University of Chicago Press.

Simons, H. C. (1948). *Economics Policy for a Free Society*. Chicago: University of Chicago Press.

Skytte, A. B., Gerdes, A. M., Andersen, M. K. et al. (2010). Risk-Reducing Mastectomy and Salpingo-Oophorectomy in Unaffected BRCA Mutation Carriers: Uptake and Timing*. *Clinical Genetics*, 77(4), 342–349. doi:10.1111/j.1399-0004.2009.01329.x.

Smith, D. (2013, July 25). South Africa Fights to Protect Rooibos Tea Name after French Trademark Bid. *The Guardian*. Retrieved from www.theguardian.com/world/2013/jul/25/ south-africa-rooibos-tea-france.

Smith, H. (2002). Exclusion versus Governance: Two Strategies for Delineating Property Rights. *The Journal of Legal Studies*, 31(S2), S453–S487. doi:10.1086/344529.

Smith, H. E. (2007). Intellectual Property as Property: Delineating Entitlements in Information. *Yale Law Journal*, 116, 1742–1822.

Spence, L. K. (2011). *Stare in the Darkness: The Limits of Hip-Hop and Black Politics*. Minneapolis: University of Minnesota Press.

State v. *Shack*, 58 N.J. 297 (1971).

Stone, B. (2009, July 17). Amazon Erases Orwell Books from Kindle. *New York Times*.

Stoppa-Lyonnet, D. (2016). The Biological Effects and Clinical Implications of BRCA Mutations: Where Do We Go from Here? *European Journal of Human Genetics, 24* (Suppl 1), S3–S9. doi:10.1038/ejhg.2016.93.

Strahilevitz, L. J. (2007). Wealth without Markets. *Yale Law Journal, 116,* 1472–1516.

Strandburg, K. J. (2005). Curiosity-Driven Research and University Technology Transfer. In G. D. Libecap (Ed.), *University Entrepreneurship and Technology Transfer: Process, Design, and Intellectual Property* (pp. 93–122). Oxford: Elsevier.

Strandburg, K. J., Frischmann, B. M., & Madison, M. J. (2017). The Knowledge Commons Framework. In B. M. Frischmann, K. J. Strandburg, & M. J. Madison (Eds.), *Governing Medical Knowledge Commons* (pp. 9–18). Cambridge: Cambridge University Press.

Sunder, M. (2000). Intellectual Property and Identity Politics: Playing with Fire. *Journal of Gender, Race and Justice, 4,* 67–98.

(2001). Cultural Dissent. *Stanford Law Review, 54,* 495–567.

(2006). IP3. *Stanford Law Review, 59,* 257–332.

(2007). The Invention of Traditional Knowledge. *Law and Contemporary Problems, 70,* 97–124.

(2008). Intellectual Property and Development as Freedom. In N. W. Netanel (Ed.), *The Development Agenda.* New York: Oxford University Press.

(2012). *From Goods to a Good Life: Intellectual Property and Global Justice.* New Haven: Yale University Press.

Sunder Rajan, K. (2006). *Biocapital: The Constitution of Postgenomic Life.* Durham: Duke University Press.

Sunstein, C. R. (1996). Social Norms and Social Roles. *Columbia Law Review, 96,* 903–968.

Surbone, A. (2011). Social and Ethical Implications of BRCA Testing. *Annals of Oncology,* 22(Suppl 1), i60–i66. doi:10.1093/annonc/mdq668f.

Tadros, V. (1998). Between Governance and Discipline: The Law and Michel Foucault. *Oxford Journal of Legal Studies,* 18(1), 75–103. doi:10.1093/ojls/18.1.75.

Taylor, D. O. (2019). Patent Reform, Then and Now. *Michigan State Law Review, forthcoming.*

Tehranian, J. (2012). Towards a Critical IP Theory: Copyright, Consecration & Control. *Brigham Young University Law Review,* 2012, 1237–1296.

Tellmann, U. (2013). Catastrophic Populations and the Fear of the Future: Malthus and the Genealogy of Liberal Economy. *Theory, Culture & Society,* 30(2), 135–155. doi:10.1177/0263276412455830.

Thacker, E. (2005). *The Global Genome: Biotechnology, Politics, and Culture.* Cambridge: MIT Press.

Tkach, J. (1997a). The Central Plank Cracks. *Transformed by Truth: Grace Communion International.* Retrieved from www.gci.org/aboutus/truth9.

(1997b). The First Reforms. *Transformed by Truth: Grace Communion International.* Retrieved from www.gci.org/aboutus/truth8.

Tomasetti, C., Li, L., & Vogelstein, B. (2017). Stem Cell Divisions, Somatic Mutations, Cancer Etiology, and Cancer Prevention. *Science,* 355(6331), 1330.

Tomasetti, C., & Vogelstein, B. (2015). Variation in Cancer Risk among Tissues Can Be Explained by the Number of Stem Cell Divisions. *Science,* 347(6217), 78.

Triangle Publications v. *Rohrlich,*, 167 F.2d (2nd Cir. 1948).

Tully, J. (1993). Rediscovering America: The Two *Treatises* and Aboriginal Rights. In *An Approach to Political Philosophy: Locke in Contexts* (pp. 137–178). Cambridge: Cambridge University Press.

Tushnet, R. (2004). Copy This Essay: How Fair Use Doctrine Harms Free Speech and How Copying Serves It. *Yale Law Journal*, 114, 535–590.

(2007). My Fair Ladies: Sex, Gender, and Fair Use in Copyright. *American University Journal of Gender and Social Policy*, 15, 273–303.

(2009). Economies of Desire: Fair Use and Marketplace Assumptions. *William and Mary Law Review*, 51, 513–546.

Tzouvala, N. (2017). Neoliberalism as Legalism: International Economic Law and the Rise of the Judiciary. In B. Golder & D. McLoughlin (Eds.), *The Politics of Legality in a Neoliberal Age* (pp. 97–115). New York: Routledge.

V Secret Catalogue, Inc. v. Moseley, 259 F.3d 464 (6th Cir. 2001).

V. Secret Catalogue v. Moseley, 605 F.3d 382 (6th Cir. 2010).

Vadaparampil, S. T., Malo, T., de la Cruz, C., & Christie, J. (2012). Do Breast Cancer Patients Tested in the Oncology Care Setting Share BRCA Mutation Results with Family Members and Health Care Providers? *Journal of Cancer Epidemiology*, 2012, 498062. doi:10.1155/2012/498062.

Van Horn, R. (2009). Reinventing Monopoly and the Role of Corporations: The Roots of Chicago Law and Economics. In P. Mirowski & D. Plehwe (Eds.), *The Road from Mont Pèrelin* (pp. 204–237). Cambridge: Harvard University Press.

Van Horn, R., & Klaes, M. (2013). Intervening in Laissez-Faire Liberalism: Chicago's Shift on Patents. In R. Van Horn, P. Mirowski, & T. A. Stapleford (Eds.), *Building Chicago Economics: New Perspectives on the History of America's Most Powerful Economics Program* (Paperback ed. ed., pp. 180–207). Cambridge: Cambridge University Press.

Van Horn, R., & Mirowski, P. (2009). The Rise of the Chicago School of Economics and the Birth of Neoliberalism. In P. Mirowski & D. Plehwe (Eds.), *The Road from Mont Pèrelin* (pp. 139–178). Cambridge: Harvard University Press.

Vatter, M. (2017). Foucault and Becker: A Biopolitical Approach to Human Capital and the Stability of Preferences. In B. Golder & D. McLoughlin (Eds.), *The Politics of Legality in a Neoliberal Age* (pp. 64–82). New York: Routledge.

Venn, C. (2009). Neoliberal Political Economy, Biopolitics and Colonialism: A Trans-colonial Genealogy of Inequality. *Theory, Culture & Society*, 26(6), 206–233. doi:10.1177/0263276409352194.

Vinaya, S. (2012). Intellectual Property Rights and the Handloom Sector: Challenges in Implementation of Geographical Indications Act. *Journal of Intellectual Property Rights*, 17(1), 55–63.

Virno, P. (2003). *A Grammar of the Multitude: For an Analysis of Contemporary Forms of Life* (I. Bertoletti, J. Cascaito, & A. Casson, Trans.). Cambridge: Semiotext(e).

VMG Salsoul, LLC v. Ciccone, 824 F.3d 871 (9th Cir. 2016).

Wacquant, L. (2009). *Punishing the Poor: The Neoliberal Government of Social Insecurity*. Durham: Duke University Press.

Wagner, R. P. (2003). Information Wants to Be Free: Intellectual Property and the Mytholo-gies of Control. *Columbia Law Review*, 103, 995–1034.

Walterscheid, E. C. (1994). To Promote the Progress of Science and Useful Arts: the Background and Origin of the Intellectual Property Clause of the United States Consti-tution. *Journal of Intellectual Property Law*, 2, 1–56.

Ware, J. H. (2006). The Limitations of Risk Factors as Prognostic Tools. *New England Journal of Medicine*, 355(25), 2615–2617. doi:10.1056/NEJMp068249.

Weiner, C. (1987). Patenting and Academic Research: Historical Case Studies. *Science, Technology, & Human Values*, 12(1), 50–62. doi:10.1177/016224398701200105

Welch, H. G., Prorok, P. C., O'Malley, A. J., & Kramer, B. S. (2016). Breast-Cancer Tumor Size, Overdiagnosis, and Mammography Screening Effectiveness. *New England Journal of Medicine*, 375(15), 1438–1447. doi:10.1056/NEJMoa1600249

Wheeler, E. A. (1991). "Most of My Heroes Don't Appear on No Stamps": The Dialogics of Rap Music. *Black Music Research Journal*, 11(2), 193–216. doi:10.2307/779266.

White-Smith Music Publishing v. *Apollo*, 201 U.S. 1 (1908).

Wieberg, S. (2005, August 23, 2005). NCAA Allowing Florida State to Use its Seminole Mascot. *USA Today*. Retrieved from http://usatoday30.usatoday.com/sports/college/2005-08-23-fsu-mascot-approved_x.htm

Wilf, S. (2008). The Making of the Post-War Paradigm in American Intellectual Property Law. *Columbia Journal of Law & the Arts*, 31(2), 139–207.

Williams v. *Gaye*, 885 F.3d 1150 (9th Cir. 2018).

Winner, L. (1980). Do Artifacts Have Politics? *Daedalus*, 109, 121–136.

Woolf, N. (2016, Nov. 18). Urban Outfitters Settles with Navajo Nation after Illegally Using tribe's Name. *The Guardian*. Retrieved from www.theguardian.com/us-news/2016/nov/18/urban-outfitters-navajo-nation-settlement.

Worldwide Church of God v. *Philadelphia Church of God, Inc.*, 227 F.3d 1110 (9th Cir. 2000).

Wu, T. (2012). Taking Innovation Seriously: Antitrust Enforcement if Innovation Mattered Most. *Antitrust Law Journal*, 78(2), 313–328.

(2013). Intellectual Property Experimentalism by Way of Competition Law. *Competition Policy International*, 9(2), 30–40.

Yu, P. K. (2008). Cultural Relics, Intellectual Property, and Intangible Heritage. *Temple Law Review*, 81, 433–506.

Yu, P. P., Vose, J. M., & Hayes, D. F. (2015). Genetic Cancer Susceptibility Testing: Increased Technology, Increased Complexity. *Journal of Clinical Oncology*, 33(31), 3533–3534. doi:10.1200/jco.2015.63.3628

Index